DATE DUE

AG 11 '94		
JY 25 '96		

DEMCO 38-296

THE
THIRD
CENTURY

*America's Resurgence
in the Asian Era*

Joel Kotkin and
Yoriko Kishimoto

IVY BOOKS • NEW YORK

Ivy Books
Published by Ballantine Books
Copyright ©1988 by Joel Kotkin and Yoriko Kishimoto

Portions of this book previously appeared in *Inc.* magazine, the *Washington Post*, the *Los Angeles Times*, the *San Jose Mercury*, the *Nikkei Sangyo Shimbun*, and *Newsweek Japan*.

ISBN 0-8041-0626-6

This edition published by arrangement with Crown Publishers, Inc.

Manufactured in the United States of America

First Ballantine Books Edition: August 1990

To Aki Tsurukame,
who never lost faith

Contents

Acknowledgments

In writing this book we have accumulated many debts. Indeed, without the help of several key people there is no way we could have even attempted this effort. Most prominent among these are Hal Plotkin, journalist-researcher and general miracle worker at Japan Pacific Associates, and Mark Benham, a brilliant editor, now a member of Citicorp Investment Bank in New York. Their tireless efforts helped develop and sharpen the key ideas in the book. To them we owe a debt of incalculable worth.

This book was, if nothing else, truly a transpacific effort. In Japan, we were greatly assisted by the thoughts and timely criticism of Jiro Tokuyama, advisor to the Mitsui Research Institute, who over the past decade has served as mentor to both of us. We also owe particular thanks to Mikio Abe of the Nomura Research Institute; Ikuo Umebayashi of the Nikkei Venture Business Center; Richard Hanson, publisher of *Japan Financial Report*; George Hara of Data Control in Osaka; Katsunaga Yamazaki of Citicorp in Tokyo; and Yoshihisa Miyanaga of Est Corporation, Tokyo, all of whom opened many doors for us in terms of both contacts and ideas. Both Sawafuji Dynameca and ADS Imaging Systems, clients of Japan Pacific Associates, also lent important assistance.

Our efforts in China and the nations of the Chinese diaspora were greatly assisted by the kind cooperation of the Chung family, especially Wing Chung and K. S. Chung, who instructed us in the wisdom of Confucianism and family values. We also would like to thank Tang Junde, of the China Science and Technology Center, and Wang Ying Ru of Cutex Corporation, both in Beijing, whose courtesy and insight contributed greatly to the making of this project. And, finally, Wong Man Sing of Action

Computer Asia, who, along with his friends inside China, shared personal odysseys from the Red Guard era to today.

In the United States we owe much to Akira Tsurukame, whose unflagging support, spiritual force and friendship was and remains indispensable to us at all times. We also would like to thank Steven Panzer, cofounder of the Southern California Technology Executive Network (Socalten) and president of Rimtech, and Robert Kelley, president of Socalten, for sharing their ideas and contacts. Similarly, we would like to thank Regina Lau, David Lam, Michael Hu, Joe Wu, and Robert Chen, of the Asian American Manufacturers Association, who opened our eyes to the power and potential of the Chinese diaspora on both sides of the Pacific. We also are grateful for the insights into Asian affairs provided us by Tom Rohlen and Dan Okimoto, both of Stanford University; Wellington Chan at Occidental College; and Yumi Kobayashi at James Sagen and Associates. Jeremy Davies of Price Waterhouse in London and Dominique Turpin of IMEDE in Lausanne also helped by contributing their unique perspectives on the new economic dynamics not only in their native Europe, but in America and Asia as well.

Our work on the changing nature of American business benefited greatly from the insights and assistance of Modesto Maidique, now president of Florida International University; James Wilburn, dean of the Pepperdine University School of Business and Management; Ed Escobedo, a consultant in Los Angeles; Ralph Whitehead of the University of Massachusetts at Amherst; Bill Bradley, political seer and publisher of the *Larkspur Report*. Hank Koehn, Los Angeles banker, consultant and futurist, also offered much early encouragement. Although he did not live to see this project completed, we hope his legacy continues, in some small measure, through the ideas we have presented.

Several colleagues from the journalism world also played an important role in sustaining our efforts with encouragement and assignments that allowed us to develop the ideas in this work. Of particular note has been the support of George Gendron, Sara Noble and Steve Solomon at *Inc*. We also would like to acknowledge the invaluable encouragement and insights of Steve Pearlstein, Joel Garreau and David Ignatius, all of the *Washington Post*, Jeffrey Klein of the *San Jose Mercury*, Gene Stone at the *Los Angeles Times Sunday Magazine*, Paul Grabowicz of the *Oakland Tribune* and Greg Critser of *California Business*. We also benefited from the many lively discussions with Andrew Tanzer of *Forbes* in Tokyo.

Writing this book took a tremendous personal toll on its authors and also on those who, by no fault of their own, found themselves impacted by it. Kayo Miyasaki, all-around assistant at Japan Pacific Associates, prevailed through the chaos with good cheer, providing invaluable assistance while helping keep the ship of business afloat. But perhaps no one felt the impact of the book more than Leland Collins and Maya, who all too often did without wife and mother while this work was being completed. In Maya, a child of Japan and America, we see the best hopes for America's Third Century. We also owe thanks to Nachiko and Yoshiro Kishimoto, Yasuo and Miyoko Kishimoto, Loretta and Mark Kotkin and Barbara Wernik for their untold kindnesses, support and love.

We never expected much in the way of support for many of our ideas from the traditional bastions of publishing in either Japan or America, yet we received many blessings for which we are thankful. Particular note must be taken for James O'Shea Wade, our editor at Crown Publishers, whose support for us and our ideas never wavered and whose criticism helped sharpen our efforts; Jane von Mehren, also at Crown; and Okihira Hattori, our editor at Sankei Publishing in Tokyo. And, most particularly, we would like to extend our gratitude to our agents, Melanie Jackson in New York and Tom Mori in Tokyo, who turned mere ideas into reality in both English and Japanese.

Joel Kotkin   Yoriko Kishimoto
Los Angeles, California   Palo Alto, California

Preface

To many observers, the signposts of the late 1980s point to the continuing decline of America and its economy. Persistent trade and budget deficits, the weak dollar and stock market turbulence, the emergence of Japan as the world's foremost financial power—all are widely seen as harbingers of a bleak future for the nation.

And, indeed, such pessimism is well justified if American business and political leaders continue to proceed as they have during the past decade. American business people will find themselves in a world increasingly indifferent to their goods, services and institutions. The oft-repeated predictions of the United States' following Britain's decline will come to fruition.

In this book, we lay out a radically different approach, one that can lead to a vastly preferable scenario for American business. This approach stems from what we perceive as the new dynamics of the world economy and the place of American business within it. In its essentials, our prescription can be seen within the context of five fundamentals that can lead to business success in the decades ahead.

We acknowledge that these fundamentals violate some of the long-cherished beliefs of many Americans. First and foremost is the realization that the Atlantic community, long the center of world economic power, is being supplanted by the nations of Asia and the Pacific Rim. In the coming decades, America's business future will lie not with our traditional European trading partners, but with the rising nations of Asia and, further into the future, with countries of what we today vaguely call the Third World. Our attempt, particularly in the early chapters, is to trace this development and, by exposing the errors of the past, present some strategies that can assist Americans in adjusting to the new economic order.

Equally important, American business must begin to come to grips with the major changes occurring *within* the nation. We are no longer merely a European "melting pot," but a mosaic of racial and ethnic groups unprecedented in world history. To many, this mosaic threatens notions of a fundamentally white, Christian America. Yet the traditional Norman Rockwellesque notion of America no longer reflects this nation's emerging demographic and cultural realities. Nor is this transformation contrary to American tradition. Throughout our history, America's racial and cultural identity has been in constant flux, reacting to each new wave of immigration. Today's immigration, primarily from Asia and Latin America, continues that pattern. Although often seen as a problem by academics and journalistic commentators, these immigrants, like the European waves before them, bring with them many assets—in terms of new domestic markets, dynamic labor forces and links to emerging nations—that can play an essential role in an American economic renaissance.

Although speaking for and about change, in no way do we suggest abandoning the core strengths underlying America's economic dynamism and political freedom. In contrast to those in government, business and academia who advocate emulation of foreign economic models, we believe America's unique entrepreneurial culture remains its most precious economic asset. Indeed, in this work, particularly in the middle chapters, we will show the often-overlooked weaknesses of the more centrally controlled foreign systems, including those existing in Japan and the European community.

None of this should be mistaken as a brief for the current strategies of American business. Despite our wealth of resources and diverse population, too many American firms have squandered their inherent advantages by surrendering the means of production to foreign companies. Despite the popularity of such concepts as post-industrialism, industrialism remains the central challenge for the American economy. Our future as the world's preeminent economic power lies squarely upon our ability to simultaneously outproduce, outconceive and outmarket the foreign competition. Going beyond theory, we discuss, particularly in the fifth chapter, American companies that, by remaining committed to the industrial challenge, have found the means to succeed in the international marketplace.

Finally, there is a spiritual point to our book. American business people like to think of themselves as the ultimate pragmatists. Yet when the United States first embarked on its historic odyssey, American companies were suffused with a spirit born of their democratic beliefs and their own sense of national manifest destiny. Today much has changed, but the need for a sense of mission, for an ethical firmament upon which to operate, remains powerful. As the Wall Street crash of 1987 all too plainly revealed, blind reliance on financial instrumentalities alone is not enough to build world-competitive companies. In the wake of the crash, American business desperately needs to consider other values, including many stemming from Asian roots, that give meaning and discipline to an enterprise.

We are acutely aware that many may be offended by the direction of this book. Outsiders ourselves, an immigrant from Japan and the grandson of Russian Jewish immigrants, we openly challenge notions of racial identity and geopolitical reality that have animated the nation's leadership for generations. As Californians, we naturally have advocated ideas that gain much of their essential inspiration from experiences in our diverse and somewhat rootless state, far from the traditional centers of American intellectual and political life.

Yet at its core, this work is not about rejecting the past, but finding a way to perpetuate America's mission—its essential message of economic, political and cultural liberty—in the coming century. For this reason we have constructed our vision for the future of the United States upon a foundation built by those who came long before our own forebears. It is to their great vision of a nation consisting of freely associating individuals that we have dedicated our efforts.

"America is the race of races"

Walt Whitman,
PREFACE TO THE FIRST EDITION OF *Leaves of Grass*, 1855

1

Post-European America

As it enters its Third Century under the Constitution, the United States confronts unprecedented questions concerning its essential character, its mission as a nation and its ultimate destiny. Until this decade, Americans comfortably identified themselves as the vanguard of a European-based Western civilization that since the 1600s imposed its will on all the other peoples of the world.

Today that once-supreme confidence in the superiority of the West no longer fits reality. In 1900, Europe itself accounted for more than 36 percent of world trade and controlled much of the commerce of Asia, Africa and North America. Its great empires now only a memory, by 1980 Europe's share of world commerce had shrunken considerably. Today the world's economic center lies not along either side of the Atlantic, but among the nations of Asia, which increasingly account for the largest share of international commerce.

This enormous shift in the center of economic gravity necessitates a redefinition of America's political, economic and cultural allegiances. In 1960, America's trade with Asia was less than half its trade with Europe; within twenty years, the total Asia-bound volume surpassed trade with all of Europe. By 1986, the transpacific commerce of the United States reached $215 billion, exceeding by over 50 percent trade with Western Europe. And by 1995, according to the President's Commission on Industrial Competitiveness, the volume will be *twice* that with the Atlantic-facing world.

1

American society itself is also going through a similar process of de-Europeanization. Today the Pacific Basin countries constitute the largest source of new legal immigrants, with Europeans accounting for barely one in ten newcomers. Currently the object of the greatest wave of immigration since the 1900s, the United States is no longer simply a melting pot of various European peoples, but an emerging "world nation," with ethnic ties to virtually every race and region on the planet. By the end of the United States' Third Century, an absolute majority of Americans may be descended from people who came from somewhere other than Europe.

For many, these changes threaten long-cherished ideas about the nation's racial identity, its traditional Atlantic ties and its ways of doing business. Identifying with the fate of Europe, some Americans see the ascendency of Asia as a harbinger of national decline. Yet the United States need not be imprisoned by its prior associations. Through the openness of its culture and its political system, its racial diversity and the entrepreneurial dynamism of its economy, America can assume a pivotal, indeed preeminent, position in the emerging post-European international order.

The first order of business in building a successful American future lies in the Pacific. Today the Asia-Pacific region represents the crucible of the ascendent new economic forces. With the highest economic growth rates in the world, this region since 1960 has boosted its share of the international economy threefold. As late as 1960, the gross national product (GNP) of Japan was smaller than that of Great Britain, France or West Germany. By 1986, the gross national product of that small island-nation exceeded that of Britain and France *combined* by over 30 percent, and is twice that of West Germany.

Today Japan stands uncontested—next to the United States—as the non-Communist world's foremost economic power. Home to eight of the world's ten largest public companies, it ranks first in industrial endeavors from steel production to consumer electronics to industrial robots. By the late 1980s, Japan also has emerged as the world's leading financial power. When Martin Mayer published his best-selling *The Bankers* in 1974, American, German, French and British banks received detailed treatment but, reflecting the general outlook of the Western nations, Japanese financial institutions were virtually ignored. A decade later, Japan had come to control over one-fourth of international banking assets—slightly more than the United States and almost three times the share of any single European nation—and boasted seven of the world's ten largest banks.

But even as Japan reaches the economic pinnacle, its place as Number One is rapidly being challenged by other ascendent Asian nations. From grinding poverty only a quarter of a century ago, the newly industrializing economies of Asia—Hong Kong, Taiwan, Singapore and South Korea—have enjoyed the developing world's fastest economic advances. Although in 1982 they represented only 2 percent of the population of the developing world, these economies accounted for almost 7 percent of the total GNP of the developing world, almost 20 percent of its trade and nearly 60 percent of its manufactured exports. Once virtually destitute, South Korea today boasts an economy larger than such industrialized European nations as Denmark and Austria. Korean officials believe this is just the beginning. "We'll overtake Britain in less than twenty years," predicts Yu Hee Yol, director of technology transfer at South Korea's Ministry of Science and Technology.

Although still desperately poor, China, the mother civilization of all the Asia-Pacific countries, is also emerging as one of the world's largest and fastest-growing economies. Between 1977 and 1985, China in real terms doubled its national income while quintupling its trade turnover as measured in dollars. In 1984 alone, China's growth was larger than the *entire* GNP of South Korea.

Owing to this rapid growth and the region's enormous population (by 1991, the Asia-Pacific region will be home to nearly two-thirds of the world's people), Asia is the most critical marketplace in America's economic future. Japan, second-largest trading partner of the United States after Canada, already represents the United States' largest overseas customer for semiconductors and semiconductor equipment, as well as agricultural products.

U.S. trade with other Asian nations has grown even more quickly. By 1986, American commerce with the economies controlled by the 46 million members of the Chinese diaspora in Taiwan, Singapore, Malaysia, Hong Kong and Indonesia had already surpassed the 1980 levels of bilateral trade with Japan. Between 1970 and 1985, the share of total U.S. exports consumed by the newly industrializing economies (NICs) of Asia— Korea, Hong Kong, Taiwan and Singapore—increased by 85 percent.

Beginning from virtually nothing a decade ago, America's trade with China has risen to approximately $8 billion in 1986. Today the United States is China's second-largest overseas trading partner after Japan. Even with its per capita income at only $400, by the mid-1990s, according to estimates made by University of Washington's Nicholas Lardy, China could rank among the four or five top trading nations in the world.

In stark contrast, American markets in Europe have been shrinking, with the continent's share of U.S. exports down by nearly 12 percent between 1970 and 1985. Nor do the prospects for an expansion of the European market seem bright. In the wake of the great "European miracle" of the 1950s and 1960s, the 1980s ushered in a period of decline on the continent, with Europe's economic growth rates falling well below those of both Asia and the United States. And despite massive "targeting" by governmental agencies, the worldwide share of high-technology industries in three top European economies (Great Britain, France and West Germany) dropped nearly 13 percent between 1980 and 1984. During the same period, the United States and Japan, the dominant global forces in high technology, increased their share by 22 percent.

Increasingly concerned with its diminishing technological leadership, Western Europe in the 1980s has become markedly more protectionist toward both Asia and the United States. Once the dominant traders of the world, Western Europeans today conduct the vast preponderance of their commerce among themselves and, increasingly, with the controlled economies of Eastern Europe and particularly the Soviet Union.

Even the much-discussed plans for European economic unification in 1992 cannot obscure the harbingers of continental decline: a decade of flat levels of industrial investment, rising unemployment, slow growth rates and fading technological leadership. Yet many residents in and admirers of Europe—the world's most brilliant economic force for nearly half a millennium—have only slowly perceived its eclipse. "Europeans do not often see their own decline," observes Jean Rimboud, chairman of French-based Schlumberger. "They do not believe in it, just as a traveler does not sense that the boat is moving down the river because the current is too regular."

And even if somehow Europe manages to correct its current economic deterioration, demographic trends seem almost certain to reduce its role as a marketplace. In its era of great expansion during the eighteenth and nineteenth centuries, Europe experienced an unprecedented population explosion, both creating a large urban work force and spurring the colonization of much of the globe. Today large-scale immigration, mostly from Asia and Latin America, keeps the U.S. population growing, but Europe's reluctance to admit newcomers consigns it to a rapidly aging, and eventually shrinking, population.

Since 1975, West Germany has suffered a net loss of 1 million people, and if present demographic trends continue, its current population of 61 million could be cut in half by the year 2050. By the turn of the next century, most other major Western European nations—including Great Britain and perhaps even Italy and France—are also likely to begin to experience population decreases. Demographers estimate that by 1990 Europe could account for less than 10 percent of the world's consumption of goods and services, a figure that could drop to little more than 6 percent early in the next century. The era of Europe as the home of the world's preeminent metropolitan areas is also coming to a close: By the year 2000, six of the ten largest cities in the world will be on the Pacific; none will be European. "In demographic terms," remarks former French prime minister Jacques Chirac, "Europe is vanishing."

Sokojikara

Nearly three decades ago a young African psychiatrist named Franz Fanon announced that with the breakup of the colonialist regime and the rise of the Third World, "the European game has ended." Yet in the wake of that decline, the United States—

a former European colony—was, in Fanon's words, itself becoming a "monster," playing a doomed role as successor to the faded imperialism of its mother continent.

As long as America continues to play Europe's "monster," or follow its model, the nation will be destined to share its fate. For many, the defeat in Vietnam at the hands of technologically backward Asians marred the beginning of America's decline as the world's premier economic and political power. In this view, the nation's best course—like that of Europe—is to protect itself from the ascendency of the non-Caucasian races by finding a comfortable but subordinate niche in the world economy. In his widely acclaimed *The End of the American Era*, published in 1970, Cornell University's Andrew Hacker argued:

> This sort of abdication is by no means unprecedented: virtually every European nation has relinquished its role as a world power and is now content to attend to ordering its domestic arrangements. There is much to be said for being a Denmark or a Sweden, even a Great Britain or France or Italy.

More recently, the nation's severe economic setbacks at the hands of a now technologically sophisticated Asia have served to increase the appeal of such views. Instead of urging that the United States rise to meet the industrial challenge of Asia, many liberal observers—including John Kenneth Galbraith; Bernard Nossiter, former London correspondent for *The Washington Post*; and the *New York Times*'s Anthony Lewis—have suggested that Americans adopt Great Britain (a nation in the midst of a century-long decline) as the model for the upcoming "postindustrial age." Similar sentiments echo in Walter Russell Mead's 1987 book *Mortal Splendor*, which details a strategy for economic and political retrenchment. Here Mead states that "Our governing assumption . . . our compass, is that the decline will continue."

Nor is this only the view of intellectuals on the nation's liberal fringe. Lawrence Krause, a former senior fellow and Asia expert at the prestigious Brookings Institution, suggests that American political and economic leaders accept a "shift to Japanese hegemony" similar to the adjustment that occurred when the

United States supplanted Great Britain as the dominant global power in the 1930s. "Japan is replacing the United States as the world's strongest economic power," Krause told the Joint Economic Committee of the Congress in December 1986. "It is in everyone's interest that the transition go smoothly."

Such views reflect a profound and dangerous misreading of both the historic strengths of the United States and the rapid changes now taking place in Asia. In dramatic ways, the United States is in the process of a major metamorphosis from a European outlook to a more multiracial, and particularly Asian, orientation. America's economy, society and culture are moving along novel and virtually unexplored paths. The United States need not share the fate of Europe.

In contrast to most Europeans, for instance, Americans are not prisoners of a national culture dependent on a specific racial identity. The United States may have flirted tragically with European-style imperialism, but its economic system and national self-image have not been bound to a now-lost dominion over the non-European world.

Simply put, America has never been a racial or cultural motherland in the sense of *La France* or *Dai Nippon*. From its earliest days, the United States always has been something of a "world nation." The notion of revolutionary America as purely Anglo-Saxon, noted Thomas Paine in 1776, was a distinctly "false" one. In revolutionary Pennsylvania, for instance, Germans represented a majority of the population while Englishmen constituted less than a third. In 1790, before the final ratification of the Constitution, Anglo-Saxons constituted slightly less than 50 percent of the nation's population. Far from viewing America as merely an offshoot of English civilization, revolutionaries such as Paine saw the destiny of the New World as the "asylum for mankind."

Equally crucial has been the comparatively free nature of the American economic system. In contrast to tradition-bound societies such as Europe or Japan, the United States always has functioned as an "open system," without a technocratic elite national bureaucracy to ensure that transitions go "smoothly" along predetermined paths. Although such transitions are often painful, the willingness to bear their impact and the ability to recover reflects a deep-seated, if often unappreciated, source of strength.

"America has the material and spiritual requirements to be a world leader for many years," notes Dr. Fuji Kamiya, a leading social commentator and professor at Tokyo's Keio University. "Vietnam may have been a major setback. For any other country it would have been fatal. It showed the reserve strength, the *sokojikara* [reserve power] and youth of America."

Sokojikara represents one of the hidden assets of the American system. In its first century, the republic exploited this reserve power through the development of the frontier and a successful defense of national independence from the powerful states of Europe. In its second century, massive waves of European immigration and capital actualized the nation's latent strength, transforming the one-time colony into the master of the Atlantic world. Today, at the dawn of the third century, *sokojikara* again expresses itself in the shift from an Atlantic-oriented, predominantly European country to a multiracial "world nation" with strengthening ties to both ascendent Asia and the Third World. This also means that the United States has a kind of communication network, particularly with Asian countries, unmatched by any other major economic power.

America's *sokojikara* rests upon ideas shaped in the nation's early history. Oswald Spengler once noted that "*underlying the nation is an Idea*" (italics original). China's "Middle Kingdom" had its Confucian system and a strong belief in its emperor. Rome's greatness was based on its sense of order and imperial destiny. Britain's empire found its justification in a belief in its own constitution and a unique "civilizing mission." The mission of America, although often obscured and even betrayed, has been, as Thomas Jefferson wrote, to serve as "an empire for liberty," a land where change takes place through the free will of its people.

Indeed, even before American independence the British philosopher John Locke, who had a seminal influence on virtually all the revolutionary thinkers, saw not a people, or a nation, but a unique opportunity to create a new kind of society out of a state of nature. "In the beginning," wrote Locke, "all the World was America." To create "this new kind of society," the founders established a political economy radically different from those prevailing in Europe. Upon seizing power from colonial authorities, for instance, the revolutionaries abolished much of what held together the rankings of European society, such as state religion and primogeniture. In opposition to the controlled systems of obligation and mercantilism of Europe, the architects of the Republic sought what their contemporary Adam Smith called "the natural system of perfect liberty." "Whether as entrepreneur or worker," observed economic historian Louis M. Hacker, "the American was again a free man: to found new towns, open his establishment, move where he pleased, and trade where and when and under whatever conditions he chose."

In these early times the open system did not often benefit the lower classes, and certainly remained out of reach of both blacks and Indians. Yet these principles remain both revolutionary and, in modern times, unique in their emphasis on the autonomy of economic life. In contrast, most modern doctrines —communism, socialism, fascism, even social democracy—seek the expansion of the controlling power of the state. "America is conservative," noted Swedish sociologist Gunnar Myrdal, ". . . but the principles conserved are liberal and some, indeed, are radical."

Even today the "radical" nature of these ideas still holds a powerful appeal, particularly in Asia and the Third World. The last few years have seen repeated drives by essentially middle-class constituencies—in countries including Korea, the Philippines and Argentina—to gain the sort of economic and political self-determination pioneered by the United States. And when 50,000 Chinese students demonstrated in Shanghai's People's Square in late December 1986, they waved banners depicting the Statue of Liberty and a Chinese dragon bound in chains. Emblazoned on the banners were calls for such values as "democracy, human rights and freedom."

This, of course, does not mean Asians have become identified any more closely with the defense or foreign-policy positions of the American government. Korean students and intellectuals have been highly critical of the "corrupting" American influence and past support for the military dictatorship. Yet many in the leadership of the opposition, including

Kim Dae Jung, have lived in the United States and received strong backing for the democratization drive from the growing Korean community in the United States.

The appeal of America's "open system" is equally profound in China, particularly among the young. To individuals such as Xu Dong, a former leader of Mao's militant Red Guard, America's appeal lies largely in the freedom granted for economic innovation and cultural expression. Involved in raising funds for a chain of video-game parlors in Beijing, Xu finds his inspiration in his "American heroes," entrepreneurs such as Walt Disney, MacDonald's founder Ray Kroc and Silicon Valley impresario Nolan Bushnell. "Of course one can learn from the socialist system," Xu explained carefully. "But the most important thing is to be independent and think for yourself."

Indeed, in times in which the leading institutions of the nation seem almost hopelessly inept and even venal, many observers raised in other countries have come to recognize America's unique self-renewing power, its *sokojikara*. "America shares equally in the crisis that afflicts all developed countries," notes Austrian-born management expert Peter Drucker. "But in entrepreneurship—in creating the different and the new—the United States is way out in front."

Fear of Asia

To take advantage of its unique strengths, America in its Third Century must undergo a radical reevaluation of its basic historical, cultural and even racial attitudes. "Each age," wrote the American historian Frederick Jackson Turner, "writes the history of the past anew with reference to conditions uppermost in its time." In its Third Century, this means reexamining the country's past relationships with non-European peoples, both at home and abroad.

There is a great need to revise historical attitudes that reflect centuries of both fear and misunderstanding of Asia. Schooled from childhood in an essentially European world view, most Americans naturally view the rising tide of Asian, or of any nonwhite, power with discomfort and foreboding. Even our language betrays us. We all unconsciously identify the United States with the "West"—the combination of Europe and North America—in opposition to the East or Asia. In an otherwise perceptive report called "Toward the Pacific Century," for instance, the *Economist* matter-of-factly describes the industrial strategy of "Japan against the West, primarily America." In both America and Europe, ascendent Asia—even in its capitalist form—is regarded as dangerous. Surveying the rise of the Asian economies, Steffan Linder, a former fellow at the Hoover Institution at Stanford and a Swedish Minister of Trade, concluded:

> There is no denying the unease felt in the West. The vitality of the Asian-Pacific countries, and the self-confidence radiating from Japan and the East Asian hub in particular, is affecting the standing of the West. . . . The Asian-Pacific advances are widely regarded as a threat.

This point of view has roots deep in the collective unconscious of Europe and, consequently, of the United States. From the days of the Roman Empire until the late Middle Ages, Europe lived in terror of Asiatic invaders. And when the earliest European explorers arrived in China, they were confronted by a society whose material and scientific achievements had been for centuries superior to their own. Up until the early nineteenth century, both China and Japan successfully restricted European entry to a few places in their homelands, usually far from the centers of power. Only advances in military technology—evidenced by the firepower of Commodore Perry's ships in Tokyo's harbor—forced the great Asian powers to allow Europeans full access to their markets.

Yet even after Europe's supremacy had been clearly established, Asia—its strange social and governmental systems, huge continental land mass and enormous population—loomed as a vague, dark threat in the European imagination. As early as 1873, English politicians fretted over the eventual industrialization of China as a potential challenge to European industrial supremacy. Even before German historian Oswald Spengler published his famous *Decline of the West* in the late 1920s, Germany's Kaiser Wilhelm worried obsessively about "the yellow races'' and was outspoken enough on the topic to propel Japanese leaders into the Allied camp.

Wilhelm's paranoia found support in the writings of a host of influential thinkers—including Houston Stewart Chamberlain, Joseph Arthur de Goubineau and Vacher de LePogue—who detailed elaborate theories about the supposed supremacy of the northern European. In its final and most perverse form, of course, this racist sentiment set the stage for the appearance of Adolf Hitler. Despite his alliance of convenience with Japan, Hitler saw as the ultimate mission of Germany to wage Europe's war against the ''lesser breeds'' of Russia, Asia, Africa and America.

Many white Americans, with their long history of antipathy toward blacks, Indians and all other ''non-Europeans,'' also resisted bitterly the presence of Asians in the United States. In 1910, Theodore A. Bell, the Democratic candidate for Governor of California, stated:

> It took our branch of the human race thousands of years to develop into our present stage of civilization. . . . it is essential that the blood of the American-European of this country who, together with their ancestors, developed civilization to its current state, should be kept pure and free from the taint of the decadent orientation of China, Japan and India. We wish them well in their own countries, but we do not want them in ours.

Through the often convoluted logic of racism, Asians in America have been attacked simultaneously as both subhumans and fearsome economic competitors. Under heavy pressure from Californians and other Westerners who feared their formidable economic drive, the Chinese in 1881 became the first race specifically banned from immigration to this country. ''The racial differences between Americans and Asiatics would never be overcome,'' explained the otherwise moderate labor leader Samuel Gompers, one of exclusion's strongest champions. ''The superior whites had to exclude the inferior Asiatics, by law, or, if necessary, by force of arms.''

With its powerful modernizing impulse, Japan was particularly terrifying to those concerned with "inferior Asiatics." Back in 1909 Homer Lea, a prominent American military officer, wrote an influential tome entitled *The Valor of Ignorance*, prophesying the eventual capture of America's West Coast by the Japanese army. Reflecting the prevailing northern European prejudice of his time, Lea maintained that the growing presence of "foreign non-Anglo Saxon" elements in the population would make the United States easy prey for a homogeneous and highly disciplined Imperial Japan. This fear was fully vented during the Second World War, when the Japanese became the only American immigrant group ever deprived wholesale of its rights and interned in concentration camps. As one U.S. senator explained:

> A Japanese born on our soil is a subject of Japan under Japanese law; therefore he owes allegiance to Japan. . . . The Japanese are among the worst enemies. They are cowardly and immoral. They are different from Americans in every conceivable way, and no Japanese . . . should have the right to claim American citizenship.

While such racially tinged ideas do not make for polite dinner conversations, much less popular literature, the emergence of Asian economic power still unsettles the consciousness of America. Lea's "samurai" has been largely replaced by the Japanese or Korean businessman in a Western suit, but the fear and resentment remain. Asian economic success—in contrast to competition from European or Latin American nations such as Brazil—provokes the shrillest political rhetoric.

The racial overtones are often not far from the surface. In 1986, a U.S. trade representative, Michael Smith, according to a *Wall Street Journal* report, openly referred to Japanese as "nippers." Texas businessman Henry C. Grover has sold thousands of bumper stickers with the legend "Remember Pearl Harbor: Save American Jobs." Explains Grover: "The Japanese have never forgiven us for whipping them in World War Two. They've been evening the score by destroying American industry."

Sometimes "Asia-bashing" also breaks out on the streets,

where incidents of violence against Asians jumped 62 percent between 1985 and 1986. In Los Angeles County, center of the nation's largest concentration of Asians, violence against Asians accounted for 50 percent of racial incidents in 1986, up from only 15 percent the previous year. And in Boston, longtime hotbed of racial agitation against blacks, anti-Asian incidents in 1986 accounted for 29 percent of racial crimes, up from just 2 percent five years earlier. In a 1982 incident, a Detroit auto worker, blaming Asians for problems in his industry, beat a young Chinese to death with a baseball bat. For his crime, he received only three years' probation and a $3,700 fine. The worker's 1987 federal jury trial for violating the Asian-American's civil rights ended in acquittal.

No such comparable hostility accompanies relations with Europe's still-potent exporters. European trade surpluses, largely the result of a neomercantilist economic policy similar to that of Japan, incite only a tiny portion of the wrath directed against the island-nation. Sales of BMWs and Mercedes might slow the production runs of Cadillacs and Lincolns, but no labor union members hack up German sedans as they have Japanese. And when a French company, Schlumberger, bought Fairchild Semiconductor, there was little outcry. But Fujitsu's attempt a few years later to buy the firm from Schlumberger ran into a series of roadblocks from both the Reagan administration and Congress, eventually clearing the way for its purchase by National Semiconductor.

The fact is that in today's supposedly cosmopolitan United States, the Europeans can invest at record rates and freely trade in American markets without causing widespread concern. But the success of a nation such as Japan, springing from such alien cultural roots, engenders a very different kind of response. As the late Theodore White commented:

> The Germans, somehow, evoke little American bitterness because we understand their culture, establish American plants there without hindrance. The Japanese provoke American wrath because they are a locked and closed civilization that reciprocates our hushed fear with veiled contempt.

The Politics of Disillusionment

In the near future, this "wrath," however misplaced, is almost certain to increase. There is, in fact no *easy* response to Asia's ascendency. Certainly the nostrums popular in the early 1980s have not provided adequate response. While Reagan's free-market economic policies have helped spark an enormous entrepreneurial and consumer spending boom, other aspects of his "politics of imperial nostalgia," as historian Joel Kreiger describes them, have caused severe, long-term problems. Centered on the seemingly contradictory policies of a massive defense buildup and tax cuts, the Reagan policies have helped cause a mounting pattern of budget and trade deficits which, noted a joint statement signed by five former Commerce secretaries, already has caused "serious damage" to the national economy and could "wreak even more havoc in the coming decades and beyond."

Under such circumstances, it is not surprising that a growing atmosphere of disillusionment and economic drift characterizes the late 1980s. The great market crash of October 1987 was a dramatic manifestation of the underlying nervousness about a wildly volatile stock market. Public confidence in the nation's leading economic institutions, bolstered in the early years of the Reagan presidency, once again have slid to historically low levels. In terms of meeting foreign competition, according to pollster Louis Harris, only one American in four believes that the nation's corporations are doing a good job, a drop from more than one in three in 1979. In 1966, 60 percent of the population had confidence in big business; by 1987, the figure had dropped to a pathetic 16 percent—below people's confidence in Congress and the Executive branch and nearly at the abysmal level of admiration accorded the legal profession.

These low opinions reflect, to some extent, a tremendous lack of confidence on the part of business leaders themselves. Even before the most spectacular rise in the trade deficit, a poll made up predominantly of leading corporate executives—conducted by Yankelovich, Skelly and White—predicted Japanese predominance into the 1990s in a host of industries from consumer electronics, steel and automobiles to robotics and semiconductors. The surveyors noted:

The leaders who were surveyed appear to betray a psychology of self-effacement. There is a subtle hint of defeatism about our prospects for success—this from many of the men and women who are and will be the architects of America's response to Japan.

Even those who are not so ready to admit the inevitability of decline insist that any future resurgence can only come at the sacrifice of much that in the past characterized American economic life. Until now the American economy has remained a remarkably open system—characterized by relatively uncontrolled access to capital, new business formations, bankruptcies and all the other messy turbulence of free-market capitalism.

In such an atmosphere, there is a growing tendency among liberals and conservatives alike to urge the basic abandonment of this "open system." The whole post-Reagan political atmosphere seems to be colored by acceptance of the superiority of foreign role models that embrace mercantilist strategies using government policy and planning to develop and maintain trade surpluses. As the economic debacle of the Depression provoked a surge of interest in such European-bred authoritarian systems as fascism and communism, today's setbacks have led to a new fascination with the industrial policies of other countries.

Kevin Phillips, a leading conservative intellectual, openly calls for a tough-minded "nationalist" business strategy roughly similar to the "neomercantilist business-government partnerships" characteristic of Japan, Gaullist France, Korea, Brazil and Taiwan. "American businessmen, facing foreign competition underwritten by business-government partnerships," notes Phillips, "must set aside old concepts of laissez-faire and adjust to—even advocate—new kinds of business-government collaboration."

At the other end of the political spectrum, Ezra Vogel's *Japan as Number One*, as one commentator noted, "opened the gates" for a generation of neoliberal thinkers. Vogel's prescriptions embody the *idealized* strengths of the Japanese system. At the core is the creation of "a small core of permanent high level bureaucrats," similar to the Tokyo University-trained elite that runs Japan's Ministry of International Trade and Industry (MITI).

These elite bureaucrats would then consult with top political, business and labor officials, proving both a "communitarian vision" and "an industrial and trade policy" for the nation.

In his *M-Form Society*, William Ouchi, author of the best-selling *Theory Z*, lays out in more precise terms how this "communitarian vision" could be implemented here in America. In his vision, Ouchi calls for the creation of "advisory councils" that would help a MITI-like bureaucracy shape economic policy. The principal council would draw exclusively from the elites of academic, business, labor and political circles. Even journalists would have their place, although Ouchi admits he would feel more "comfortable" if on the more important councils membership would be restricted only to editors of sufficiently established major publications such as the *New York Times*.

Such a program has a natural appeal to those already in high positions within the nation's most powerful institutions. But for entrepreneurs—one of the crucial catalysts of America's *sokojikara*—it could prove disastrous. With its emphasis on behind-the-doors consultation and bureaucratic elites, the political-economic system in Japan, as Vogel himself points out, tends to "tilt" policy toward corporate stability and big business rather than encourage the economic turbulence that fosters new, emerging companies.

But such a predominance of institutions over entrepreneurs is of little concern to most who share the "communitarian vision." Recalling the logic of John Kenneth Galbraith's *New Industrial State*, many of today's new statists reject the traditional American faith in the individual entrepreneur as the engine of economic growth. Walter Russell Mead, a strong though pessimistic advocate of the "new statism," dismisses entrepreneurs as "baby dinosaurs" set for extinction.

Similarly, Robert Reich, perhaps the most influential of the new statists, urges Americans to abandon the legend of Horatio Alger, the central *leitmotif* of the American economic dream and leave "the myth of the self-made man" behind forever. The new realities of international trade, Reich argues, have made the entrepreneur—with his limited capital and human resources—a poor economic risk. Because he "short-circuits progress," "opportunistic individualism" is no longer appropriate to "our place in the world."

To meet the challenge of world competition, Reich maintains, Americans should discard their traditional faith in individuals and turn instead to "the stewardship" of government and business leaders. Rather than look toward the American "open system," Reich and other new statists maintain that the best blueprints for the future lie in ministerial and corporate offices in Tokyo, Bonn and Paris. Through superior control and organization, Reich argues, these nations have found the means for an economy to "adjust" from declining industries:

> The recent progress achieved by Japan and several European countries, and America's relative decline, require no convoluted explanations. For largely historical reasons these countries are organized for economic adaptation. And for largely historical reasons America is not.

The Open System

To a nation once certain of its unique historic mission, the widespread yearning for foreign models represents a major psychological watershed. Yet to scrap the "open system" would amount to discarding not only a prime source of the nation's self-renewing *sokojikara*, but also much of the American political heritage.

As victims of the mercantilist state of George III, the founders of the Republic instinctively sought to prevent the pervasive intermingling of commerce and government. Control and protection of industries by quasi-governmental agencies circumscribed colonial commerce. Hatters, nail makers and other British industries had succeeded in banning competitors in the colonies. Under such circumstances, it is understandable that frustrated colonial entrepreneurs such as Benjamin Franklin railed against "the extreme corruption" of Britain's "old rotten state" with its "numberless and needless places, enormous salaries, pensions, perquisites, bribes, groundless quarrels, foolish expeditions, false accounts and no accounts, contracts and jobs [that] devour all revenue. . . .''

To assure that the young United States would not follow the path of Britain, the shapers of the Republic developed an ''open system'' designed to prevent the overconcentration of economic and political power. Economic growth, although affected by government, was left largely in the hands of the entrepreneur and to the marketplace. And rather than seek a politics based on a ''communitarian vision,'' the framers of the Constitution sought a government that would regulate the competition between factions, rather than impose harmony upon them. James Madison, for instance, recognized ''the inevitability of contention'' as part of the natural order of things. Such acceptance of diversity and competition, observe historians Nathan Rosenberg and L. E. Birdzell, provided an ideal basis for the future capitalist expansion of the nation.

Against better organized and centralized force, however, the ''open system'' often has appeared a poor match for more centrally directed powers. Nazi Germany and Imperial Japan—or, more recently, the mercantilist nations of Europe and Asia—all made quick early gains at the expense of America's relatively unfettered political economy. Yet in the long run, the centralized states tend to lack the crucial *sokojikara* to adjust to changing conditions through the development of new technology and competitive environments.

In the early national period, a comparatively weak America seemed easy prey for the centralized economic and military powerhouses of Europe, who often considered the new United States as an embarrassing and even dangerous revolutionary presence. ''For a century after the American Revolution,'' writes historian R. R. Palmer, ''. . . partisans of the revolutionary or liberal movements in Europe looked upon the United States generally with approval, and European conservatives viewed it with hostility or downright contempt.''

Faced with such ''contempt,'' America's early leaders had to take strong steps to defend their ''empire for liberty.'' Britain— which Madison called the ''Leviathan . . . which aims to swallow all that floats on the ocean''—posed a particular problem. Through such things as the ''dumping'' of products, the unlawful seizures of U.S. vessels and mercantilistic exclusion of American entrepreneurs from its vast colonial markets, Britain seemed determined, as Secretary of State James Monroe put it, to "recolonize our commerce."

Like the Japanese in the years just after World War II and the Koreans more recently, Americans—despite the antimercantilist sentiments of Jefferson and even Alexander Hamilton—resorted to baldly protectionist measures, including high tariffs and embargos. Yet it would be invalid to suggest, as have Robert Reich and other advocates of a "communitarian vision," that America's prosperity was largely the product of governmental intervention beginning with Hamilton's days at the Treasury. As Keiji Tajima—a Japanese scholar of the early national period—points out, such a conclusion is invalid since Hamilton's oft-cited program of targeted industrial development was never implemented.

This is not to say that the government did nothing. Pressed by Henry Clay and his American System, Congress did provide some degree of tariff protection for American industry while diplomats struggled for "reciprocity" in order to improve U.S. access to overseas markets. Governmental bodies also invested in the development of the vast nation's transportation infrastructure, although even here the bulk of financing was arranged privately or through the various states, with most of the actual capital flowing from private sources.

The crucial difference between European and American economic development lay in the obtrusiveness of the government role. At a time when government bureaucracy grew to massive proportions in European capitals (the French government in the first half of the nineteenth century took *four times* the share of gross domestic product in percentage terms than its counterpart in the United States), Washington grew less quickly than did the rest of the nation. The attorney general in the Jeffersonian era, for example, did not even have a clerk, and worked out of his home.

Where the ideals of the Revolution and the reality of the early United States tended towards decentralization, in Europe after the French Revolution, as Alexis de Tocqueville noted, the irrevocable tendency was toward "centralization." Largely unrestrained by the Constitutional notion of limited powers, European central governments played a far larger role, as business historian Alfred D. Chandler has observed, in national economic development. At the famous London Crystal Palace Exhibition of 1851, for instance, most European exhibits were funded from government sources, while their American counterparts, as exhibitor Benjamin P. Johnson recalled proudly, were virtually alone in being *"without aid or assistance"* of the state. The success of the exhibition, Johnson maintained, reflected "the peculiar advantages of our free institutions in the development of the energies of the people. . . ."

And, indeed, far more than the controlled systems of Europe, America's "open system" sparked rapid economic change. Old methods of production were constantly overturned through the immigration of craftsmen and skilled mechanics from Europe—a sort of human "technology transfer." The lack of government monopolies and social restrictions common to Europe led to the rapid application of these techniques, often by men outside the established classes. All this provided the conditions for what the Austrian economist Joseph Schumpeter would later call "creative destruction." America's pace of change, entrepreneurial vigor and social mobility staggered European visitors. As de Tocqueville wrote in the 1830s:

> I know of no country, indeed, where the love of money has taken stronger hold on the affections of men and where a profounder contempt is expressed for the theory of the permanent equality of property. But wealth circulates with inconceivable rapidity, and experience shows that it is rare to find two succeeding generations in the full enjoyment of it.

America's European Era

After the conclusion of the Civil War, the American economy began attracting the first great flows of foreign capital. A primary focus was railroad stocks. In 1853, Europeans held a bare one-tenth of all U.S. rail securities. By 1870, the figure had doubled to 20 percent, and, at century's end, it reached as much as one-third, with the lion's share—some $2.5 billion—controlled from London. Even Andrew Carnegie's fortune as the ultimate American industrialist derived largely from his role as agent for U.S. firms in placing bonds with British and German financiers. So great were America's financial ties to the mother continent that Karl Marx, with some justification, could call America "economically speaking" a "colony of Europe."

An even more crucial import from Europe was people, now coming from outside the traditional origins in the British Isles and the Germanic countries. While the native-born population grew sixfold between 1840 and 1930, the population comprised of immigrants and their children—from the largely depressed regions of southern and eastern Europe—expanded by thirteen times. By 1930, these newcomers constituted one-third of the American nation.

The dawn of the twentieth century saw the economy of the United States clearly surpassing for the first time its financial colonizers, with American GNP growth from the period between the Civil War and World War I more than twice that of England and three times that of France. Yet even as it surpassed Europe by draining its excess capital and restless population, the United States began trying on the imperial garb fashionable among the nations of the mother continent. Continental imperialism had long been at the center of the national character; the American version pushed west, displacing the Indians, Mexicans and, occasionally, Europeans. But when its continental empire was assured at the turn of the century, this "empire for liberty" started looking for other lands and peoples to dominate. With European imperialists controlling much of Asia, Oceania and Africa, many Americans felt it was time to join in the expropriation of the nonwhite world.

Navy captain Alfred Thayer Mahan, who was to become one of the great theorists of the new imperialism, saw in the American "impulse toward expansion" part of a "sentiment that has swept over the European world within the last few decades." Thus America would become a true "European power," intervening with impunity in Latin America, establishing colonies in Asia and vassal states in supposedly "liberated" lands such as Cuba. Much the same spirit also animated a Princeton academic named Woodrow Wilson. The future president, and hero of liberals, believed firmly in the basic prerogative of Europeans to dictate to non-Europeans. Writing in the *Atlantic Monthly* in 1910, Wilson said:

> The East is to be transformed . . . the standards of the West are to be imposed upon it; nations and peoples who have stood still for centuries through are to be quickened, and to be made part of the universal world of commerce and of ideas which have so steadily been a-making by the advance of European power from age to age. It is our peculiar duty, as it is also England's, to moderate the process in the interests of liberty: to impart to the people thus driven out along the road of change . . . our own principles of self-help; *teach them order and self-control* in the midst of change. [Italics original]

By the end of the First World War, the process had come full circle. At Versailles, Paine's "asylum for mankind" worked in concert with both the great European imperial powers and a newly emergent Japan in carving up the former colonial possessions of the defeated Germany and Turkey. For the first time, national interests and aspirations locked firmly on a European beacon. "Our real competition, the competition which means most to us," noted *Nation's Business* in 1925, "comes from Europe."

This European tilt reflected economic realities of the time. Although Europe's economic power was perceptibly fading in comparison to both North America and Asia, the continent still clearly dominated the world economy. As late as the early 1930s, Europe and its vast colonial possessions accounted for over half of world trade, while America's transpacific trade in 1929 accounted for only one-fourth of that with Europe.

Even when Japan launched a direct attack on U.S. territory, these long-standing economic ties—along with powerful social and cultural ones—lent the European theater a greater urgency and higher priority. Throughout the war, U.S. Pacific Commander General Douglas MacArthur complained bitterly about the "North Atlantic isolationism" of the War Department. The southwestern Pacific theater benefited from only about 15 percent of America's total war expenditures while accounting for over one-third of its casualties.

This movement toward Europeanization was accelerated as many of the continent's leading academics, artists and scientists—including Albert Einstein, Leo Szillard, Hannah Arendt and Thomas Mann—migrated to the United States. Many of their less famous compatriots took up key positions in academia, the arts and journalism. This "Europeanizing of American culture," as Laura Fermi described it, was perhaps most strongly felt in New York. Populated with the wholesale importation of European talent, by the end of the war New York effectively replaced London and Paris as the world's leading cultural center while remaining very much in the traditional European cultural mold.

The fusion of the nation's self-image with Europe—along with fear of Russia—became even more evident after the war. Although President Roosevelt embraced the traditional American values of anticolonialism, his successor Truman, supported by the dominant Eurocentric faction in the State Department, tragically chose to support the return of Asian colonies to their former masters. Secretary of State Dean Acheson believed that America's interests in the colonies "coincide with the interests of European metropolitan countries." With an ease born of a misapplied sense of European *realpolitick*, Acheson saw "no clear moral 'rights' and 'wrongs' " in the colonial question.

This European bias also expressed itself in the direction of American aid and investment. American net foreign aid to Germany between 1945 and 1952 reached over $3.7 billion, far above the $2.1 billion given to more populous Japan. Overall, Europe received nearly $28 billion, over four times the amount allocated for all of Asia.

Even the American view of the Communist threat in Asia was dominated by European prejudice. Mao and his Red Army had seized China largely on their own, but Dean Rusk, later to be secretary of state, then assistant secretary of state for Far Eastern affairs, could only see "a Slavic Manchukuo." In the estimation of many American policymakers, Russia now led the "Asiatic hordes." The notion that Asian Communists might seek to direct their own fate, independent of the Soviet Union, was barely considered.

Eventually all Americans would pay dearly for such views, with John F. Kennedy's advisors—men David Halberstam would later call "the best and the brightest"—carrying into the 1960s views about "the East" enunciated years earlier by their high-minded precursor, Woodrow Wilson. But Asians—Communist or not—were no longer willing to listen to the good schoolmasters from America. For two decades, with helplessly deepening commitment, the United States tried to impose its will on Vietnam, in the end, as historian Barbara Tuchman has noted, succeeding only in "betraying" its own traditions:

> In the illusion of omnipotence, American policy makers took it for granted that on a given aim, especially in Asia, American will could be made to prevail. . . . "Nation-building" was the most presumptuous of the illusions. Settlers to the North American continent had built a nation from Plymouth Rock to Valley Forge to the fulfilled frontier, yet failed to learn from success that elsewhere, too, only the inhabitants can make the process work.

The Third Century and Beyond

To date, a similar inability to grasp Asian realities also has characterized the American response to the region's rising capitalist economies. Throughout the first two decades following the close of the last world war, America's corporate elite persisted in a single-minded fixation on the European market. By 1966, American business had invested over $16 billion in Europe, but during the same time period investment in the vast Asia-Pacific region spanning Japan, Southeast Asia and India amounted to a mere $4.2 billion.

In contrast to their enthusiasm for even devastated enemy countries such as Germany and Italy, American investors were, *Business Week* reported in 1953, "wary" of opportunities in Japan. The nation was seen as weak, vulnerable to Communist subversion and plagued by chronic trade deficits. Ravaged by war and bereft of overseas investment, Japan was decidedly a weak link, ranking fifteenth in world trade, behind even Belgium and the Netherlands.

Even in the early 1960s, when Japan's economy clearly had recovered, smug American and European business leaders continued to view the Japanese with condescension, echoing the opinion of French president Charles DeGaulle, who after a 1962 encounter with Japanese prime minister Hayato Ikeda remarked, "I had the impression I was meeting a transistor salesman rather than a Prime Minister." Like the Vietnamese guerrilla in black pajamas, Japanese—and later Korean and Chinese—entrepreneurs were frequently underestimated by American and European executives. Even as Japanese corporations were taking the market share from American companies around the globe, executives like Simon Ramo, then vice-chairman of TRW Corporation, continued to believe that this country had an unbreakable lock on the economic future. "Only the United States," he predicted confidently, "has the unique combination of resources, the people, the science and technology to respond."

In the emerging reality of its Third Century, such attitudes can only assure a continuing progression of humiliations and setbacks. America's Third Century—the era of Asia—has arrived. The nation's prime economic challenge and its greatest future opportunities now arise from the lands bordering the Pacific. With international trade, including both imports and exports, presently accounting for nearly a quarter of the American *industrial* economy, up from less than 10 percent in 1960, Americans can scarcely afford not to address the aspirations and needs of their largest potential competitors and overseas trading partners.

Yet all too often American business people act as if the world economy were still dictated by the Anglo-American, the European and the white man. Many Americans simply find it easier to concentrate their activities in markets at home and in more familiar Europe. When the U.S. Census Bureau's Center for International Research published a report on consumer trends in China, for instance, only a handful of Americans paid the $500 fee for the information, while at the same time over 700

Japanese companies signed up. Similarly, a 1987 mailing by the Taiwanese government concerning its market opportunities sent to 2,000 firms in New York State received only fifteen responses.

To succeed in its Third Century, the United States must engineer a radical reappraisal of its world view. The moment approaches when the future must be confronted—or forever lost. Decisions to concentrate on protecting status-quo markets, either domestic or in Europe, may seem to make sense in the short run, but assure almost certain obsolescence in the world now being born.

Already the Japanese, masters of international marketing, are moving aggressively into the expanding new markets of Asia. Between 1970 and 1982, Japan increased its share of exports to Southeast Asia by almost 13 percent and now accounts for two-fifths of the region's imports. While American firms like General Electric have been reducing employment in locations such as Singapore, Japanese investment in these countries has been rising rapidly. In 1986, Japan's total investment in the region outpaced investment by the United States by 50 percent, with over 1,400 Japanese-affiliated firms building textile, steel, auto and other plants.

In India, where English is the language of both business and government, Japan is rapidly eroding the United States' long-held position as their largest non-Communist trading partner. In 1970–71, the United States accounted for over 27 percent of India's total imports. A little over a decade later that figure had shrunk to under 10 percent, while Japan increased its share from less than 5 percent to 7.5 percent. Despite its poverty, India is a significant market for American business. With a GNP growth rate between 1973 and 1985 of over 4.3 percent, India already boasts a larger economy than Spain. Its expanding middle class, although still only 7 percent of its millions, already outnumbers the *total* population of France.

But when this Indian middle class begins buying cars, it is likely they will be of Japanese design. By the mid-1980s, firms such as Toyota, Nissan and Suzuki maneuvered themselves into a key position as suppliers of parts, technology and components for India's infant automobile industry. And even in General Motors' fledgling venture with Hindustan Motors, the cars will use engines from yet another Japanese manufacturer, Isuzu.

Indeed, as American automobile companies seek out Asians to supply their own domestic market, their Japanese competitors have been busily staking out strategic positions as suppliers to the young Korean, Taiwanese and Malaysian car industries.

Much the same process is taking place in China. Once a relatively minor force in Hong Kong, which is the chief entrepôt to the vast Chinese mainland, Japan today exports more to the Crown Colony than any nation except the People's Republic of China. It has also stepped up its investment activity. In 1986 Japanese investment in the Crown Colony jumped to $502 million, a more than threefold leap from the previous year. As recently as 1976, only one Japanese department store maintained an outlet in the world's shopping paradise. By 1988 more than half a dozen different Japanese store chains had established local operations, sharing among them a combined 30 percent of the local market.

This emphasis on emerging Asian markets was even more plain when the Japanese in the early 1970s—at a time when firms from virtually every other country had written off China's consumer market—launched advertising campaigns to promote electronics and household goods. By the early 1980s, Japan emerged as China's dominant overseas trading partner, accounting for roughly one-third of all its imports—more than the share of the United States and the European Economic Community combined. Even with the post-1985 cutbacks owing to changes in Chinese government policy, Japan remains China's dominant source of consumer durable imports while at the same time the Japanese are playing a central role in the development of China's own growing manufacturing capacity. One joint venture between China and Hitachi, for instance, already accounts for 27 percent of China's total domestic television production.

In its refusal to break with its past marketing strategies, American business is playing demographic suicide. "When U.S. firms spend their resources fending off intrusions from Asia and focusing their marketing strategies on Europe, their view is

shortsighted,'' warns Doris Walsh in *American Demographics*.
"The Japanese leave no stone unturned. Once the Japanese have
a hold on a growing market, it will be hard for American companies to compete."

Yet despite such setbacks, there exist within the nation today
many of the elements that can lead to a renewed American preeminence in its Third Century. The large influx of new immigrants from India, China and Southeast Asia provides the United
States with unprecedented social, cultural and economic ties to
most of the ascendent nations of Asia. Through their complex
interactions with the rest of American society, these newcomers
can also help shift the nation from its traditional European moor-
ings toward a more multiracial and multicultural identity.

The new Americans from Asia give the United States the
energy, connections and knowhow required to break down many
of the barriers that long have stood in the way of profitable
relations with the nonwhite world. Many immigrants, for instance, bring with them an Asian-bred capitalist dynamism.
Through them, Americans can learn many effective management ideas, born of Confucian roots, particularly with regard to
the importance of commitment to employees, customers and
suppliers. By synthesizing ideas bred in Japan, Hong Kong,
Taiwan or Korea with the entrepreneurial spirit of the United
States, American business can forge an effective economic response.

Indeed, despite the notions of American decline fashionable
among many in the intellectual establishment, the United States
has at its disposal the tools for a new ascendency. The dawning
of new industrial powers does not necessarily mean the setting
of the American sun. Drawing on the "open system" be-
queathed by its founders, enriched by its status as a world nation
and the favored area for foreign investment, the United States
can flourish anew in the age of Asia. In the words of Stephen
Vincent Benét:

> *Call on the great words spoken that remain*
> *Like the great stars of evening, the fixed stars*
> *But that is not enough.*

*The dead are mighty and a part of us
And yet the dead are dead.
This is our world,
Our time, our choice, our anguish, our decision.*

2

The Pacific Crucible

As a young man growing up during the 1950s in the drab tenements of Glasgow, Scotland, Bill Elder looked out at a world that seemed to be dying. Both the old Murray and Sons steel mill down the street and the Upper Clyde Shipbuilders five miles to the south, the latter once among the world's premier shipyards, were in the midst of rapid consolidation. As more of the business shifted overseas, more of the great bays grew rusty from disuse.

Even as he studied engineering at Paisley Technical College just outside of town, Elder made plans to emigrate to America. After working a couple of years at the Upper Clyde Shipbuilders, Elder boarded an airplane for San Francisco, where he hoped to find work in one of the key centers of America's shipbuilding industry. Yet when he arrived at Hunter's Point, he found the once-proud shipyard closed. America's shipbuilding industry—like that of his native Glasgow—had fallen victim to the relentless drive of Japanese industry.

After working at California Blue Shield and rising rapidly through the ranks, Elder joined Fairchild Semiconductor in 1970, then a leader in the still-emerging integrated-circuit industry. When Fairchild set up a consumer-products division, Elder was sent to Hong Kong as head of production. There Elder was impressed that, amidst the crowded and dreary living conditions, the economy seemed to be growing at an amazing rate. "I was dazzled by the tremendous dynamism, the efficiency I saw there," Elder recalls. "In spite of having all that congestion and poor housing, the economy just throbbed. The attitude was totally different from that in Glasgow. Everyone was trying to make it. In Glasgow, people accepted the status quo and went on the dole. In Hong Kong, if you didn't work you'd sleep on the street.''

In 1977, Elder signed on to become vice-president of the Kasper Instruments Division of Eaton Semiconductor Equipment. Suddenly, dealing with Asia took on a quite different dimension. American semiconductor wafer-processing equipment was then the accepted technological world leader. Yet despite this edge, in Japan—where semiconductor-manufacturing capacity was growing the fastest—he could hardly make a sale. Even worse, the company's one-time Japanese partner had begun manufacturing a suspiciously similar piece of equipment. He would fly two or three times annually to Japan, but to no avail. ''I could not get any results in Japan,'' he recalled. ''I hated Japan. I dreaded going there.''

In 1981, Elder founded Genus, a firm specializing in highly advanced equipment used in the manufacturing of high-density semiconductors. Despite his earlier aversion, Elder now found he could no longer avoid Japan, which between 1981 and 1986 emerged as the world's leading producer of semiconductors. Under such conditions, Elder had to sell his chemical wafer-processing equipment—at between $500,000 and $800,000—in Japan, or fold up his operation. He saw the Japanese share of the wafer-fabrication-equipment market jump one-third between 1982 and 1985, accounting for nearly 40 percent of the world total.

To break into Japan, Elder reached an agreement with a division of C. Itoh and Company. Rather than merely dispatch a marketing man to the island nation, Elder went himself, three times a year, to develop a close personal relationship with the C. Itoh executives. Today that investment in time, and understanding, has paid off. Now over one-third of his sales are to Japan alone, with significant and growing sales to Korea and Taiwan—each of which contributes as much revenue as does all of Elder's native Europe.

In the future, Elder believes Genus's survival will depend increasingly on his success in selling to Japan, Korea and Taiwan, the nations that will, along with the United States, dominate the microelectronics industry in the decades to come. "The key will be winning in Asia," explains Elder. "If we lose our market share in Asia, it will be the end for us. Japan forces us to be on the cutting edge. If we cannot do it, then we will lose out, not only there but everywhere. We Americans must face Asia or end up as a second-rate country."

A Hawk Hides Its Claws

To survive in America's Third Century, U.S. business must first understand the economic spirit behind Asia's dramatic bid for industrial hegemony. This spirit expresses itself in a thousand, often seemingly contradictory ways. Authoritarian generals in Korea, Communist cadres in China, Chinese entrepreneurs in Taiwan and Japanese corporate executives may differ in many of the essentials, but they are united by a common desire to see their peoples *restored* to what they regard as their rightful role on the stage of human history.

Today's Asian renaissance—like Europe's earlier hegemony—is based largely on the strength of its manufacturing. Some observers, such as *Megatrends* author John Naisbitt, see nothing ominous in this rapid industrial ascendency. Naisbitt even urges American companies to abandon the "declining sport" of manufacturing to the Asian countries. In his view, Asians can be left to perform the mundane tasks while Americans reap rich profits by dominating such "postindustrial" fields as high technology, banking and other services. The New York Stock Exchange, in a 1984 proclamation, echoed this ideology, claiming "a strong manufacturing sector is not a requisite for a prosperous economy."

Such beliefs perhaps represent the greatest contribution of the United States to the continuing ascendency of East Asian nations. Because it forgot the connection between production and the entire cycle of creating new product ideas, marketing and the long-term creation of wealth, American business has been caught by surprise by the new muscle of Asian companies—particularly in banking, securities, real estate and insurance—who are now free to spend the wealth accumulated through their proficiency at Naisbitt's "declining sport." Less than three years after the issuance of its anti-industrial *pronunciamento*, the total value of shares traded on the New York Stock Exchange fell to second place behind those on Tokyo's exchange. At the same time, America's electronics trade balance with Japan approached levels earlier associated only with such smokestack industries as automobiles.

In this context, the rapid movement of Asian nations into ever higher value-added production represents perhaps the most significant economic fact of America's Third Century. As recently as the late 1960s, Americans concerned about the future of science-based industries considered as their primary competitors the Soviet Union and the nations of Western Europe. And even by the early 1970s, when Japan's technological sophistication could no longer be denied, *Forbes* described the other nations of Asia as "economically speaking, children, who need to be cured of childhood illnesses and taught many skills, some of them elementary."

And for the most part, Japanese and other Asians have been generally content to parrot back American stereotypes about how incapable they are of innovation, fit only for sweatshop subcontracting, as the assembly house for prototypes from the United States. "You do what you do best and let us do what we do best," suggests George Koo, managing director for the international division of Hambrecht and Quist. A man long involved in soliciting American companies for Taiwanese high-tech manufacturing ventures, Koo remarked, "Americans are great at inventing and marketing products, but we are the ones who know how to manufacture well and cheaply."

Yet in their careful, often self-deprecating comments these Asians reflect the old Japanese proverb that "the true hawk hides its claws." Although nations such as Taiwan and Korea have clung to the favorable trading terms accorded to developing nations, these economies increasingly have little in common—except to serve as bracing role models—with their struggling brethren in Latin America, Africa and the Indian subcontinent.

Taiwan's industrial ascendency up the value-added scale epitomizes the nature of the manufacturing-based Asian rise. Once known largely for its cheap garments, which accounted for 35 percent of overseas sales in 1971, Taiwan in the 1970s—mostly thanks to large investments from American companies such as RCA—emerged as a major producer of consumer-electronics products such as radios and television. By 1980, following the path established by the Japanese, Taiwan's garment industry represented less than one-fifth of all its exports, while high-technology products began to edge out consumer electronics. In 1985, Taiwan's sales of computers, peripherals and components reached over $1.3 billion, a number the government predicts will more than triple by the end of the decade.

But simply making computers does not fulfill the ambitions of many Taiwanese entrepreneurs and government officials. Now the target is the very areas—involving innovation, research and development—that hitherto have been considered the special domain of more advanced industrial economies. Even as their American salespeople extolled a natural "division of labor," by the end of 1987 Taiwanese government officials spent well over $200 million to turn a favorite offshore "manufacturing platform" into a center for new research and development.

In part this is a response to a remarkable success that has driven factory wages up over 15 percent annually during the early 1980s and the rapid migration of labor-intensive jobs to lower-cost locales such as Malaysia and Thailand. Long known as the technology "piracy capital of the world," Taiwan now increasingly stresses the development of homegrown technologies. No longer able to sell cheap labor, the country's over 350,000 corporations now seek to sell their brainpower rather than cheap labor. They can offer engineering expertise for a third of the cost of comparably skilled Americans. In an attempt to lure back some 50,000 foreign-educated expatriates, the bulk of whom live in the United States, the government is offering a package that includes grants and tax awards, and even has built a sparkling new Silicon Valley-style science park in Hsinchu, an hour from Taipei and complete with jogging tracks and condo clusters. Says Choh G. Li, director general of the Hsinchu facility: "This is the cradle of the new Taiwan."

The undisputed role model for this rapid movement up the value-added scale remains Japan. For over four decades the Japanese protected their domestic markets from foreign competition and investment while systematically moving up the value-added scale. As recently as 1960, textiles accounted for nearly one-third of all Japanese exports. During the next ten years the nation expanded rapidly into such fields as shipbuilding, steel and consumer electronics. In the wake of the 1973 oil shock, Japanese leaders, concerned about the costs of their own energy consumption, accelerated their move into newer, more technologically intensive fields. In 1974, Masaya Miyoshi, chief economist of the Keidanren, the nation's most influential business group, declared that Japan would now "challenge the long-established position of America and many European countries in products of high technology. We have no choice."

And, indeed, since the mid-1970s, Japan's net exports of technology have surpassed its imports; by 1977, Japanese firms were filing three times as many patents as those in West Germany and over 50 percent more than those in the United States. By 1980, Japan depended on textiles for only 5 percent of its exports; for the first time it passed West Germany to become the world's second leading exporter of high-technology products. By 1986, Japan produced almost four times as many semiconductors as did all European countries combined, and had also established worldwide leadership in such key future sectors as robotics, fiber optics and magnetics.

Perhaps the most accomplished student of the Japanese example has been its former colony, Korea. A quarter of a century ago, Korea had a per capita annual income of only $87, ranking among the world's poorest societies. But by the 1970s, Korea, like its role model, started making dramatic progress up the value-added scale. Though largely dependent on food-based products, textiles and raw materials for much of its exports in 1970, within six years the machinery and transportation-equipment component of Korea's exports had more than doubled. Aided by cheap government loans and subsidies, Korea's dominant *chaebol*—large trading and industrial conglomerates similar to Japan's *keiretsu* groupings—launched a major drive into heavy industries such as steel and shipbuilding. By the early 1980s, Korea—a nation the size of New York State—boasted both the world's largest ship and steel structures yard as well as its most efficient steel mill. By 1985, Korea's per capita income had reached nearly $2,000—among the highest in the developing world.

More recently, Korean *chaebol* such as Hyundai have shocked the world with their success in the complex and competitive automobile business. Within one year after entering the Canadian market in 1984, Hyundai's Excel—with its Japanese engine—was that nation's leading imported car. In 1986, the company entered the car-seller's bazaar of the United States and, selling over 160,000 cars, broke a first-year record for an import. By the end of 1987, Hyundai—only two years after entering the market—was expected to pass Volkswagen, Suburu and Mazda to become the nation's fourth-leading imported car. And true to their higher-value-added strategy, Hyundai officials now seek to add more profitable middle-market lines to augment the compact Excels. "Within three to five years," said Hyundai of America's Max Jamiesson, "we'd like to have a range of models like that enjoyed by Honda."

Automobiles are not the only field in which the Koreans have challenged Japanese supremacy. Ever since the early 1970s the Koreans, like the Taiwanese, have been focusing much of their attention on the electronics field, with Korea emerging by 1986 as the world's sixth-largest manufacturer of electronic goods. By that time, Korean manufacturers provided nearly one-tenth of all the consumer electronics imported by the United States, including almost one-third of all televisions. And although they have captured only 5 percent of the VCR market, their lower costs are already leading some Japanese electronics firms to abandon the lower end of the market, while hoping to continue their lucrative role as key components suppliers. "The Koreans have had an absolutely major impact on the consumer electronics market," observes Robert Gerson, editor of *This Week in Consumer Electronics*. "The impact has been almost twice as big as the Japanese had in the early days."

Japanese also have reason for concern about Korean progress in semiconductor production, where in 1986 Koreans increased their exports by 42 percent to $1.4 billion. By linking up with American firms—including Advanced MicroDevices, AT&T and Micron—they have gained the technology that is cutting into the Japanese market share in such fields as dynamic RAMs. "In the less advanced end of the business there is an opportunity for them to play a big role,'' admits Yasuo Miyauchi, a senior managing director of Hitachi. "They will be competitors with us.''

But like Taiwan, Korea has no intention of remaining in "the less advanced end.'' Previously, Korean companies had been largely content to depend on technology imported from Japan, with whom they have concluded more than 1,500 technology licensing agreements, and to a lesser extent from the United States. But more recently Korean officials and *chaebol* executives increasingly have emphasized the development of their homegrown technological prowess. Spending on research and development between 1981 and 1985, for instance, rose fivefold to over 2 percent of GNP. Firms such as Samsung Electronics and Daewoo Telecom now spend as much as 10 percent of sales in research and development, a figure comparable to that of their U.S. and Japanese rivals.

As they move into such advanced industries as semiconductors and computers, these firms make up a ripe market for the sort of sophisticated equipment sold by Bill Elder's Genus. But even this dependency, insists Kang Bak Kwang, a leading official of the national Ministry of Science and Industry, could soon be broken as the nation attempts to telescope the industrial progress of Europe, Japan and America into less than twenty years. "Right now we have to send students abroad to get adequate manpower in science and engineering,'' Kang explains. "We also have to buy all our equipment abroad. But in a generation we will have our own.''

One indication of the seriousness of this potential can be seen in the rapid development of Daewoo's Telecom subsidiary. Between 1980 and 1986, the unit's sales rose from $3.5 million to over $150 million. Using technology licensed from such companies as Fujitsu, Sanyo and Northern Telecom, Daewoo is making strides where even the Japanese have met only limited success. Its personal computer, marketed as The Leading Edge, was described in 1986's *Consumer Reports* as "the best buy among IBM compatibles,'' taking in that year a share of the business PC market equal to the leading Japanese exporter, Epson, which had been working assiduously since 1982 to penetrate the U.S. market. Although to date the market share of the

Koreans remains relatively small and their products generally uninspired, their aspiration is to supplant what has been one of the brightest industrial performers in the American economy. "In a very short time Korea will be the base for personal computer manufacturing in all of the world," boasts B. C. Lee, founder of Qnix, a small software and accessory firm.

Such claims may be a bit grandiose for a nation of 41 million, with a limited industrial infrastructure and severely unstable political conditions. But the great Asian drive toward higher-value-added products and services is also spreading to China, whose vast market and resources—despite its current poverty and burdensome Communist bureaucracy—make it a potential economic superpower.

Nowhere is the potential of China more developed than in the vast region between Hong Kong and the Chinese provincial capital of Canton. Though many of Hong Kong's entrepreneurs fear the 1997 reunification with China, these inveterate capitalists also provide 60 percent of the direct foreign investment inside China. Spurred by massive investment—over $1 billion poured into the Shenzhen border region economic zone in just eighteen months during 1985–86—neighboring Guangdong Province now boasts per capita incomes three times the Chinese national average and, in 1986, overtook Shanghai to become the leading exporter among all of China's provinces. "This isn't China anymore," notes an American consular official in Canton. "It's the new Hong Kong and it wants to become the new Los Angeles." One sees the very landscape along the Pearl River being leveled to make way for shiny, California-style industrial parks.

In the process of pushing once-sleepy Guangdong into an industrial megalopolis, Hong Kong's growing links with China are accelerating its own rapid movement up the value-added scale. Once heavily dependent on low-cost manufacturing, the Crown Colony—with its large cadre of English-speaking, highly educated Chinese—now finds its growth centers more on high-technology and fashion design, as well as banking and trade services. Between 1975 and 1985, for instance, the manufacturing share of Hong Kong's gross domestic product dropped to 22 percent, roughly similar to that of the United States. Since the early 1980s, manufacturing jobs dropped nearly 10 percent, but

Hong Kong's unemployment rate remained low owing to an upsurge in service jobs, which grew nearly 30 percent during the same period. Over the ten years between 1975 and 1985, the Crown Colony's total service exports jumped fivefold, to over $6 billion.

The China connection is also transforming the nature of the manufacturing that takes place in the Crown Colony. In the garment and textile industries, for example, which now account for more than 40 percent of Hong Kong's industrial employment and exports, there has been a dramatic shift in emphasis. For decades, the bargain basements of America have been stocked with clothes labeled ''Made in Hong Kong.'' But today it is just as likely that those cheap garments are made in China, where labor rates are as little as one-third of those of the British possession. In fact, many of these Chinese factories were started in collaboration with Hong Kong firms such as synthetic leather maker Wong Po-yan's United Overseas Enterprises, S. M. Ko's Grace Garments and Soco Textile Hong Kong.

While Chinese-based factories take over the low end of the garment trade, Hong Kong's local industry has been moving decidedly upscale. Today, Hong Kong already has become the manufacturing center for high-fashion lines such as Giorgio Armani, Abercrombie & Fitch and Christian Dior. Like Japan in the late 1970s, Hong Kong is also developing its own fashion designers and stylists. Demand for Hong Kong Polytechnic's fashion-design courses outpaces available slots by nine to one. And some prominent designers, including Patrick Lung and Diane Freis, the latter an expatriate from Los Angeles, already boast their own lines. Prominent U.S. companies such as Esprit, which have traditionally relied on the the sewing skills of the locals, now hire Hong Kong-based designers as well.

Few people from Hong Kong epitomize these changes more than Eddie Lau. Born into a working-class family, Lau left school at thirteen to work in one of the city's garment factories. After a brief stint to study design in London, he returned to Hong Kong in his early twenties, and started designing and sewing clothes for Hong Kong's secretaries, working in his own 100-square-foot studio. Now in his mid-thirties, Lau currently designs high-fashion clothes, manufactured in local factories, for trendy boutiques as far away as Europe and Japan. But increasingly his most important client is the Chinese government, which is seeking to develop an original look for its own burgeoning garment industry.

"Together, Hong Kong and China will emerge as the new fashion center," predicts Lau as he sits in his posh Kowloon boutique. "When China takes over, we will have an identity to match with our skills. China will need designers to reach out to the world, and they will find them here."

Many Chinese, once confined to the monotony of Mao jackets and drab Stalin-era clothes for women, are certainly anxious to emulate Lau. His lectures in Shanghai and other Chinese cities draw overflow crowds. Nor is it likely that these suddenly fashion-conscious Chinese will wish to depend for long on their Hong Kong cousins. At the 38th Middle School in Canton, the most popular class is fashion design. A factory attached to the school produces Pierre Cardin jeans, but for the teenagers studying old *Vogue* magazines in their dank classroom, the future means more than a job bent over a sewing machine. "Their older brothers and sisters were happy to get a job in the factory making clothes," notes Chen Yi, the school's principal. "The younger ones want to design them."

A similar process of interaction between the two economies is also taking place in technology. Hong Kong electronics manufacturers want to make the same move into the research and new-product field already being pioneered by the Taiwanese and the Koreans, with their labor-intensive operations shifting to China. "We are perfectly placed to provide the interface between China and the West," notes Stephen Cheong, a lawyer who is a key member of Hong Kong's "Establishment." "For thirty years, we have developed and absorbed modern technology while China was cut off. Now, we have the educated people, the technicians and the managers to tap China's resources and markets. This is our future role."

Perhaps even more than the people of Hong Kong and Singapore, the Chinese are sensitive to issues of economic imperialism, especially from Japan and the West. In the short run, the new managers of the Chinese economy will probably be content to offer a manufacturing platform for more developed trading partners, both in Asia and in the West. But like their capitalist cousins in Taiwan and Hong Kong, they look with confidence to the day when they will be designing, developing and marketing their own product lines, for both internal consumption and export. During the first six months of 1987, China's electronics output expanded nearly 50 percent, while shipments of its locally built microcomputers increased more than fivefold.

The Cambridge-educated Cheong is already preparing for his own movement up the value-added line. Along with his associate Alan Lee—a former high-ranking executive with Ampex Corporation in the Far East—Cheong has built a new factory in Dongguan, a city once known mainly for its excellent lichees, to produce laminates for printed-circuit boards. For the first time, the factory gives the People's Republic a capacity to produce printed-circuit boards that meet IBM's standards, setting the stage for entree into the huge, multibillion-dollar Far East market for such products.

Although the partners approach the joint venture with different ideologies and interests, their purpose remains the same: to build a world-class high-technology corridor from Hong Kong to Canton. By the twenty-first century, believes Cheong, the entire Pearl River Delta will rival such areas as the industrial corridor between Tokyo and Osaka, the northeast corridor or the southern California industrial megalopolis.

"We will start with just the assembly, the simple part," predicts Wang Guorun, a high-ranking Communist cadre and vice-mayor of Dongguan. "Then we will move on. We are building the firm foundation for a major electronic industry here. We want to produce it and design it all right here. We will make that leap in a very short time."

The Triumph of the Confucianists

The rapid progress of the East Asian economies reflects not only recent changes, but the continued transmission of their ancient value system to the modern world. Centered on Confucian precepts concerning the sanctity of social relationships and the importance of order, these values forged societies that often surpassed the economic and technological development of Europe.

Asians have a deep consciousness of their past predominance. Even as the Hellenistic and Roman empires blossomed, China built its own *imperium*. And when Europe collapsed into semi-barbarism, China developed the world's most advanced civilization, as the originator of paper, gunpowder and the printing press. Even as late as the mid-eighteenth century, admiring Europeans such as Leibniz and Voltaire considered the Chinese Confucian system a role model which European monarchs should, in the words of Voltaire, "admire and blush—but above all imitate."

The habits bred by such long-standing superiority led many in China at first to reject European-style science, industry and capitalism. Although some Chinese intellectuals advocated the abolishment of Confucianism in their societies—equivalent to abolishing all Christian influences in the United States—a more predominant view held that Western ideas and the Confucian system were utterly incompatible. "The barbarians do not recognize the moral obligations between ruler and minister, father and son, elder brother and younger brother, husband and wife," argued Chu I Hsin, an important late-nineteenth-century Confucian scholar. "Barbarian institutions are based on barbarian principles."

Yet over time many Asians—impressed by the superior material and military power of the Europeans—sought ways to blend Confucian precepts with modern European economic systems. Rather than accepting the Lockean concept of a "state of nature," the Asian societies have generally tended toward careful cultivation, insulating and controlling their social and economic conditions to the greatest extent possible. Even with the massive flows of products, information and capital across the Pacific, the ancient virtues still find expression.

At the center lies an attempt to maintain the traditionally strong cocoon of social and psychological supports. Rather than being an unalloyed pursuit of profit, capitalist motives are often interwoven with an evolving set of duties and obligations. Among the over 46 million overseas Chinese who have little in the way of strong political loyalties, the key emphasis is on serving the interests of the family and its trusted retainers.

K. S. Chung, an entrepreneur reared in Canton and Singapore, learned the Confucian fundamentals at home. Today he instructs his children and grandchildren in the same principles. At eighty-three, Chung heads over thirty family-owned enterprises spread from Bangkok and Hong Kong to Los Angeles and Zurich, with 1986 sales of over $100 million. A man of simple tastes and unpretentious appearance, Chung rejects the "Western notion" of the totally self-interested entrepreneur who considers his success proof of basic superiority. In truth the "superior man" achieves the Confucian quality of *jen* by being gentle, responsive, charitable and selfless in the service of others:

> The highest duty of man is to create and produce. You should not think you are lucky, due to the environment's whimsical position, to be placed in the responsible position of planning a productive project. To be successful, you have to enlist other people's willing cooperation. . . . In other words, according to Confucian humanism, all men are born spiritually equal though they may not be materialistically the same. You have to treat everyone with respect and dignity. . . . This will encourage him to contribute his best effort in cooperation.

According to Chung, the entrepreneurial attainment of personal material goods is secondary to the promotion of a common interest with others, particularly within the clan and its followers. This approach explains much of why entrepreneurs throughout Asia—whether in controlled systems or in the free-for-all of Hong Kong—often approach their enterprises with a longer-range, fundamentally group-oriented mentality. Within the Chung operations this has meant a willingness to absorb losses for as long as five years in developing such diverse new businesses as growing tobacco in Thailand or selling microcomputers in mainland China. Large sums are also set aside to send family members, and trusted retainers, for advanced training at schools in both Europe and the United States.

"Our goal is not just to make money this year or next," notes

Chung's son and heir apparent Wing, an engineer trained at the University of California at Berkeley and at Columbia University. "We think in terms of passing the company on to our children and their children. Nothing we do really makes sense unless you see it in the context of the family." These attitudes are not confined to Asia; our new immigrants bring them to business and life in the United States.

In Japan, Korea and some other Asian states, this profound sense of long-term commitment often has been made to extend to the nation as well. Confronted by foreign Western powers armed with vastly superior economic, military and technological power, the samurai behind the 1868 Meiji Restoration overthrew the decaying shogunate and consciously sought to remold the social structure to encourage commerce and industry, the pursuit of money, as being the best way to defend the nation. Yet they, too, recoiled at the prospect of becoming "Westernized."

The Meiji leaders' solution was "Western technology, Eastern spirit." The reformers essentially turned the pursuit of profit, previously classified as despicable, into a noble pursuit—the balance-sheet equivalent of the samurai sword. Yet the ethics remained, as in the Chung family, founded on something other than short-term ego gratification. Profits were necessary, but not primary. Even as they urged adoption of the latest Western technologies and economic systems, the Meiji leaders sought to preserve traditional Confucian values. As Eiichi Shibusawa, one of Japan's earliest industrial leaders, wrote in 1873:

Those who return from abroad . . . cite how much better than in Japan is everything in those countries, not only their cities, their currencies, land reclamation methods and commerce, but their armies, scholarship, parliamentary processes, laws, steam and electrical power, clothing and machines. For the advancement of our civilization, they declare that Japan must emulate the West in all these things. . . .

Yet if the form of things is given too great an emphasis and the substance is neglected, government will go against its people; institutions will thrive while the people are impoverished, and living standards may rise while the strength of the nation withers. For all the merits of foreign things, the nation itself will risk bankruptcy before it even has seen success. . . .

The kind of capitalism created by men such as Shibusawa allowed for continuation of many of the hierarchies that have characterized Asian societies for millennia. Rather than adapt the profit-seeking, transactional mentality of the British or American entrepreneur—guided only by Adam Smith's "invisible hand"—the Asian entrepreneur was expected to inculcate many of the values of the Confucian gentleman or feudal samurai. In either of those systems, making money for money's sake was tantamount to unethical behavior. As the old samurai teaching put it: "Nothing is more important to the samurai than duty. Second in importance comes life, and then money."

This commitment to broader national goals was further strengthened by a web of dependent relationships between entrepreneurs and the state. From the earliest Meiji period, government directly subsidized some activities, such as building a merchant fleet, while using its procurement policies to openly favor domestic producers.

Individual citizens were urged to purchase Japanese rather than foreign goods whenever possible. Key industries, such as shipping firms and railways, were kept out of foreign hands, and even purchases of capital goods, long imported from Europe or America, were reduced substantially. In 1930, for instance, Westinghouse was encouraged to sell its Japanese operations to Mitsubishi Denki Kabushiki, since Japan's big-three electrical equipment makers—the other two being Shibura (the prewar predecessor of Toshiba) and Hitachi—were now deemed sufficient to serve the Japanese market and even to export.

As the nation prepared for war, the concentration of power in the hands of giant *zaibatsu*, or "money cliques," such as Mitsubishi was seen as crucial to laying the foundation for the sort of heavy, world-class industry needed for modern warfare. By the outbreak of war, about a dozen of these *zaibatsu* controlled 80 percent of Japan's industrial, commercial and financial enterprises.

With substantial modification, this system survived the attempts of postwar Occupation authorities to create more of an American-style "open system." After World War II, occupation authorities broke up the traditional *zaibatsu* groupings, widely seen as at least partially responsible for Japan's aggressive overseas adventurism and antidemocratic tendency. But soon the old hierarchies and ideas began to reassert themselves. This was in part strengthened by developments during the war which, as Kiichiro Sato, the former chairman of Mitsui Bank, once noted, made it "second nature with us to uphold a planned, controlled economy."

When the American authorities started to abandon their reform policies, the traditional elites reasserted themselves. A rejuvenated Japanese bureaucracy immediately returned to the old policy of concentrating the nation's then-scarce resources of capital, technology and government contracts into large corporate groupings, or *keiretsu*, albeit this time under the control of managers rather than family hierarchs. By the late 1960s, the prewar Mitsubishi group, which included the manufacturer of the renowned World War II Zero fighter, was ascendent once again under the direction of management rather than family, controlling better than 10 percent of the nation's exports. In each of the twenty major industries in Japan, firms affiliated with the former big-three *zaibatsu*—Mitsubishi, Sumitomo and Mitsui— accounted for between 30 and 100 percent of total production. Today, however, no one in Japan wields anything like the power of the original *zaibatsu* families.

Small business was also encouraged but largely relegated to the position of captive subcontractors, dependent on the large groups even for financing, or as "mom and pop" retail operations. To keep away the still vastly more powerful American multinationals, the new leaders also followed the Meiji model of protecting domestic industry from foreign products and investment. They kept Japan a *sakoku*, or closed country, while allowing local companies to compete fiercely for the growing domestic market as a precondition for later export activity.

Out of the economic crisis of the postwar period arose a system that found career bureaucrats steering the professional politicians in the basic development of the economy. Faced with chronic trade deficits, the elite bureaucrats guided the economy through tax incentives, loans and direct consultation between business leaders and government. "Throughout the 1950s the Japanese government operated and perfected what is recognized as a model of the state-guided capitalist developmental system," explains Chalmers Johnson of the University of California at Berkeley, a leading expert on Japan's economic and political development. "This system worked phenomenally well in Japan."

As usual, success soon bred its imitators. Other Asian nations—including Taiwan, Singapore and Korea—soon looked increasingly toward Japan as a model of development. Sharing the same basic Confucian traditions, these nations all laid out elaborate, albeit differing, strategies for following the Japanese example. Even Communist China, with a historical loathing for Japan, at times has looked to Japan as its model of state-nurtured, yet market-driven economic growth.

But the most astounding student of Japan has been Korea. As subjects at one time of the Japanese, the Koreans had long, first-hand experience with its methods of economic management. And certainly the problems facing the nation's leaders after the Korean War—a devastated infrastructure, huge military budgets and almost total dependence on loans from overseas—were no less daunting than those of the Japanese following the Second World War.

The Koreans also feared returning to the status of an economic colony of Japan. To forge their own independent economy, the Koreans emulated the very strategy the Japanese used to wean themselves from American and other foreign interests. In a manner far more authoritarian than in Japan, Korean government technocrats, many educated in America's top universities, took firm hold of Korea's economic destiny, assuming complete command of all the nation's banks.

Unlike their Japanese counterparts, the Korean bureaucrats even had to help create a local capitalist class. As subjects of Japan, Koreans previously had few opportunities to engage in anything more than small-scale trading. And since assets had previously been in the hands of their Japanese masters, the distribution of the lands, plants and also credit were all political and business allocation decisions. In these circumstances the government chose to favor a small handful of *chaebol*, or general trading companies, who often secured expropriated Japanese assets at what two leading experts on the period, LeRoy P. Jones and Il Sakong, have described as "ridiculously low prices." These *chaebol* also received cheap government-backed bank loans, tax assistance, tariff protection and import protection. By 1985, the five largest *chaebol* had sales of over $50 billion, or more than half the nation's GNP, and they employed nearly half a million people.

Without this support from the state, the *chaebol* could not have achieved their extremely rapid pace of development. Woo Choong Kim started his Daewoo group in 1967 with $9,000, five employees and a small order for inexpensive shirts. Twenty years later the company—with operations spanning shipbuilding, aerospace and microelectronics—boasted sales of over $10 billion. Hyundai, now a $15 billion conglomerate, had in the 1950s a similarly humble origin as a motor-vehicle repair shop.

Government support also plays a key role in the *chaebol*'s move into the high-technology arena. When *chaebol* such as Lucky Goldstar or Samsung entered highly competitive fields such as microelectronics, their entrepreneurial courage was fortified by over $500 million in direct government grants. More recently, the government joined forces with Daewoo, Lucky Goldstar and other companies in a $70 million program to produce a Korean superminicomputer. Another government-backed development scheme calls for capturing, by the year 2001, 10 percent of the expanding world market for work stations.

This continuing reliance on governmental generosity has created among the *chaebol* leadership an ethos more reminiscent of Meiji industrialists such as Shibusawa than the more sophisticated and internationalist-oriented leaders of contemporary Japanese *keiretsu*. Lee Hun-jo, president of the Lucky Goldstar group, for instance, admits that his corporate decisions are, at root, "guided by the national interest." As Woo Choong Kim, founder of Daewoo, explains:

> I had a dream that the best way to serve my country would be to build a great company. This company would create jobs

for our youth, and contribute to the prosperity of Korea. I did
not see business primarily as a way to make money.

The subsequent success of the Daewoo group has provided a sense of accomplishment. This has motivated me
to lead the company further and faster, into challenging
new areas. The realization that business can serve society
has given me the energy to continue working hard.

America's Lost Opportunities

Against this ethos, American business often has seemed all
but helpless. In one generation, U.S. business has lost its predominance in industries like steel, textiles, automobiles and
consumer electronics. As the various Asian economies move
relentlessly up the value-added scale, no field—even such traditionally American bastions as microelectronics, computers and
financial services—seems safe.

Some observers already believe that these recent setbacks
presage the inevitable decline of the United States and its eventual replacement as the world's economic superpower. Geohistorian Immanuel Wallerstein, among others, sees the relationship
between Japan and the United States today as similar to that
existing between America and Great Britain in the years before
the Second World War. While the United States represents ''the
old leading power,'' Japan presents the figure of ''lean, aggressive, confident economic growth.'' Wallerstein predicts that,
through its deepening economic penetration of China, with its
vast resources and manpower, Japan is the leader of a new Asian
alliance destined to supplant the economic hegemony of the
United States.

And Wallerstein's vision may well become true, unless U.S.
industry undergoes a major reevaluation of attitudes and approaches toward Asia. Throughout most of the past century,
Americans have often underestimated the strength of Asian societies and their strong desire for self-determination. Unable to
see in Asian struggles for independence the parallels with their
own nation's struggle for independence, U.S. policymakers
since the late nineteenth century all too often have approached

Asia with the instincts of European imperialists, leading ultimately to foreign-policy disasters from China to Vietnam. Similarly, the reluctance of U.S. business interests to accept Asians as economic equals led Americans to supply them with the tools—in terms of technology, markets and production contracts—with which they would later bury much of American industry. And now, Americans who think they understand what is happening in Asia often overemphasize Asian strengths, creating in the process a self-fulfilling prophecy of American failure in that part of the world.

Ironically, the earliest American contacts with Asia displayed a surprising degree of savvy. A new nation, suddenly cut off from its mother country, the United States had a natural need to find new markets and trading opportunities. In 1784, only one year after the signing of the Treaty of Paris ending hostilities with England, the *Empress of China* sailed from New York Harbor for Canton. Yankee traders had undertaken at least nine other journeys to the Far East by the time the Constitution was ratified. By 1800, Salem, Massachusetts, was doing so much business with the East Indies that it had assumed the title of "World Emporium of Pepper." Five years later, American traders were second only to the British in the burgeoning Canton tea market, carrying almost ten times as much of the precious cargo as all other European nations combined.

As this trade expanded, so too did the American desire to gain direct access to the Pacific Coast. Lewis and Clark's mission to the mouth of the Columbia River was, in the words of Thomas Jefferson, designed to find a direct route "for the purposes of commerce" with Asia. In line with this desire, American businessmen such as Asa Whitney and John Jacob Astor set up trading operations in the Pacific Northwest, where they procured sea otter and seal pelts much valued in Canton. Eventually, through both conquest and negotiation, the United States took actual possession of the Pacific Coast, with the full expectation of furthering its Asian trading relationship.

This period represented the first great American opportunity in Asia. Rejecting the primacy of Europe, early American nationalists—Thomas Jefferson, Missouri Senator Thomas Hart Benton, journalist William Gilpin—saw expansion to the Pacific as a means of escaping dependence on what Benton decried as "the English seaboard." A disciple of Thomas Jefferson and Andrew Jackson, Benton held that "access to Asia becomes a symbol of freedom and national greatness."

A non-European identity also provided Americans with a special advantage in Asia. Although it took nearly twenty years for news of the American Revolution to reach cloistered Japan, many liberal samurai, including some of the architects of the Meiji Restoration, came to regard the American struggle for independence as something of a role model. Nagazane Motoda, who later drafted the Imperial Rescript on Education for the Emperor Meiji, considered George Washington a figure on the level with the legendary emperors of China. Shonan Yokoi, a key progressive intellectual, believed the United States' anti-imperialist past made it by far the best power for Japan to cooperate with.

Chinese officials shared a similar point of view. While English and other European merchants tended to press their interests heavy-handedly, often backed up by warships, Americans usually came to China simply as traders or missionaries. Lin Tse-hsu, chief Chinese official in Canton in 1835, described the Yankee traders as "good barbarians" who were far more respectful of local laws and customs than their European competitors. Tseng Kuo-fan, perhaps the most prominent official of mid-nineteenth-century China, wrote in 1861 that "Americans are of pure-minded and honest disposition and long recognized as respectful and compliant toward China."

By that time, the United States had established a major presence in the Far East, capturing more than half the trade through the port of Shanghai and emerging as Japan's leading trading partner, a role it maintained well into the early 1930s. For visionaries such as New York's Senator William H. Seward, it was in Asia that the nation would achieve its ultimate destiny. Seward, who later became Abraham Lincoln's secretary of state and architect of the Alaskan purchase, proclaimed:

The Pacific Ocean, its shores, its islands will become the great theatre of events in the world's hereafter . . . henceforth European commerce, European thought and European connections, although becoming more intimate, will nevertheless sink in importance.

But in years following the Civil War, American business lost sight of Seward's prophetic view. Competition with superior industrial goods from Britain as well as the rise of other European competitors, each content with carving out its own special sphere of influence in China, damaged American prospects as did the rising power of Chinese entrepreneurs. But perhaps the most significant factor was the growth of better investment opportunities closer to home. The fortunes of Yankee traders—made in the high-risk trade with Asia during the first half of the century—now found more advantageous investment opportunities in such domestic enterprises as New England cotton mills, western railroads and mines.

As a result, by the early twentieth century, the United States had lost much of its once-promising Asian role, particularly in China. "The old China trade had helped build America," comments China scholar John K. Fairbank, "but what it left was not a great American vested interest still present in East Asian trade and power politics . . . but rather a nostalgic sentiment, a New England tradition represented by Brattle Street chinoiserie. . . ."

While the China trade stagnated, the United States also squandered its political capital by discriminating against Chinese immigrants, from the 1840s on. This annoyed and then infuriated their countrymen back home. The passage in 1904 of a bill excluding *all* Chinese immigration spawned a boycott of American goods by merchants in both Shanghai and Canton. As diplomatic historian A. Whitney Griswold has noted, the discrimination against Chinese in the United States "dissipated" much of the goodwill created by the nation's traditional support for China's territorial integrity and commercial "open door."

Similar restrictions on Japanese immigration—pushed mostly by Californians such as the editors of the *San Francisco Chronicle*, who feared the "complete Orientalizing of the Pacific Coast"—did perhaps even more serious damage to U.S. relations with an increasingly powerful Japan. The decision by San

Francisco school officials to place Japanese children in separate schools constituted, in the words of instructions by his government given to Japan's ambassador in Washington, "an act of discrimination carrying with it a stigma and odium that is impossible to overlook." Particularly exasperated was President Theodore Roosevelt, an admirer of the ascendent Asian nation, who feared that the United States would someday "pay the consequences" in a future war with the nation's leading Pacific trading partner. So angry was Roosevelt that he complained bitterly to his cabinet that California "was too small to become a nation, and too large to put into a lunatic asylum."

For three decades the extreme prejudice against Japanese immigrants embittered the Japanese. By 1930, Japan had emerged as the United States' third-leading trading partner, and several major American corporations, such as General Electric and IBM, had established operations there. But the racist overtone of the U.S. immigration policy continued to impede closer relations. "The issue of Japanese immigration," noted historian Griswold in 1938, "hung like a cloud over the Pacific." When the Pacific war broke out, racial antagonism provided much emotional fodder for Japanese propagandists, who exploited the issue in an attempt to win over other Asiatics to their side. "To scores of millions of participants the war was also a race war," observes historian John W. Dower in his *War Without Mercy*. "It exposed raw prejudices and was fueled by racial pride, arrogance and rage on many sides."

Miscalculation also led to the squandering of yet another opportunity, this time in China. Sun Yat-sen, the leader of the Chinese movement for a Western-style revolution, had lived in Hawaii and raised large sums of money for his cause among Chinese throughout the United States. He heard of the initial 1910 uprising against the Ch'ing Dynasty while staying at the Brown Palace Hotel in Denver. An admirer of American political institutions, many of which he planned to emulate in China, Sun Yat-sen expected American aid against the reactionary forces who seized power shortly after the initial revolution. But when the Nationalist regime took control of customs revenues in Canton, several Western powers, including the United States, sent naval vessels. Embittered, Sun turned increasingly toward the young Soviet Union for assistance, explaining:

> America was the inspiration and example when it started the revolution to abolish autocracy and corruption in high places . . . We might well have expected an American Lafayette would fight on our side in this good cause. In the twelfth year of our struggle towards liberty there comes not a Lafayette but an American Admiral with more ships than any nation in our waters.

With its refusal to aid the revolutionaries, the United States, in the words of Ambassador Jacob Gould Schurman, was locked into a position of ''benevolent hopelessness.'' From then on the United States became identified not with the more revolutionary Sun Yat-sen tradition, but with the conservative, even reactionary wing of the Kuomintang, led by Chiang Kai-shek.

Based largely on a Eurocentric world view, American policy failed to provide an appealing alternative to a Communist ideology which at least superficially supported Asian aspirations. As early as January 1922, the Comintern's Gregori Zinoviev was propounding Lenin's view that Europe constituted ''only a fraction, a little corner on the map of world revolution.'' Soviet ideology, at least until the 1950s, maintained that Asiatics would emerge as ''a new and mighty factor in international relations. . . .''

By offering Communism as the means to achieve Asian national self-determination, the Soviets outmaneuvered their American rivals, who found themselves on the losing side of the Chinese Revolution, with the Soviets finishing in the predominant role when the Communists seized power. When, on October 1, 1949, Mao Tse-tung stood at the Gate of Heavenly Peace in Beijing and proclaimed the People's Republic, Sun Yat-sen's widow, Ching-ling, stood at his side.

The inability to assess properly the dimensions of the Asian desire for self-determination affected American fortunes in other areas as well. The once-strong support for Japan's ''Greater East Asian Co-Prosperity Sphere'' had foundered on the rocks of that nation's racism against its fellow Asians and stubborn insistence on subordinating all other interests to those of the supreme *Yamato* race. But Asians, having seen the Europeans knocked off their colonial perches, also had no desire to see them return. Like Sun Yat-sen before them, they looked anxiously toward the United States as both liberator and role model. When U.S. troops came to Malaysia, for instance, they were welcomed with signs reading "Nippon Go—America Come."

But when it became clear that the United States would not resist a return of British colonialists, this goodwill quickly dissipated. Obsessed by its friendship with the European imperialist powers, the United States simply turned its back on both Asian nationalists and its most fundamental, basic, historical traditions. Asia experts such as John Carter Vincent, the director of Far Eastern Affairs at the State Department, urged the United States to follow its historic anticolonialist position in Asia. But George Kennan, the department head of policy planning and one of the originators of the postwar theory of containment, countered that a far higher priority had to be given to maintaining "the morale" of European nations such as France, whose deflated wartime pride could not stand the loss of its longtime colonial possessions. "America's Indochina policy," writes historian George C. Herring, "continued to be a hostage of its policy in Europe, the area that Truman and Acheson assigned the highest priority."

The ironies here would be comic if they did not prove so tragic in their consequences. Asians did not see Europe as "the highest priority" and expected the United States, as the leading noncolonialist power, to support their move for independence. When Ho Chi Minh declared independence from France in 1945, he borrowed liberally from Thomas Jefferson, opening with the words: "We hold these Truths to be self-evident, that all Men are created equal. . . ." At ceremonies marking independence, American warplanes flew overhead and U.S. military officers stood on the reviewing stand with General Vo Nguyen Giap, while the Vietnamese band played "The Star Spangled Banner." Even the Emperor Bao Dai, who had abdicated in favor of the new Democratic Republic, warned that "this desire for independence . . . is in everyone's heart and no power can overcome [it]."

Many other new Asian countries based their declarations of independence on the American model. In such beginnings, the United States had an ideal chance to identify with the new Asia and work out mutually profitable economic as well as political ties. But the U.S. State Department chose instead to ally with reactionaries and colonialists in virtually every country of Asia. "It was in the power of the United States in August of 1945 to have assisted in the revolutionary birth of Asia, to have acknowledged the inevitable change in the status quo and to have led the revolt," noted journalist and old Asia hand Robert Payne in 1949. Instead, Payne wrote, "nearly every action taken during that year seemed almost willfully to have been taken with an instinctive sense of fatality, of going against the grain of history."

As a result of such policies, the United States time and again alienated virtually every ascendent force in Asia. In China, the United States refused to deal with Mao Tse-tung's Communists. Instead, the nation poured some $2 billion into a sinkhole of a Kuomintang regime which Secretary of State George Marshall himself described as both "weak" and "lacking in self-discipline and inspiration." While the United States stubbornly clung to its defeated ally on Taiwan, Great Britain and eventually other allies, including France and Japan, rushed in to cement at least some early trade ties with the incipient Communist regime.

Part of this blindness toward Asian aspirations was based on political considerations at home. Many experienced Asia hands were forced out by McCarthyite persecutions, leaving policy firmly in the hands of Cold War ideologues. All other considerations, including the nation's own political traditions, were cast aside in order to bolster Europe. To gain political capital for the massive Marshall Plan, Eurocentric policymakers such as Paul Nitze and Dean Acheson purposely, as they later admitted, "chose to exaggerate the Russian threat" in order to steer American resources into Europe.

With Mao's victory in China, the defense of Europe also took on an all-too-familiar racial tinge as well. Now the Soviets and the Chinese appeared to be joining together in something akin to an "Asiatic horde." "What is happening is obvious," said a Berlin postman quoted approvingly in *Newsweek* in 1949. "The

Russians have failed to overrun the western sectors of Berlin from the East, so now they are trying to do it from the other direction, by way of China.''

Japan, Inc.: Made in USA

Such attitudes would ultimately turn the greatest American success story in Asia—the occupation of Japan—into yet another lost opportunity. America's occupation of Japan represented both America's most splendid accomplishment and its greatest economic blunder. The changes, notably land reform, instituted by General MacArthur helped turn Japan into the most progressive, democratic society Asia has ever known. Yet at the same time, the abandonment of reform dissipated a splendid opportunity to create in Japan a deeper rooted ''open system'' such as exists today in Hong Kong. Indeed, in many respects the creation of the much-feared ''Japan, Inc.'' was in large part a function of American foreign policy.

In the years immediately after the war, American occupation forces under General MacArthur worked assiduously to lay the foundations for the development of an American-style ''open system'' in Japan. A peculiar combination of autocrat and committed democrat, MacArthur made dramatic changes in traditional Japanese institutions. He recognized women's rights, initiated large-scale land reform, legalized unions and established the beginnings of a democratic electoral system.

MacArthur also sought to break up what he called the prewar *zaibatsu*-dominated ''socialism of the monopolies.'' By forcing the holding companies and families at the apex of the *zaibatsu* structure to sell their stock on the public market and by imposing a tough antimonopoly law, MacArthur gave life to the beginnings of an economic ''open system'' in Japan. At times incompetently administered, the anti-*zaibatsu* laws contributed to the economic confusion characteristic of postwar Japan. But in banning many of the former top *zaibatsu* leaders, the measures breathed new life into old institutions by allowing younger managers to take the helm. Reform also helped clear the stage for the emergence of new companies such as Honda Motor Corporation and Sony, which would later rise to worldwide prominence.

These reforms, however, offended many large American corporations and conservatives, including such groups as the U.S. Chamber of Commerce and the National Association of Manufacturers. Adding to the antireform clamor were many former "Japan hands" who now yearned to exploit their ties to the old *zaibatsu* structures. A 1947 report to President Truman from James L. Kaufmann, a legal advisor to firms such as General Electric and Standard Oil with strong prewar ties to established Japanese interests, urged the abandonment of democratic reforms Kaufmann deemed to be "anti-American," "socialistic" and likely to lead to the "communization of Japan."

Besides the self-interest of the old Japan hands, the antireform drive, notes Japanese historian Takeshi Igarashi, also resonated with the "Moscow-centered views" of Kaufmann and influential diplomats such as George Kennan, head of Secretary of State Marshall's Policy Planning Staff. The on-site observers of the Occupation knew of Japan's indigenous anti-Communist and anti-Russian traditions, but Kaufmann and influential allies such as Kennan insisted that the island nation could prove fertile ground for Communism. MacArthur, through the force of his powerful will, maintained his reformist policies for the time being, but eventually the conservative Cold War point of view prevailed.

Eventually, Japanese conservatives exploited this American obsession with the Communist threat to reactive the latent components of the prewar corporate state. Under the leadership of conservatives such as Prime Minister Shigeru Yoshida and his successor, Ichiro Hatayama (a right-winger purged by MacArthur for writing a prewar book praising both Hitler and Mussolini), Japan resuscitated much of its prewar economic policy including blatant protectionism, strict restrictions on foreign investment and government subsidization of "target industries." With antireform elements in control, the new *keiretsu* groups—including such direct descendents of prewar *zaibatsu* as Sumitomo, Mitsubishi and Mitsui—once again assumed powerful, if not dominant, positions.

One obstacle blocking the reascendency of these forces lay

in the new Communist regime in China, long a major trading partner for large Japanese firms. Eager to reopen this enormous market, some Japanese corporations began pressuring their government to reach an accommodation with the Chinese Communists. Anxious to deflect such a prospect, the United States satiated the Japanese need for expansion by offering its own huge domestic market without demanding any reciprocal rights. Similar approaches toward other Asian nations, notably Taiwan and South Korea, ultimately created other deadly trading relationships, in which ideologically compatible regimes could restrict American products while exporting the bulk of their goods to the vast and rich U.S. markets.

In an atmosphere of almost blind assumption of American omnipotence, by the early 1960s Japanese firms operating from the safety of their own protected domestic markets already were taking market share from such key American industries as shipbuilding, textiles and steel. But Washington policymakers—obsessed with "strategic" considerations—refused to force the Japanese into opening their economy. Reflecting the hubris characteristic of the Camelot administration, McGeorge Bundy, President Kennedy's national security advisor, once described the United States economy as "the locomotive at the head of mankind, and the rest of the world the caboose." To such men even the suggestion of a possible economic threat from our Asian allies would have seemed preposterous.

So while the American regime placed its primary emphasis on Europe, the Middle East and, most tragically, the escalating war in Southeast Asia, the executives in the Japanese economic "caboose" focused on the United States. While Japanese corporate executives assiduously studied American technology, management and markets, the United States, for the most part, ignored Japan, giving Japanese election campaigns far less attention than it gave to those in relatively minor European states.

The Japanese were not so neglectful. To protect their interests in Washington, the Japanese *keiretsu* hired powerful lobbyists and lawyers, including former Republican presidential candidates Thomas E. Dewey, Richard Nixon and Richard Allen, who, before serving as Ronald Reagan's first national security advisor, represented clients such as Nissan and Toyota.

As Japanese and other Asian countries began penetrating deeper into industries once dominated by Americans, Washington turned up the political rhetoric but did little to force Japan into opening either its consumer or investment markets. Faced with a hostile and often totally closed economic system, American corporations such as RCA, Dupont and Ampex simply sold off their technology to Japanese manufacturers. By 1958, American firms were garnering about $25 million annually from such licensing arrangements, leading *Business Week* to exult that U.S. firms were driving a "hard bargain" that allowed them to "share" in Japan's economic boom.

Yet by August of 1959, the United States suffered its first peacetime monthly trade deficit since 1937. This licensing of technology, which would reach $19 billion by 1980, provided Japan with what Shigeo Nagano, chairman of Nippon Steel, called "the cream of the world's technology." The Ampex deal, for instance, helped lay the basis for Japan's total domination of the VCR industry, while other licenses helped develop expertise in such critical areas as electrical machinery, communications equipment, machine tools and chemicals.

"Whenever we found out about a new technology, we could not rest until we went out and bought it. We rejoiced even when we knew it was useless technology. . . . But we have found that the winner in almost any technology-purchase relationship is the buyer," noted Koji Kobiyashi, chairman of NEC Corporation in 1982. America's "hard bargain" of 1959 ultimately proved, in the words of one business consultant, "the greatest fire sale in history."

3

The Third Century Economy

Orange County, California, conjures up images of freeways, Ferraris and blondes at the beach. Home to both Disneyland and some of the nation's most conservative political activists, it has epitomized the suburban homogeneity of the "Ozzie and Harriet" 1950s and an economy dominated by commuters working at the sprawling defense plants of greater Los Angeles.

Into this bastion of homogeneity came three young men from Asia: Tom Yuen and Albert Wong hailed from the crowded tenements of Hong Kong; Safi Qureshey was the son of a Pakistani foreign service officer, raised in Karachi. Although they had been brought up in the backwaters of Asia's colonial past, their aspirations were American. "My school was British, but it seemed foreign to me," recalled Wong, who emigrated in 1970. "But America was different. It was *our* culture; the movies, TV and Pepsi were everywhere. The Gemini program, Apollo—they were what we talked about back home."

The son of a schoolteacher, Wong had done well in his English school, but not well enough to gain entrance into the highly competitive Hong Kong University. Discouraged, he wrote to California schools and, filing through brochures, picked out Orange Coast College. After transferring to Cal State Fullerton and getting his degree in electrical engineering, Wong went to work for General Instruments Corporation, where he met Qureshey, a young engineer who had arrived in 1971. In 1980, the handsome and well-spoken Qureshey introduced the technically gifted Wong to his friend Tom Yuen, a young Chinese engineer with a salesman's outgoing personality.

The talk among the young engineers turned to the new microcomputer business just taking shape 400 miles to the north, in the Silicon Valley. Although the industry was in its infancy, they decided that here was their opportunity. All they had at the start was a notion that the IBM PC, then in development, would create a huge market for add-on boards to enhance memory and other functions. If they could deliver the right products, they might ride IBM's coattails to success. "We had a good idea what to do but we were barely out of our twenties, and we really didn't know what it was to run a company," remembers Safi Qureshey. "We didn't even have a formalized business plan. We just did what felt most comfortable."

Albert Wong, the technical genius of the trio, pored over the early specifications released by IBM for their new computer and handled the basic engineering tasks; Tom Yuen directed the marketing and sales effort; Qureshey took on the formal title of president, and handled the administrative and planning functions. When it came to making the product, all three pitched in, soldering the boards together in Tom Yuen's garage.

When sales broke $400,000 in 1982, the young company—named AST Research, after the first names of the founders—resorted to traditional Chinese methods. Albert Wong called in members of his sprawling family, who in turn recruited their friends. When the production runs got larger than the family could handle, they recruited hundreds of Vietnamese, Chinese and Latinos who had begun to concentrate in the poorer sections of the county.

Today AST, with sales in excess of $206 million, stands as the world's leading independent producer of add-on boards for personal computers. It boasts strong links with such giant companies as IBM, Apple and AT&T. And with sparkling new plants in Hong Kong and Irvine, California, the company now makes over one-quarter of its sales overseas, mostly in Europe and Southeast Asia.

Still in their mid-thirties, the AST founders have moved aggressively to expand their operations, adding their own laser printers and microcomputers to a growing list of products. Once the ultimate outsiders, they are now comfortably part of an Orange County scene that is rapidly shifting from a monotonic suburbia to a multicultural mecca in which one out of five residents is non-Caucasian. In the years ahead, they plan to become a permanent fixture not just in Orange County, but in a new and revitalized American economy. "Our goal is to build an organization for the long term, a company like Hewlett-Packard or an IBM," explains the thirty-six-year-old Qureshey, dressed in a red AST tee shirt.

Economic *Sokojikara*

The process that allows three immigrant engineers to become industrial leaders in less than a decade reflects the fundamental changes now sweeping the American economy. Even as many of the nation's largest companies have retreated before the mounting competition from Asia, other firms, including many founded by immigrants from those same countries, are creating new industries and companies at an unprecedented rate. In the nation's Third Century, these children of America's "open system" represent the most crucial asset, the key ingredient for prevailing over ascendent Asia.

Indeed, nowhere is America's reserve power, its *sokojikara*, more evident than in the rapid evolution of the structure of its economy. In 1970, United States-based multinational corporations dominated both the nation's business and much of the world's, as well. Nineteen of the world's twenty largest corporations were American based. The American "colossus," as Jean-Jacques Servan-Schreiber put it, included three of the world's four largest automakers, as well as the largest steel, chemical and aluminum firms.

These firms were widely considered then the ultimate form of economic organization. And their performance was certainly impressive. In only two years between 1954 and 1976 did more than five of the hundred-largest American industrial companies lose money. European nations perceived these American giants as powerful enough to threaten national independence itself. In his 1966 book *The American Challenge*, Jean-Jacques Servan-Schreiber warned, "We are simply letting European business be gradually destroyed by the superior power of American corporations.'' The only way to meet their challenge, Servan-Schreiber suggested, was consciously to build similar ''big industrial units'' in Europe.

Two decades later, however, the once overwhelming ''superior power'' of the 1960s' generation of American giant corporations had faded considerably. Between 1959 and 1978, the world market share of the top U.S. companies dropped between 30 and 50 percent in such key fields as pharmaceuticals, chemicals, electronic products and aircraft. Some of America's great companies—notably IBM, Hewlett-Packard and 3M Corporation—remain as world leaders, but competitors, mostly from Asia, clearly have seized the initiative.

In the process, some of America's largest companies have either fallen to mergers and breakups or, in some cases, been simply wiped out, with nearly 30 percent of all Fortune 500 companies falling from the list between 1970 and 1981. Particularly hard hit has been that ultimate expression of 1960s-style corporate giantism, the conglomerate, which attempted to overcome the dislocations of the business cycle by diversifying into scores of unrelated businesses. A 1987 study by Harvard University's Michael Porter of thirty-three large-company diversifications between 1950 and 1986 found that most had a ''dismal'' track record, with over half of the acquisitions made by 1980 divested by January 1987. Particularly revealing has been the downward trajectory of ITT, the ultimate conglomerate, from its 1974 ranking as the world's eleventh-largest corporation, to forty-fourth in 1985 and totally off the Fortune Top 50 the following year.

In another country without America's unique *sokojikara*, such a development could have proved disastrous. When Britain's great corporations—such as British Steel, British Leyland and the Upper Clyde Shipbuilders—began failing in the years after World War II, so also did the British economy. But America's experience has proved different. Although plagued by trade deficits, owing in part to mercantilist policies of trading partners in Asia and Europe, the American economy in the 1980s has revealed surprising strengths. Once beset by relatively high unemployment and persistently sluggish growth, the United States has more recently been outperforming most of its major industrial competitors.

From 1959 to 1976, for instance, unemployment in West Germany stood at only 1.2 percent—less than one-fourth of the American average. France, Italy and even the United Kingdom enjoyed levels of joblessness at least 50 percent below that of the United States. By the mid-1980s, however, U.S. unemployment rates stood at least one-third lower than those of Europe.

GNP growth has revealed a similar pattern. During the 1960s and 1970s, with the exception of Britain, the United States suffered the lowest rate of economic growth of any major industrialized country, while Japan's economic growth averaged nearly 8 percent—more than twice the American average. By the mid-1980s, however, the situation had changed drastically. Between 1980 and 1985, the American economy expanded 75 percent faster than its European counterparts, and since 1983 generally has matched or exceeded that of Japan.

Behind this renaissance lies the emergence of a host of new growth companies such as AST Research, which have risen to a rapid prominence unparalleled in any major industrialized country. Even as Fortune 500 firms such as Crown Zellerbach, Sperry and Kaiser Steel fell from the ranks of the elite, new firms—often in totally novel industries—developed to take their place. Between 1979 and 1986, nine companies from *Inc.* magazine's list of the nation's 100 fastest-growing small public firms—running the gamut from computer manufacturers Tandem and Apple to service firms such as Federal Express and Southwest Airlines—vaulted their way to the ranks of the Fortune 500.

The structure of the economy as well as the cast of characters has changed dramatically. Once dominated by a seemingly irreversible process of consolidation, the economy in the 1970s began generating record numbers of new businesses. In 1985, over 700,000 new corporations were registered in the United States, up from 200,000 twenty years earlier. Between 1977 and 1985, American firms with less than 100 employees generated 89 percent of the roughly 18 million new jobs created. In contrast, larger companies, after increasing payrolls in the late 1970s, lost 2 million positions in the first five years of the 1980s.

Although the power of large corporations may once again reassert itself in some future period, today for the first time since the 1920s many economists are beginning to doubt their inevitable preeminence. In 1986, the revenues commanded by the Forbes 500 ranked by sales actually *decreased* 2.3 percent. Even the profitability of large firms has been falling. Since 1980, the profits of even the 500 most profitable companies in the country have risen only 18.8 percent, well below the 28 percent pace of inflation. As Dale Jahr, senior economist of the Joint Economic Committee of the Congress, explains:

Perhaps large corporations don't have the competitive edge anymore. In a dynamic and high-tech economy "bigness" may be an impediment to adapting to rapidly changing business conditions. Liquidity and mobility are natural advantages; massive amounts of sedentary capital tend to rust or rot.

The End of the Galbraith Era

The recent patterns of corporate development in the United States contradict much of the fundamental economic wisdom of the last century. Virtually all the major economic thinkers of the past 100 years—from Karl Marx and Friedrich Engels to Joseph Schumpeter and John Kenneth Galbraith—have pictured the entrepreneur as, in Galbraith's words, something of "a diminishing figure in the industrial system." In Galbraith's view, the smaller company could inhabit only the world "of the independent retailer, the shoe repairman, the bookmaker, narcotics peddler, pizza merchant and that of the car and dog laundry."

Corporate executives in the Galbraithian era prided themselves on being professional managers and aspiring administrators in an increasingly oligopolistic economy. "To a surprising degree, American businessmen and writers have [stopped] interpreting our cooperative society as individualistic [and have stopped] concealing our quest for security in phrases like competition," noted *Fortune* magazine in a 1976 profile of Fortune 500 executives. "It is a rare chief executive . . . who would consider himself an entrepreneur or capitalist."

Today, corporate ambitions are changing. In response to the competitive challenge from both overseas and domestic entrepreneurial firms, many companies have restructured after unsuccessful diversifications. Even Gulf & Western, a quintessential conglomerate of the 1960s, has rapidly divested a large number of its myriad divisions—in products ranging from foods to auto parts and cement—to concentrate on a new core of information-related enterprises.

The dismantling of conglomerates and other corporate restructurings has also served to reduce the payrolls and cause a rapid increase in the use of contractors, often smaller companies. A 1987 study of 375 large North American corporations found that the share of work done by outside contractors had grown from roughly 5 percent of total employment to over 15 percent between 1983 and 1986. Today such "contingent workers," according to economist Audrey Freedman, may account for as much as 25 percent of the total U.S. work force.

The new, more enterprise-oriented mood is also reflected by profound changes within corporate management. Companies as proud as IBM, NCR and Memorex have attempted to "entrepreneurize" by breaking their organizations down into smaller units. At venerable Campbell Soup, for instance, president Gordon McGovern saw sales of his company's traditional line of "red and white soups" and Swanson TV dinners declining, largely as a result of a growing trend toward high-quality specialty foods produced by smaller firms. Faced with the prospect of continuing decline, McGovern broke his company into fifty small business units. For inspiration about marketing, for instance, he turned to entrepreneurs such as Murray Lender of Lender's Bagels and Mo Siegel of Celestial Seasonings. In the words of McGovern: "We sensed the world was changing. If we didn't pick up what the entrepreneurs were doing, we figured we'd end up like the dinosaurs. . . . We were scared of getting wiped out."

Perhaps nothing violates the Galbraithian world view more than the increasingly crucial role of entrepreneurs in the growing technology-intensive fields. Galbraith, for instance, maintained that only large firms possessed the resources, the management acumen and the marketing skills to enter advanced technology-based markets. "Size," Galbraith proclaimed, "is the general servant of technology. . . ."

This view is still widely accepted, and is often cited by advocates of a more "communitarian" American economy. Walter Russell Mead argues that the rising costs of new plants and equipment place serious technological development beyond the reach of entrepreneurs, who in maturing industries can play the role only of scavenging "hyena" feeding on the leftovers of the corporate "pride of lions." Like Mead, Robert Reich holds that, "America's economic future depends less on lonely geniuses and backyard inventors than on versatile organizations."

Yet contradicting such assertions are small and midsize firms that are increasingly providing leadership in the key emerging industries. One of the postwar era's most significant fundamental technological innovations—the microprocessor—was not developed at a giant firm like IBM or Bell Labs. Of the two firms that patented the microprocessor in 1971, Intel was a one-year-old start-up company and Texas Instruments had only recently shifted itself from its traditional emphasis on the oil business. Today these and a handful of other American firms—including relative newcomers such as Zilog Corporation—control as much as 90 percent of the world market for the latest generation of microprocessors.

Much the same pattern persists throughout key high-technology sectors. Cray Research and ETA (a start-up financed by Control Data Corporation) have dominated the supercomputer business despite the efforts of such firms as IBM and Fujitsu. In the expanding superminicomputer field, young companies such as Pyramid Technologies and Convex Computers are among the industry leaders. The rapidly expanding biotechnology industry, born of the marriage between university research and the nation's entrepreneurial infrastructure, has been paced by more than 200 small, independent companies, including such leaders as Amgen, Genentech and Chiron.

And as they have from the beginning, entrepreneurs have continued to lead in the application of microprocessor technology. It was precisely "backyard geniuses" such as Steve Wozniak, Steve Jobs, George Morrow and Adam Osborne who developed and popularized the personal computer, now a $35 billion industry worldwide. Wozniak even proposed the idea of commercializing the personal computer while working at Hewlett-Packard, but management chose to reject the suggestion. As Adam Osborne wrote in 1979:

> Can anyone explain how established computer manufacturers—and there were more than 30 of them in 1974—missed such a market? Why was the entire industry left to reckless entrepreneurs, lucky amateurs and newcomers to computer manufacture? The answer is that this new market was too bizarre to fit any predictions made by established means. And over the next 30 years, we will see similar scenarios—again and again.

By 1982, Osborne's own firm, after reaching sales of over $100 million, went bankrupt, but the industry remained very much under the entrepreneurial sway. Even with IBM's forceful entrance into the market, young firms continue to dominate much of the microcomputer-related industries. The preeminent "giants" of the world's microcomputer software industry—Microsoft, Ashton Tate and Lotus—all were launched after 1975 and in the United States.

The progress of relative latecomer Compaq Computer Corporation perhaps best reveals the continuing importance of entrepreneurs in the microcomputer industry. Founded in February 1982 by three Texas Instruments engineers at a Mexican restaurant in Houston, Compaq introduced its first products after both Apple and IBM had established dominant market positions. Like those produced by more powerful competitors such as AT&T, Epson-Seiko, NEC Corporation and Fujitsu, their machine was built to be IBM-compatible. Yet over the next four years, Compaq not only withstood a determined challenge from IBM, but surpassed AT&T in worldwide sales. By 1986 Compaq had garnered more revenue in dealer sales in the hotly competitive market for business computers than AT&T and all the Asian manufacturers combined. In April of the same year, four years after its inception, Compaq joined the Fortune 500—on the list faster than any other company in history.

In the semiconductor industry, well over 134 new American

start-ups have formed since the late 1970s, including such major successes as LSI Logic, whose sales jumped from $34 million in 1983 to almost $200 million four years later; Integrated Device Technology, which grew between 1982 and 1986 from $4 million to over $100 million; and Cypress Semiconductor, which four years after its founding in 1982 achieved sales in excess of $50 million. As L. J. Sevin, a lead investor in Compaq and chairman of Cypress Semiconductor, remarks:

> People have developed a mythology of technology. Nobody thought a company like Compaq could survive against IBM and the Japanese, but it did. . . . The same is true of semiconductors. I heard [Intel founder] Bob Noyce quoted fifteen years ago when he was still at Fairchild tell a bunch of guys there'd be TI, Motorola and Fairchild and there wouldn't be room for other semiconductor companies. It would end up like car companies. It proved to be an irrelevant comment.

So "irrelevant" is the concept of the inevitable consolidation of technology-based industries that large American corporations are emerging as major financial backers and strategic partners of entrepreneurial firms. Between 1980 and 1984, corporate venture investments in smaller companies, according to *Venture Economics*, rose from $100 million to nearly $500 million. In the semiconductor field, for instance, giant firms such as Rockwell International, Johnson Controls and Wang have all cemented relationships with small Silicon Valley chipmakers. Rather than buying out companies in the increasingly discredited conglomerate style of an ITT or Gould Corporation, top corporate executives, including some in Japan and Europe, are seeking ways to borrow the entrepreneurial energy of smaller firms without quelling their spirit.

"If you want a new technology, it doesn't make sense to go out and buy a start-up," notes Jim Keyes, vice president and chief financial officer of Johnson Controls, a $1.7 billion maker of building controls and energy products that has an alliance with LSI Logic. "All that you accomplish is to make the founders rich and lose their people. And it is the people and the skills that you needed in the first place."

Return of the Artisan

One common complaint concerning the jobs created by small business is that they tend to be both low paying and in the service field. Though a large proportion of new jobs created since 1979 have been low paying and in the service field, the biggest percentage increases have been in executive, managerial, technical and professional fields. The proportion of low-wage workers, according to the Joint Economic Committee, declined between 1973 and 1985 to only 31.4 percent of all new jobs, a historically low ratio.

Chagrined by the loss of many jobs in unionized large corporations, some economists such as Barry Bluestone and Bennett Harrison of MIT have equated the rise of small business with the "de-industrialization" of the American economy. This view is also shared by heralds of the "postindustrial age," such as John Naisbitt, who link the decentralization of the economy with the demise of manufacturing.

The reality, however, is not that manufacturing is dying, but that its structure is changing. Seen by the Galbraith era as the ultimate province of giant companies, manufacturing—which accounts for roughly the same 22 percent share of GNP as it did in 1947—is now being increasingly dominated by entrepreneurial firms, many of whom focus on small-niche markets. Indeed, it is largely owing to entrepreneurial companies that the United States remains very much an industrial power, with small and midsize firms accounting for virtually all the nation's new factory jobs since the early 1980s.

We may only now be seeing the effects of this transition. Even as some experts were writing obituaries for the nation's manufacturers, American industry by the late 1980s started to become *more* productive. The increase in the annual rate of output per man-hour, for instance, which had sagged throughout the 1970s and early 1980s, had tripled by the latter half of the decade and by 1986 was outgrowing virtually all the nation's advanced industrial competitors. Indeed, rather than being a "declining sport," industry today is spawning many new and aggressive young companies, with manufacturing firms accounting for nearly half of *Inc.* magazine's 1987 list of the nation's 100 fastest-growing public companies.

This pattern applies as much to the so-called low-tech industries as it does to computers or biotechnology. Between 1976 and 1982, small firms with under 100 employees even registered strong gains in industries—primary metals and lumber products—that suffered overall reductions in employment. In fact, between 1970 and 1984 large companies shed themselves of some 1.4 million manufacturing jobs, yet during the same period 41,000 new manufacturing companies created enough new jobs to offset those losses. As a result, companies with fewer than 250 employees now account for 46 percent of the manufacturing work force, up from 42 percent a decade ago. If the trend continues, small-scale manufacturing should pass the 50 percent mark in the 1990s.

Often dependent on producing small runs of highly customized products, these small low-tech firms generally display a greater tendency than their giant rivals to incorporate the latest technology. A 1987 study by the Boston-based Yankee Group, for instance, projected that computer purchases by small manufacturers have been rising by 35 percent each year—twice the rate of the largest companies—a pattern they expect to continue into the 1990s.

Perhaps the most outstanding example of the expanding entrepreneurial role in American manufacturing has been the rapid emergence of the "minimill" sector of the steel industry. At a time when U.S. Steel, once America's largest corporation, divested much of its steelmaking operations and changed its name to the anonymous USX Corporation, these smaller operations invested heavily in the latest steelmaking technology, such as continuous casters and electric arc furnaces. Now numbering fifty, these minimills have increased their share of the American steel market from 3 percent in the early '70s to over 20 percent in 1986.

Like Compaq, the success of these firms is based largely on the superiority of their execution. For instance, Nucor, based in Charlotte, North Carolina, now produces twice as much steel per hour as its giant U.S. counterparts. From its new Pilgrim, Utah, plant, Nucor has also started penetrating deeply the West

Coast markets dominated by the Japanese and other Asian steelmakers. In late 1986, the firm began an assault on the steel-fastener market, at present 90 percent controlled by foreign firms, and in the following year started construction of a technically advanced plant outside Indianapolis to produce flat rolled steel, thus threatening one of the last bastions of the giant integrated firms. As John Jacobsen, steel analyst for Wharton Econometrics, put it: "What's at stake here is the survival of the traditional integrated companies."

In sharp contrast to the executives of his giant competitors, Nucor president Ken Iverson, who took over the company in its infancy back in 1965, believes in economic *sokojikara*, even in one of the world's most overbuilt, fiercely competitive industries. Convinced that free competition can lead to renewal, Iverson opposes protectionist or adjustment measures. "Unless you're under intense competitive pressure and it becomes a question of the survival of the business to do it, you're just going to lapse back into your old ways," believes Iverson, whose firm in 1985 achieved sales of over $750 million. "There's no other answer. But out of all this will come a lot of things that are beneficial: more of an orientation toward technology, greater productivity, certainly a lot of changes in management structure."

But much of the most dramatic growth in the emerging Third Century economy comes from firms in the service sector. Even as America's product balance of trade declined, U.S. exports of services—such as transportation, advertising, engineering and entertainment—have tripled over the decade from 1975 to 1985 to $150 billion, posting a surplus of over $20 billion. Although many service firms remain in retailing and consumer-oriented activities, the fastest-growing sectors in the past decades have been in entertainment, business and professional services, which generate wealth by attracting dollars from outside a community or outside the nation as a whole.

As in technology, the service sector is not necessarily a "servant of size." In fact, often it is very small firms, sometimes sole proprietorships, which seem best suited to providing many of the business and other services increasingly in demand. While back in 1969 a study by the Institute for the Future even predicted that self-employment would practically vanish by 1985, the numbers of self-employed persons, mostly in the service field, have increased every year from 1970 to 1984, more than doubling over the period.

Nowhere is this new dynamic more evident than in San Francisco. Over the past decade consolidations, relocations and lay-offs among the city's major corporations have cost the city some 46,000 jobs. Using conventional Galbraithian perspectives, much of the city's political and business establishment saw these developments as the harbingers of decline. Mayor Dianne Feinstein rushed off to Japan, hoping to lure new electronics factories to the city. Roger Boas, former chief administrative officer, proposed a major program aimed at attracting new large corporations to replace those already gone.

Yet behind the hysteria lay a surprising reality. Though large corporate employment had dropped significantly, smaller firms in the city had more than compensated for the loss. Between 1981 and 1985, according to a study conducted by the *San Francisco Bay Guardian*, small firms with under 100 employees created virtually all the city's new jobs with three out of four of these new jobs originating from firms with less than 20 employees.

Some of this growth came from traditional small-business activities such as the restaurant trade, always a big industry in this heavily tourist-oriented city. But the more spectacular gains were registered in business services such as advertising, health care, accounting and legal services. Headed often by highly trained professionals—many of them former executives with large companies—these firms did not fit the marginal niches assigned to small business by Galbraith; they recalled nothing so much as the artisans of Western Europe in the thirteenth century—the weavers, carpenters, money changers and merchants—who helped shape early capitalist economies such as Venice and Antwerp.

These "white-collar artisans" specialize in a wide variety of fields, ranging from technological services (computer leasing, software development and consulting) to specialized investment banking functions, such as raising capital from Asia or handling Brazilian investment funds. Still others provide services to larger firms which find it more economical to purchase expertise from entrepreneurs than to develop it within their own corporate structure.

Although the firms frequently are small, sales per employee are often not low. Peterson and Dodge, which produces business publications and annual reports for such large companies as American Express, AT&T and the U.S. subsidiary of Audi, with only ten employees enjoys 1987 sales of over $1 million. As cofounder Linda Peterson explains: "Good 'craft people' don't flourish in large corporate settings. Creative people don't handle depersonalization very well. A more intimate environment promotes creativity."

Despite the gloomy reports focusing on the loss of large corporations, artisan companies such as Peterson and Dodge are creating the basis for a new San Francisco prosperity. By the summer of 1987, San Francisco's unemployment rate—traditionally above the national average—was among the lowest for any major metropolitan area in the country. With a per capita income of over $21,000 San Francisco in the same year was also the nation's richest city.

The European Syndrome

The phenomenon of a city losing its established corporations and getting rich in the process epitomizes the often unrecognized—particularly by the public-policy establishment—self-rejuvenating power of the American economy. Over the past decade, on the other hand, the oft-praised European system, with its bureaucracy-directed "adjustment" policy, has shown little of this dynamism.

Indeed, in its almost monomaniacal search for security and certainty, European society seems to have opted for a closed system dominated by government, large companies and, in some countries, trade unions. This closed system marks a major point of divergence between Europe and the United States, reflecting profound differences in the nature of democracy on opposite sides of the Atlantic. While in the United States democracy has long been associated with autonomy of the individual or corporate entity, on the continent—owing in part to its feudal past—

democracy has tended generally to what Swiss historian Jacob Burkhardt called "lawless centralization," in which the state emerges as "sole guardian of rights and public welfare."

Following these nineteenth-century patterns, European governments have grown to play a larger and more intrusive role in their economies than is the case in America or its Asian counterparts. As latecomers to the industrial revolution, France, Germany and Italy all relied heavily on government subsidies and direction in their drive to catch up with Great Britain. By the 1930s, even Britain, its industrial decline by then acute, had abandoned the remnants of its past commitment to entrepreneurialism and unstructured change. In 1935, Conservative leader Stanley Baldwin declared laissez-faire to be as dead as "the slave trade." Harold Macmillan, then a young party radical and later prime minister, envisioned a society that would replace "individualism and laissez-faire" with "that organic conception of society that was the distinct contribution of medieval thought." The Labour party, of course, had an even more jaundiced view of unregulated economic change with its vision of forging a socialist postindustrial England characterized by state-owned industry and an extensive welfare state.

Whether in the guise of socialism, Toryism or Gaullist nationalism, Europe has developed a deep commitment to government absorption of economic wealth that is unparalleled in the United States or even the most statist capitalist economies of Asia. In 1984, government spending accounted for over 30 percent of gross domestic product (GDP) in West Germany, well over 40 percent in the United Kingdom and France and an astounding 58 percent in the Netherlands. In the United States—despite its massive military budget—government spending accounted for only 24 percent of GDP. Japan, Korea and Singapore significantly also stood substantially below European norms.

With government control too firmly a part of the European syndrome, the prospect of this state-dominated system's dissolving seems remote. Even in Thatcher's Britain, a 1985 *Survey of British Attitudes* poll found that two-thirds of the people still believed government has the power to produce higher living standards; a similarly large percentage also favored price controls, while only 5 percent wanted government cut back. Eric Willenz, a senior European affairs specialist at the State Department from 1956 to 1984, traces Europe's welfare-state orientation to the class antagonisms originating with the industrial revolution:

> In the eyes of West Europeans, the construction of the welfare state above all else has enabled them to preserve democratic institutions in the wake of World War Two and after the disasters of the interwar period. . . . Their aim has been to shore up a still precarious domestic balance among competing sociopolitical forces that in the interwar period frequently faced each other across unbridgeable ideological and political chasms.

In the early postwar period, when the European economy was taking off, this welfare-state orientation may well have served its historical purpose. But more recently, nonwage labor costs—including high costs of layoffs, rigid work hours, job security guarantees, social security and premature tenure—have crippled European competitiveness. Although American admirers celebrate Europe's rise in industrial productivity, they rarely discuss the impact of these nonwage costs on real labor costs, which grew five times as fast in Europe as compared to the United States from 1979–84. Employers in Germany, France and Italy pay social security taxes two to three times larger than those paid by their counterparts in Japan or the United States.

Under the slow growth conditions of the 1980s, these rigidities, argues MIT economist Rudiger Dornbush, has turned "hiring an extra worker . . . [into] a near irreversible investment." Such conditions, Dornbush asserts, helped slow Europe's employment growth rate during the late 1970s to only one-fourth that of the United States. While the American economy created 18 million new jobs between 1974 and 1984, the Common Market countries lost 3 million positions. By early 1987, nearly 19 million Europeans—one out of every four youths—were jobless. Unemployment in Italy has risen to double-digit levels and is nearly 60 percent among youths. These figures are closely followed by similar ones from such oft-cited economic role models as France and West Germany.

The situation elsewhere in Europe is, if anything, worse. By the late 1980s, Ireland, Holland and Spain have suffered unemployment rates around 15 percent, levels usually associated with those of Third World nations. Just a few years ago, the Irish Development Authority proudly billed its nation as "the best business base in Europe," luring over 800 multinationals to set up operations on the island. To show off Ireland's large, and relatively young, educated work force, the authorities ran advertisements with a picture of twenty proud recent university graduates. But with competition for overseas investment growing in Europe and elsewhere, such promotions simply could not make up for a lack of homegrown entrepreneurs. Less than a year after the picture was taken, seven of the graduates had left the country, joining the nearly 100,000 other Irish people who emigrated between 1984 and 1986. By 1987, nearly 200,000 more of their countrymen had applied for visas to the United States.

Perhaps the key difference lies in the concept of the entrepreneurial function on opposite sides of the Atlantic. While self-employment is well entrenched in all European societies, small firms tend to be primarily conservative, family-oriented and highly specialized, not the kind of entrepreneurial growth ventures that generate new jobs and innovations. In France, for instance, legislation assisting small businesses often means protecting small shopkeepers through such regulations as forbidding larger discounts for bulk buyers.

This approach helps the corner *charcuterie* or dressmaker, but also precludes the rise of entrepreneurial ventures such as Trader Joe's, Ross Stores or the Price Club. It prevents the disruptive 8 percent turnover characteristic of American small business, but stands in the way of the sort of risk-taking that creates the companies that end up in the *Inc.* 100, the *Venture* 100 or the *Forbes* "Up and Comers." "Attitudes are totally different there," notes Jean Deleage, a former French government official and now a leading venture capitalist in San Francisco. "The small businessman wants to live well on his business with his family. He doesn't want to be diluted, only to pass the business on to his children.''

This self-limiting nature of European small proprietorships may well explain the tremendous difference in the vitality of entrepreneurialism between the United States and even countries such as Italy, whose economy is the most small-business-oriented on the continent. Attempts to break out of the narrow niches assigned to small business are often thought of as not worth the risk. While Steve Jobs or William Gates are like matinee idols to many young Americans, they have little appeal to European youths, who often maintain strong socialist leanings. ''Profit is a dirty word here,'' notes West German venture capitalist Karl Heinz Fanselow.

Nor would Germany's more conservative business leaders look upon such activities with favor. ''Apple would still be in a garage here,'' said Bernd Ertl, head of a Munich investment bank specializing in small issues. Accustomed to the comforts of the welfare state and employment in large, stable corporations, Germans who wish to break out of the pattern often find themselves at odds with basic social attitudes. Klaus Neugebauer recalls the reaction of family and friends when he left his job in 1971 to found Softlab, G.m.b.h.:

I was treated with great reservation, even by my wife. People thought I was a money-grabber, that I only wanted to be rich. I was stamped as a gambler.

In America you can fail and start again. But here, when one fails, he is branded as a failure for the rest of his life. It's always in his record. When you try to do something again, people are afraid to do business with you. We must learn to live with flops.

This failure ''to live with flops'' may have much to do with why the Europeans—in sharp contrast to the United States—have largely been unsuccessful in generating jobs from their small-business sector. According to a study conducted by MIT's David Birch, Britons are two and a half times less likely to create jobs by starting a new business than are their American counterparts. In Sweden, small business creates only 15 percent of all new jobs, one-sixth the U.S. rate.

At a time when small business is mushrooming throughout the world, the lack of entrepreneurship in Europe, as David Birch notes, constitutes "an exception rather than the world norm." And it is an exception for which present and future generations of Europeans may pay dearly. "If we stick to the same policies and mentality," says Manuel Martin, the European Economic Community's Commissioner for Social Affairs and Employment, "more than 10 percent of the Community's work force will continue to be unemployed in 1990."

Despite the setbacks, there is little prospect for change in the "policies and mentality" of most European governments. Like the French generals who tried halting Hitler's *blitzkrieg* with the heavily fortified Maginot Line in 1940, European governments seem determined to fight American and Japanese domination with strategies more appropriate to the era of Servan-Schreiber's *American Challenge*. European industrial policy remains very much a patchwork of large joint-venture projects, massive government subsidies and protective measures.

Although frequently hailed as paragons of "adjustment" by American statists like Robert Reich, such programs have had a dampening effect on entrepreneurial development in Europe. Almost by its very nature, large-scale government intrusion in industry, in the words of Arthur Schlesinger, tends to serve as "a weapon of future conservatism," favoring the large, the established and the politically well connected. As Peter Drucker has noted:

> "Planning" as commonly understood is actually incompatible with an entrepreneurial society and economy. Innovation does indeed need to be purposeful and entrepreneurship has to be managed. But innovation, almost by definition, has to be decentralized, *ad hoc*. . . . It had better start small, tentative and flexible.

Nowhere has the dampening effect of planning on entrepreneurial growth been more evident than in the high-technology field. "The almost unquestioned assumption of European industrial policies,'' noted the London *Financial Times* in its summer 1987 technology survey, ''has been that sheer size is the answer to the American and Japanese challenge.''

This mentality has produced an almost limitless array of government-sponsored inter-European initiatives designed to counterattack American and Japanese technological supremacy. The Airbus program, for instance, has gained significant market share, but only at the cost of direct grants and subsidized loans between 1971 and 1986 amounting to over $7 billion, with additional commitments of nearly $3 billion in the pipeline. Other more recent projects—with such names as Megaproject, BEP, Esprit, RACE, BRITE, BAP, and Comett—have sought to pool the resources of various European firms and governments to awaken the continent from its technological slumbers. At the same time, Europe's largest industrial power, West Germany, did not even open its first small-business park until 1983.

Indeed, the relative weakness of new high-tech industries in West Germany, Europe's premier economic power, reveals what could have happened to the United States if technological development had been left totally in the hands of giant corporations. Hugely successful in their chosen fields of steel, production machinery, chemicals and automobiles, the German companies—with the remarkable exception of the late Heinz Nixdorf and his Nixdorf Computers—simply slept as the Americans and Japanese seized the initiative in high technology. ''A young man with an idea in Germany faces mainly skepticism and reluctance,'' notes Munich management consultant Manfred Brede.

In the emerging Third Century economy, such attitudes have done great damage to Europe's technological standing. European governments have spent twice as much on research and development as the Japanese, but in recent years companies on the continent have filed only one-quarter as many patents. Various European governments in the late 1970s and early 1980s spent an estimated $500 million on microchip research and development—again twice the Japanese figure. Yet between 1982 and 1986 the European share of global microchip production fell nearly one-tenth, accounting for a mere 10 percent of world output. As Rudolph Sprung, an official of the West German Economics Ministry, puts it: ''We lag far behind the development of other countries, particularly the U.S. Some talk of being twenty years behind.''

Some American public-policy figures praise Europe's heavily targeted approach, in Robert Reich's words, as ''trying to guide their economies into higher-value-added production.'' And certain heavy subsidies and protectionist measures do allow Europeans sometimes to win sales abroad or keep jobs at home. But it has done little to improve overall competitiveness. A 1985 study by the Kiel Institute of World Economics found that European businesses had gained market share against the United States and Japan only in ''fortress Europe,'' where they benefit from such strong protectionist measures. In key Third World markets such as Southeast Asia, European firms lost 33 percent of their market share while largely unsubsidized American and Japanese companies improved their performance.

In fact, Europe's government-guided shift to high-value-added production has contributed even further to turning the continent into a technological backwater. Europe's technological failures, according to estimates by Robert Sheaf, the European Economic Community (EEC) liaison officer in London, have cost the continent as many as 3 million jobs. An attempt to ''Europeanize'' America's technology-based industries, notes New York University economist Melvyn Krauss, would amount to nothing more than ''a call to catch up with the losers.''

This link between statism and technological backwardness is clear to many European technologists. With governments obsessed with challenging entrenched leaders such as IBM or, more recently, Japanese firms such as NEC Corporation, there has been little of the *ad hoc* entrepreneurialism characteristic of the United States. Instead, executives have been forced to cope with governmental logic for choosing ''winners,'' a logic that, observes Pierre Costa-Marini, a former executive with French government-owned Bull, sometimes seems to take its inspiration from pages of *Alice in Wonderland*.

''If someone had a good idea, they'd ask 'if it's such a good idea why hasn't IBM done it?' '' Costa-Marini has recalled. ''And if IBM hadn't done it, how could it be a good idea? I always figured that it would be better to do what IBM wasn't doing, since once they decided to go into something, it was too late.'' Costa-Marini adds that the ineffectiveness of the approach can be seen by the fact that IBM, the object of so much French government concern, in 1985 enjoyed a share in the European computer market four times larger than its largest local competitor.

The targeted approach also has made it virtually impossible for the indigenous development of the sort of niche-filling computer companies so prevalent in the United States. This lack of entrepreneurialism in hardware may even threaten the future of the French software industry, long the acknowledged European leader. With American personal computers controlling 80 percent of the European market, French firms will be hard pressed to make inroads into the fastest-growing sectors of the software industry. Phillipe Sahut d'Izarn, technology advisor to the Banque Nationale de Paris, admits: ''Most of the software used in France's personal computers will be American.''

Such sentiments reveal not a lack of patriotism, but a frank admission of the limits placed on entrepreneurial development by Europe's ''closed system.'' When Jean Auricoste returned to France in 1955 with a master's degree in electrical engineering from MIT, his goal was to help build a computer industry in his homeland. In the early 1960s, as an executive vice-president at Compagnie Internationale pour l'Informatique (CII), Auricoste developed a computer that was roughly equivalent to the new minicomputers then under development by Digital Equipment Corporation (DEC).

As DEC would later prove conclusively, the minicomputer was a commercially viable concept. But the government of France, anxious to create its own answer to mainframe-maker IBM, ordered CII to concentrate on the technically advanced but virtually unmarketable mainframe. ''We couldn't have ever been a European IBM,'' Auricoste—who, like Costa-Marini, left the government-owned sector to found his own small software service firm—recalls bitterly, ''but we could have been a European DEC. Unfortunately we had 'help' from the French government.''

Can Japan Be "Americanized"?

As Europe's failure slowly dawns upon advocates of a "communitarian vision," they are beginning to turn their gaze toward more successful models such as Japan. Yet, ironically, at the same time there is a growing desire throughout the Japanese and other Confucian economies to adopt the economic self-determination that is characteristic of America's "open system." "Asian societies are at a turning point," notes Yasanobu Nagura, an Osaka-based business consultant who has worked with more than 500 firms in both Japan and Taiwan. "There is a new spirit, a willingness to dare new things. We are becoming Americanized."

By "Americanization" Nagura refers to the growing desire throughout Asia to emulate the United States' pattern of "creative destruction," which has allowed the development of high-growth companies like Compaq Computer or Federal Express while allowing older firms to fall by the wayside. And indeed Asia—particularly the economies of the Chinese diaspora—already exhibits far more entrepreneurial vigor than Europe.

Owing to its dominant international presence, the Japanese economy is most cited by advocates of a more closed economic system. And in fact, despite its relatively low levels of government expenditures, Japan's system has remained largely a closed one, with a government and business establishment restricting the emergence of powerful new players. Increasingly, however, many in Japan today recognize that the nation's long-term future depends not on the maintenance of this system, but on its "Americanization." As Naohiro Amaya, former vice-minister with Japan's Ministry of International Trade and Industry (MITI) and one of the leading strategists of Japan's postwar economy, observes:

There is one more modernization that needs to be promoted. While a powerful government controlled by a highly capable elite corps may be essential in the early stages of economic development, everything possible should be done to encourage the functioning of natural, uncontrolled market mechanisms once a society has taken off. Economy and politics alike should be gradually democratized and the government shrunk.

In many ways, people such as Amaya in Japan seek to recreate the sort of "open system" first implemented by the American occupation. Under American influence, the *zaibatsu* groups temporarily were broken up and old monopolistic practices outlawed, creating a brief period when conditions were ideal for the emergence of a new group of entrepreneurs, including Soichiro Honda, Konosuke Matsushita, Masaru Ibuka and Akio Morita. "The new freedom," observed British historian G. C. Allen, "kindled many fires."

However, as a coalition of conservative Japanese and American interests succeeded in reversing the original occupation policy, the situation worsened for entrepreneurs. In the rush to industrialize and catch the United States, government officials sought to create ever-larger industrial units, including the reconstituted portions of the old *zaibatsu* groups.

Almost immediately the bureaucrats fell into conflict with the new entrepreneurial forces. When Sony applied in 1951 for a $25,000 licensing fee for transistors from Bell Laboratories, MITI demurred. "The bureaucrats," Morita later recalled, "could not see the use for such a device. . . . MITI thought that such a small company [as Totsuka, Sony's original name] could not undertake the enormous task of dealing with brandnew technologies." It took six months to get an approval which, over time, gave the first boost to Sony's, and later, to Japan's dominance of the consumer-electronics business.

But perhaps no entrepreneur has been more at war with the bureaucracy than Soichiro Honda. Throughout his remarkable career Honda was forced to battle MITI bureaucrats at virtually every turn. In the 1950s, for instance, MITI tried to block access to capital for expansion of motorcycle production which the bureaucrats thought "bordered on insanity." Later, MITI also tried to block Honda's earliest forays into the automobile business, claiming that Japan needed fewer, not more, automakers.

"Probably I would have been even more successful had we not had MITI," says Honda, who was forced to wage a bitter struggle against the agency in order to launch his car division.

"MITI was incapable of building cars, but I was. . . . If the Japanese government was a private corporation, it would certainly be deep in the red."

For the most part, however, few entrepreneurs managed to overcome the giant-oriented mentality of the Japanese bureaucracy. In their eyes, small firms were generally deemed worthy of only a minor supporting role. While MITI promoted consolidation through "administrative guidance," the equally powerful Ministry of Finance made certain that the vast majority of loans flowed toward the giant firms. Even in the mid-1980s, 11 percent of all Japanese corporations received nearly 50 percent of all corporate loans.

Under these circumstances, it became extraordinarily rare for even outstanding small companies to raise the funds necessary to break out of the narrow role assigned them by government bureaucrats, corporate chieftains and bankers. As Masasuke Ide, a leading expert on the Japanese financial system and associate dean at the Nomura School of Advanced Management, explains:

> The Ministry of Finance and the major banks are like father and children. The Ministry protected the big banks and the big industrial groups from competition [from outside this group]. The system was regulated to protect the status quo, and made it very difficult for entrepreneurs to start something but easy for one of the big groups to launch new business.

As a result, Japan's over 800,000 small and medium-size manufacturing companies, which produce a greater proportion of output and employment than their American counterparts, nevertheless increasingly find themselves captives of the larger companies. Indeed, by 1980 over two of every three small manufacturing firms were classified as *shitauke*, or subcontractors. Dependent on orders from their oligopolistic customers, these companies often seek to establish some degree of independence by developing new technologies and products. But all too often *shitauke* find their innovations ending up in the hands of their corporate overlord. Among Osaka-area subcontractors, for example, electronics giant Matsushita is widely referred to as *maneshita*, incorporating the Japanese word "to copy."

"The big contractors like Matsushita control everything, even the ideas of the small companies," complains one Osaka banker specializing in lending to small firms. "But the small firms are afraid to say anything, because they'll get thrown out if they do."

In the past, Japan's apologists, both at home and abroad, accepted such inequities as a necessary price of the nation's phenomenal economic ascent. Yet today Japan faces a new set of challenges—protectionism, rapidly changing technologies and rising competition from other Asian states—that require the adoption of drastically different tactics and new role models. "Coordination is all right if you're building steel and cars on the model of other people," argues Jiro Tokuyama, a leading Japanese economist and cofounder of the Nomura Research Institute, the nation's leading think tank. "But now we're in the era of fast change, of integrated circuits and microprocessors. I don't think our large organizations can move quickly enough to make the changes. We must find our model among the entrepreneurs such as those in the Silicon Valley."

The central problem facing Japan, notes Tokuyama, lies in the basic inability of its central institutions to adjust to such changes. Whereas the United States, with its "open system," has undergone a massive, often wrenching change—with large-scale bankruptcies, corporate spinoffs and growth in new ventures—Japan has experienced relatively few such shocks. Attempting to preserve the giant *keiretsu* structure at all costs, Japan's business elite has tried to do internally what in the United States has been more effectively accomplished by the formation of new, highly focused entrepreneurial ventures. The American economy spawns new niche-oriented firms, such as Cray Research, to develop such sophisticated products as supercomputers. In Japan the lead has been taken by vast, integrated electronics giants like Hitachi. Attempts over the past decade by giant Japanese firms to create breakthrough technologies and brand-new industries, as the United States did in biotechnology, already have proved disappointing.

One central problem for these firms has been the tendency of the *keiretsu* to follow almost identical corporate strategies. Following deep-seated patterns of conformism—reinforced by government "targeting" as well as the often uniform educational and social conditioning of the elite executive class—large Japanese firms traditionally have focused on identical technologies and product areas. In the early 1980s several competing giant firms targeted videotape technology. After refining their products in the hothouse environment of the home islands, these firms then went out to conquer world markets.

But in an era increasingly marked by the diffusion of technology, a proliferation of competitors and rapidly quickening product life cycles, this logic has begun to unravel. One clear example can be seen in semiconductors, often cited as the ultimate example of Japan's industrial supremacy. With the encouragement of MITI, several major Japanese electronics firms attacked the dynamic-memory portion of the semiconductor market with fearsome determination. By outspending and outproducing American rivals, they hoped to duplicate earlier successes in automobiles and consumer electronics. Yet in the end they ended up competing against not only themselves but also rising Asian competitors such as Korea and Taiwan, so that the price curves for even recently developed products were quickly driven below cost. As a result, within two years of establishing leadership in such devices as 64kdRAMs and 256kdRAMs, the semiconductor divisions of such major Japanese producers such as Hitachi, Fujitsu, NEC and Toshiba suffered revenue drops in excess of 40 percent. "Business was not so good last year," admitted Yoshio Egawa, a Fujitsu official, in early 1987. "We didn't get much of our bonuses. Maybe we'll get paid in semiconductors." (See Note, page 100.)

While the Japanese firms and similar U.S. companies were absorbing huge losses, a host of upstart American firms were concentrating on smaller but more profitable technically advanced niches such as very high speed CMOS (complimentary metal oxide semiconductors), microprocessors, gate arrays and application-specific chips. The giant Japanese firms are attempting to shift into these fields, but the American entrepreneurs seem almost always a step ahead, reaping the profits that accrue to the technological leader. Atsuyoshi Ouchi, senior executive vice-president of NEC Corporation, once thought American "boutique" semiconductor producers would not survive into the mid-1980s. Today he jokes that if he could move to California, he might be tempted to start one himself.

"You cannot deny the role of small American firms, because the semiconductor industry has changed," Ouchi, one of the prime architects of the Japanese industry, admits. "In the past, the number of products was small; now it is enormous. In that kind of market, it's very difficult for us to cover the customer's demands."

Indeed, Japan's tragedy, ultimately, is that a capable executive such as Ouchi cannot or would not start his own firm. Despite several sporadic efforts over the past decade, the *keiretsu*-dominated economy and society have so far been resistant to the drastic changes in attitude that would allow the creation of independent "boutique" semiconductor producers. The problems associated with rising costs in Japan have led the *keiretsu* to choose the strategy of offshore production, with the objective of lowering cost, rather than the longer-term strategy of spurring innovation through new entrepreneurial endeavors.

Perhaps most telling of all has been the rapid decimation of Japan's technology-oriented "venture businesses," once widely hailed as the successors to such occupation-era entrepreneurial firms as Honda and Sony. In the first six months of 1986 alone, nearly thirty of these firms, backed by Japan's $1 billion venture capital industry, went bankrupt. Among the failing venture businesses have been such highly regarded technology start-ups as Nihon Electric, Kangyo Denki, Dainichi Kiko, and Japan Soft and Hard Corporation.

These bankruptcies testify to the still-powerful grip maintained by the *keiretsu* on smaller Japanese business. Work in the large corporate groups may be limited by bureaucracy, but lifetime employment provides a sense of security unmatched in small companies. Although engineers and inventors sometimes can be lured into small companies, top-management talent still tends to channel into the larger firms. Under such circumstances, it is difficult for these firms to provide the kind of talent that flows from large American firms such as IBM and Texas Instruments into promising start-ups like Compaq.

Indeed, even the most successful venture businesses, such as Nippon Densan Corporation (Nidec), are hard-pressed to hire talented young executives, even right out of college. Shigenobu Nagamori, who founded the high-precision small-motor manufacturer in 1973, often has to resort to visiting graduates' mothers in order to persuade their sons to join his firm:

A certain freshman [recent graduate] was interested in joining our company. But he said his mother is interested that the son join the company which is being publicized on TV commercials. So, he chose Toyota. Is he designing Toyota motor cars? No, no. He is working as a service engineer in a local city. He is nearly a salesman. But the mother is proud: He is working for the great Toyota. The neighborhood is impressed: Oh, your son is working for Toyota. . . . That's why it's very difficult for Japanese venture businesses to recruit the very good human resources.

Such a severe lack of talent has retarded the progress of Japan's venture businesses, particularly in comparison to those in the United States. A 1984 study conducted by Hosei University professor Tadao Kiyonari, which compares the twenty top, young, growth companies in each country, found that American firms less than ten years old grew in revenues on average *ten* times the rate of their Japanese counterparts. The leading enterprise on the Japanese list enjoyed growth less than that of the twenty-first–ranked U.S. firm on Kiyonari's list—Compaq—then in just its first year in operation.

But when it comes to crushing entrepreneurs, Japan's corporate giants remain the most effective weapon of all. Kangyo Denki, which caused a stir by raising over $3 million in venture capital and $23 million from a consortium of banks syndicated by the prestigious Japan Long Term Credit Bank, was widely publicized as one of the superstars of the new innovative Japan. But two years after raising its funds, the company found the market for its patented ultra-thin motors intruded upon and then dominated by large companies such as Asahi Chemical and Matsushita, forcing Kangyo Denki into bankruptcy.

But perhaps the most significant failure was Sord, the company that once saw itself as "the Sony of the personal-computer age." Founded in 1970 by Takayoshi Shiina, the company became the first in Japan to produce an integrated-circuit–based small computer. It broke new ground again when it pioneered the first easy-to-learn computer language in Japan, Pips 1. By 1984, the company enjoyed sales of $100 million and controlled over one-fourth of the Japanese personal-computer market as well as an expanding presence in Europe.

Then, Shiina recalls, Japan's elite forces closed in. Suddenly someone started spreading the word to MITI that "Sord is shaky." These rumors, which Shiina calls "fatal," ultimately undermined the company's ability to raise money and attract new customers. As his resources became stretched, the *keiretsu* entered the market with the full force of their immense resources and captive customers. Eventually Sord was acquired by Toshiba, the equivalent of Apple being swallowed by General Electric. Not surprisingly, Shiina looks back at his experience with more than a little bitterness:

> Big companies have a pump to re-circulate money but we smaller companies were little better than naked—no place to go but begging to the bank. We found the market was also conservative and closed. . . . The old *zaibatsu* have a defensive posture. You can probably count the number of large customers who are unaffiliated and independent. Toshiba and NEC and other large companies were our customers early on, but as soon as their groups started making personal computers. . . .

> I had hoped we would be treated better; not cut off at the bud.

The Jews of Asia

In the future the most impressive Asian economic gains may come not from Japan, or even the United States, but from the various Chinese-dominated economies of the region. From their tiny enclaves in Hong Kong and Taiwan to virtually all the developing countries in Southeast Asia, the 46 million members of the Chinese diaspora represent the dynamic cutting edge of Asia's economic renaissance.

Even Korea, which has so closely patterned its development

on that of Japan, looks increasingly to these Chinese-dominated economies as models. For the past decade, of course, Korea's dominant *chaebol* have represented astounding entrepreneurial success stories, albeit with massive government assistance. But today some prominent Koreans are beginning to question the driving assumption behind the *chaebol*, in which, in the words of one former executive, "to be small is something criminal."

For instance, it is increasingly clear that the top-heavy nature of the Korean industrial structure has exacerbated the nation's staggering dependence on Japanese firms for components. Whereas the Japanese model allowed, and even encouraged, the growth of hundreds of thousands of small subcontractor firms, Korea's single-minded adherence to giantism has caused the share of smaller firms in the export and import field to drop to about 33 percent in 1981. Without their own network of local suppliers, the *chaebol* have been forced to rely on Japanese components that constitute as much as 30 percent of the cost of Korean exports, from autos and heavy construction equipment to videocasette recorders. Complains finance minister Jang In Yong: "Most of what we earn in the U.S. goes out of our pockets to Japan."

Korean government planners also wonder increasingly whether the heavily leveraged, large, capital-intensive industries such as steel and shipbuilding are capable of producing jobs for a youthful working-age population that devours half a million new jobs per year, a work force that includes an estimated 100,000 college graduates. By the mid-1980s, some of these industries already were suffering from overcapacity and shrinking foreign markets. To promote more economic diversity, in recent years the government has enacted antimonopoly laws, tax breaks for entrepreneurs and a rule encouraging all banks, including foreign ones, to steer at least one-third of their loans to smaller firms. "In all countries," admits Kim Kihwan, a top official with the powerful Economic Planning Board, "you find the innovative jobs are created by small and medium-size businesses. In many ways we take Taiwan as our model."

And, indeed, Taiwan shows clearly the advantages of a diverse and flexible economy dominated by small and medium-size firms. With a population less than half of Korea's, Taiwan boasts both three times as many companies and a per capita GNP that is 50 percent higher than Korea's. And whereas Korea's giant-dominated economy remains burdened with nearly $50 billion in foreign debt, by 1988 Taiwan held foreign exchange reserves nearing $80 billion—greater than Japan's and expected soon to be the world's largest.

In the past, this remarkable performance has been largely the product of small, family-owned companies that flourished in a free-wheeling environment which would be the envy of Japanese or Korean entrepreneurs. But Taiwan more recently also has begun to generate a host of ambitious new growth companies, particularly in the nation's ascendent high-technology sector. Young firms such as Compeq Company, Norplex-Oak, Cadac Electron, and Unicap Electronics International have made Taiwan the fourth-largest printed-circuit-board production center in the world, following only the United States, Japan and West Germany. And with large new investments in advanced technology and facilities, boasts Charlie Chen, marketing and sales director of Norplex-Oak, these companies constitute "a definite threat to overtake the front-runners."

But, characteristically, Taiwan's entrepreneurs are not restricted to microelectronics. Y. C. Wang, Taiwan's leading industrialist, started out with $200 borrowed from his father, a poor tea merchant, to open up his first rice mill. From rice Wang moved into lumber before branching out into plastics in 1954. Today his Formosa Plastics is a multibillion-dollar concern, with fifteen plants within the United States alone. Evergreen Marine, once a relatively obscure container shipping firm, now has reached international prominence, shipping 200,000 containers a day and handling as much as one-third of the shipping through the bustling harbor of Osaka, Japan's second-largest city. After looking over Evergreen's operations, the head of Honda Motor Corporation's transportation division observed: "It reminded me of Honda in the fifties. I really felt the young, invigorating energy."

Yet unlike Japan, where precious few new ventures have flourished since Honda, Taiwan continues to generate an ever-growing number of dynamic new firms, with the number of new manufacturing companies between 1971 and 1981 doubling. Attempts to merge companies, sometimes by government officials, have usually been rebuffed by the individualistic entrepreneurs. As Park Sung-Kyou, executive vice president of Daewoo Telecom, puts it: "If you go to Korea, you see a group of people working. If you go to Taiwan, you see individuals working."

This individualism is even stronger, if possible, in Hong Kong, a free-trade haven where a mostly Chinese population lives under economic conditions that even Adam Smith might see as a "natural system of perfect liberty." By 1980 there was one business establishment for every twenty people in the British Crown Colony, a rate of entrepreneurship *twice* that of the United States. Over 95 percent of these firms had under 100 employees and virtually all were family owned.

Such atomization is a unique feature of Hong Kong's vast manufacturing infrastructure. Indeed, between 1954 and 1984 the average size of a Hong Kong factory dropped by more than 50 percent, to slightly over eighteen employees. Although largely subcontractors for firms overseas, Hong Kong manufacturers—in sharp contrast to Japan's *shitauke*, or subcontractors—tend to be exceptionally independent minded. With 95 percent of their financing from family and friends, Chinese subcontractors are more likely to switch customers, or product lines, in the best interests of their clan than to accept even the suggestion of an outsider's suzerainty. "You can predict the number of executives in a Chinese company by counting the founder's sons and sons-in-law," notes Jerry Wasserman, a vice president of Arthur D. Little and Company with long experience working with entrepreneurs from the Chinese diaspora.

This family-oriented entrepreneurialism has its roots deep in the history of the overseas Chinese. The decades-long dispersal of entrepreneurs—largely in response to political and economic chaos in China—has lent the Chinese way of capitalism a radically different character from that of other Asian peoples.

Both Korea and Japan, for instance, also borrowed much of their ethical system from Chinese Confucian philosophy. But whereas the Japanese maintained the Confucian concepts that extended the social hierarchy from the family unit to the state and emperor, the political chaos in China shattered the Confucian links beyond the family unit. "The Japanese state had an enormous stability that allowed it to identify with larger entities while all that was left to the Chinese was the family concept," notes Wellington Chan, a native of Hong Kong and a leading expert on the business history of his fellow overseas Chinese. "The Japanese deeply care about the corporate house or the country, not only the blood relationships. But the Chinese could trust only the family."

The family-first principle gained primacy during the last decades of the Ch'ing Dynasty. Descendents of Manchurian warriors from the far northern plains who seized control of the imperium in the seventeenth century, the Ch'ings were widely regarded as foreigners and barbarians by the indigenous Chinese. As their rule grew ever more corrupt, the Ch'ings lost so much credibility that many Chinese—in sharp contradiction to their traditional respect for authority—began yearning for their overthrow.

The anti-Ch'ing sentiment was particularly pronounced in the South China province of Guangdong. Thousands of miles from the centers of power in Beijing, the Cantonese were the classic outsiders of their time. They spoke a local dialect so distinct that few Mandarins in the north of China—or most anyone else—could understand them. Described by one imperial official as both "industrious" and "obstinate," the Cantonese were natural entrepreneurs in a society still dominated by anticommercial, feudal attitudes.

When economic conditions worsened noticeably in the mid-nineteenth century, the cantankerous, impatient Cantonese were the first to seek opportunities elsewhere, accounting for the vast majority of Chinese who came to California during the Gold Rush and the building of the railroads. Hundreds of thousands of others, along with many from neighboring Fujian Province, emigrated to the new colonial regimes established by the Europeans in Southeast Asia.

Few of these emigrants left with much more than the shirt on their backs. The vast majority worked as simple laborers or domestic servants. But a handful established small shops and trading firms, mostly to serve the local Chinese settlement. Later some started expanding into enterprises that served broader markets. In the American West, for instance, Chinese were prominent in the establishment of such service businesses as restaurants and laundries. In the less competitive colonial societies of Southeast Asia, they often emerged as a dominant force in all aspects of commerce, becoming widely known as "the Jews of Asia" and sometimes surpassing in wealth their colonial masters.

Like their Caucasian counterparts, the overseas Chinese turned their diaspora networks into business assets. With family members spread throughout the Pacific Basin and in such key Atlantic centers as New York, Chinese entrepreneurs created a remarkable informal information network on a global scale. Like the famous Jewish trading families—the Rothschilds, Sasoons and Kadoories—they often arbitraged this information to their advantage.

This peripatetic activity, however, was not only the product of business savvy. The wanderings of the "Jews of the Orient" were also in part the result of a consistent pattern of oppression. In the United States during the late nineteenth century, for example, Chinese were denied property rights, victimized in anti-Asian pogroms, and ultimately excluded from future immigration.

Unfortunately, such oppressions are not merely remote history. Just two decades ago, hundred of thousands of overseas Chinese—ironically, despised both for their business savvy and for their supposed ties to the Communist regime in Beijing—were slaughtered by rampaging Indonesian mobs. After the Communist takeover in Vietnam, and particularly in the wake of a brief but bloody undeclared war with China, local Chinese suffered tremendous repression, with many forced out of the country. And even today, Malaysia's large Chinese community, envied for its economic achievements by the indigenous Malays, has suffered under strict quotas intended to reduce its dominant position.

These oppressions—as well as the homeland's own turbulent recent history—made Chinese entrepreneurs a rather suspicious lot. They tended not to trust government officials or anyone else outside the immediate family group. This suspicious attitude explains why even successful Chinese entrepreneurs—including such major Hong Kong capitalists as Y. K. Pao or Kenneth

Fung—often are reluctant to give the reins of power to persons outside the family group, sometimes with disastrous results.

For the most part, these attitudes have tended to make Chinese-owned businesses both undercapitalized and rather small. Nor is this pattern likely to change in the near future. Despite its surging economy, Taiwan remains an island deeply aware of the claims placed upon it by the larger, more powerful Communist regime on the mainland. The fear is even more palpable in Hong Kong. Despite Beijing's promises of autonomy, most local businessmen fear deeply the scheduled Communist takeover now only a decade away. As they have for generations, the Chinese entrepreneur today has ample reason to keep his or her international contacts current, assets liquid and bags packed.

"They remain the victims of their history and the trials and tribulations that come from living in that part of the world," sums up Wellington Chan. "They always have to be prepared to yank up their roots and move. They remain, as they have for generations, entrepreneurs on the run."

Yet in a world marked by extreme economic turbulence, being "entrepreneurs on the run" has its advantages. When K. S. Chung arrived in Bangkok, he certainly had schooled himself in survival economics. Since the 1930s he had built several businesses—ranging from commodity trading in Malaysia and restaurants and newspapers in Canton, to a Hong Kong steel business and a flourishing postwar Japan-China trading company—only to see them perish because of corrupt officials, wars and civil insurrections.

"I started with a failure and had many others," Chung recalls, sipping a cup of hot tea on a muggy Bangkok afternoon, "but that's how the family got its training. Setbacks are not really bad. They make you grow up in your business philosophy."

Such attitudes might violate ethics in societies such as Germany or Japan, where failure is considered a disgrace, but they work in entrepreneurial societies, whether in Asia or the United States. Starting virtually from scratch, and with thirteen children to support, Chung opened a small cookie shop and set up a company shipping Thai produce to Japan. Although Bangkok, where one person in ten is of Chinese descent, remains among the most congenial locales for members of the Chinese diaspora, Chung took no chances. He sent many of his children abroad for schooling and today Chung family members hold citizenships in the United States, Canada, the United Kingdom and Switzerland.

Alternating between his base in Bangkok and a new trading firm in Hong Kong, Chung took full advantage of the family's dispersion. While the Bangkok-based family members developed a profitable tobacco and produce business in Thailand, son Kim—married to a Swiss woman and living in Zurich—opened a European textile and watch-importing business. Another son, Wing, moved to Los Angeles, where he helped launch a new microcomputer firm.

To a casual observer it is almost impossible to make sense of the far-flung Chung empire. There are no clearly delineated chains of command, and although there's a board of directors, no one can recall its ever being convened. But according to K. S., such formalities are unnecessary. What the Chungs are selling, he explains, is not things like wristwatches, computers or tobacco, but a sprawling informal network of contacts shared by the widely scattered family. "Our assets are not our expertise or money, but the family members themselves," he explains. "By keeping them in different places, we maintain the maximum flexibility to do our trading, no matter what happens in any one place."

For the future, however, the place K. S. is focusing on is his native China. When China began opening its doors to outsiders in 1972, K. S. seized the opportunity to gain exit permits for several family members still on the mainland. While son Wing was badgering the bureaucrats, he also started to conduct business, arranging for the first shipments of U.S. tobacco to China since the Korean War. Soon some of the very family members who had been rescued from poverty in China were sent back, this time with American or Canadian passports, to exploit their old contacts within the Communist bureaucracy. By the mid-1980s the family owned a taxicab company in Canton, sold American computers to the Chinese government and started shipping a host of products—ranging from silk lingerie to plaid lumberjack's shirts—back through their worldwide network.

The opening of China unlocks a vast new opportunity for the entrepreneurs of the Chinese diaspora. Europeans, Americans and Japanese may hesitate because of shifts in government policy, but Chinese entrepreneurs, although often fervently anti-Communist, are likely to continue pushing ahead in their drive for a large slice of their ancestral market. "In the end they are Chinese and they will see the logic of our ways. After a lifetime abroad, I can say our future will be in China," says K. S. "China is opening up and there's no turning back. It will, of course, take time. Not for me, maybe even not so much for my children, but for the grandchildren. But it will happen. And the family will be there."

Note (see page 89): Since the writing of this chapter, this situation has changed, largely as a result of the U.S. government's agreement with Japan aimed at stopping the "dumping" of such memory chips. By restricting supplies to American customers, the agreement inadvertently boosted the prices of the chips, providing a return to profitability for many large Japanese semiconductor firms.

4

The Refinancing of America

The Utage Lounge is unremarkable in the extreme—a glitzy little bar with dark leather seats, bright lights and hostesses in slinky cocktail dresses. The wallpaper showing scenes of forests seems almost ludicrous given its somberly dressed clientele of urban Japanese businessmen.

Yet for the boys from the bank, Utage—which means "banquet" in Japanese—is a refuge, a place where the mildest-mannered of them can let loose, take up a microphone and belt out a syrupy love song from back home. One can even get a cocktail waitress to flirt with along with the beer, priced at a mere $50 each. Choose a girl from back home or a tall California blonde. It's all harmless fun—a night on the town *nihon shiki*, Japan style.

"I feel very comfortable here," says Nobuyuki Tateno, as he downs his beer. "Many Japanese say Los Angeles is the twenty-fourth ward of Tokyo [which is divided into twenty-three wards]. When my wife writes a letter home she puts a return address that says Los Angeles, California, twenty-fourth Ward. We can have any kind of Japanese product or food here. In fact, sometimes we think the Japanese life here is better than at home."

Such familiar surroundings are important to the men who run Japan's banks, which these days also tend to be the world's largest. Spread like financial Jesuits around the globe, they proliferate in the old Atlantic banking centers of New York and London, as well as the new Pacific financial bastions such as Hong Kong and Singapore or in Los Angeles, where Asian faces proliferate, as do bars, restaurants and shops that cater to Japanese. In such places there are always small nooks and crannies, places where Japanese is the predominant language, the tunes are familiar and the style of business reminiscent of that found in the bars of Maronouchi, Japan's financial district.

Unlike their American cousins, Japanese bankers don't leave to catch the five o'clock train at Grand Central or rush onto the freeway to get home for dinner. For them, the workday often extends late into the night, as they eat and drink with colleagues or customers. "We usually don't say 'see you tomorrow,' but 'see you today' because it's usually after midnight when we get home," jokes Tateno, a vice president at Dai-Ichi's downtown Los Angeles headquarters.

Across the room another Japanese executive has just gotten up. Across the negotiating table he would seem as dour as a Puritan tradesman. From a metallic-sounding recording comes a tune unknown to an American's ears. The businessman takes off his coat, grabs the microphone. Sweat is pouring down his reddened face. He starts screeching out a tune that would sound terrible in any language.

"We feel guilty getting away early," explains Koichi Yoshimine, a colleague from Dai-Ichi's San Francisco office, with a slight air of resignation. "We always worked after the war to survive. We are here to work, to establish ourselves. This is our job. We feel we must work all the time. Our leisure time is only sleep."

As the clock moves toward the midnight hour, the Utage Lounge is filling up. At the table with the Dai-Ichi men, an argument rises over the high-pitched singing of a Japanese hostess. Like many disagreements among Japanese today, it revolves about their vastly increased importance in the world. Some seem ready to fit into the role of banker to the world, the new Asian cosmopolitan. Nobuyuki Tateno feels quite at home in California. Like many Japanese businessmen in Los Angeles, Tateno— along with his wife, Yayoi, and three children—have grown accustomed to the California life-style. Happy in their spacious tract house in Torrence, they have little desire to return to the teeming, concrete blocks of Tokyo.

"In Tokyo it felt like I was living in a prison," Tateno recalls with the look of a man facing an extended sentence. "Everything was very small—only two rooms. The dining room sat next to the toilet. If we went back to Japan, I wonder how we could survive there with no garden, no trees, no birds. Our life is so much better here."

Yoshimine, the fellow from the San Francisco office, finds all this somewhat disagreeable. He seems weary of his American sojourn and anxious to return to familiar surroundings, back where Dai-Ichi Kangyo is a household word and where business relationships are nurtured for decades, over drinking bouts and golf games at $500 a head.

"I feel very isolated here," complains Yoshimine, a thin, ascetic-looking man whose English shows traces of his graduate education at the University of Manchester. "We just don't have the relationship with these Americans. We have a hard time doing business with people with whom we don't have a relationship."

Yoshimine also wonders how long the Americans will put up with Japan's financial occupation. They already resent the longer waiting lines at the local golf courses. "I see their anger when we have twenty people on the golf course, yelling in Japanese," he says. "I am always embarrassed because I am a foreigner."

A Japanese, he believes, can never be Japanese outside of the home islands. The rush, the crowds, the humid, rainy months, the comforting web of *giri*, of obligations, of ancestors—that's what makes a Japanese. Not the fact that the *sushi* in LA may be just as good as in Tokyo. "We can't stay here permanently," Yoshimine maintains, sipping his beer. "If I stay I fear I lose myself. I want to hold on to my national characteristics."

Yoshimine's predicament reflects that of his country. From its earliest beginning, Japan's "national characteristics" have been predicated on the exclusion of outsiders. Yet money is the international language, and the Japanese have more of it than anyone else. Used to scrimping and saving on their resource-poor island, Japanese suddenly find everyone turning to them for a piece of the action.

"Back home we live modestly in a neighborhood with the policeman or supermarket worker, and then one day you wake up and find out that you own the world," Yoshimine noted, his voice almost drowned out by one of the slightly inebriated bar-side crooners. "Then everyone accuses you of doing something wrong. All we've been doing is working very hard with our nose to the grindstone. We don't know what to do."

Up until then Michio Yamada, a vice-president at Dai-Ichi's downtown Los Angeles office, had been conspicuous only by his silence. But as Yoshimine talked, Yamada drained his beer and politely waited his turn. "Maybe," he said, "it's time for us to change, Yoshimine-san. We have to take a greater sense of leadership."

This question of "leadership" is a nagging one for a whole people who now, rather unexpectedly, find themselves the new mandarins of the world financial system. Looking quite depressed, Yoshimine turned to the one Caucasian in the group: "We have always been following the leaders and now we are treated like the leaders. But we don't feel like leaders; we've never done it before," Yoshimine explained, for the first time some emotion breaking through his carefully chosen words. "Maybe we're not ready for leadership. It's a very dangerous position to be in, but it's here. Nothing else can be done."

Beyond the Cash Nexus

Japan's new financial "leadership" reflects a broad sea change in the nature of the relationship between the world's two largest capitalist economies. For the last two decades Japanese corporations—proving imitation can be the most profitable form of flattery—have seized one industry after another from American manufacturers. Today the era of Japan's product-led "invasion" has reached its zenith. The soaring yen, tough new competitors such as Korea and growing protectionism are reducing Japan's market share on the industrial battlefield. Slowly but inexorably, Japan's manufacturers will be forced to shift more of their operations to other countries, particularly the United States.

Yet as the manufacturers fade, they leave behind a legacy of financial power. Until recently, America's interface with Asia has been largely one of products, but in the years to come this will spread to virtually all aspects of American economic life. Long after all the Sony TVs and Toyota cars have been replaced by products made in Korea, Malaysia or the United States, Japan's growing financial power—and eventually that of other Asian countries—likely will have a major impact on the business climate, interest rates and credit availability in virtually every American city.

The speed with which Japan has achieved this financial hegemony is almost shocking. Back in 1947 a destitute Japan needed a $60 million loan to rebuild its devastated textile industry. When Eastern banks balked, the loan package was rescued by California's Bank of America, then the world's largest bank. Exactly forty years later, a desperate and failing Bank of America found its own survival riding on the possibility of selling $130 million worth of notes to a consortium of thirteen large Japanese banks.

This turnabout represents one of the fastest financial ascendencies in world history. As recently as 1960, not one Japanese bank ranked among the world's fifty largest. Only fifteen years ago, Japanese trading companies coming to the United States had to resort to "standby credit" from the Bank of America before receiving loans from other U.S. banks. And even in the mid-1970s during the oil crisis, according to Teruhisa Shimizu, president of Sumitomo Bank of California, bankers from Tokyo were routinely charged a "Japanese premium" whenever they sought to raise capital at the then-dominant New York and London money markets.

Today it's more often the once-haughty Anglo-Americans—including the debt-ridden U.S. government—who go hat-in-hand to Tokyo, home to four of the world's five largest banks. With current foreign assets of over $129 billion and expected to surge to $400 billion by 1990, Japan is now the world's dominant financial power. By 1995, according to the Nomura Research Institute, Japan will hold net assets in excess of $558 billion, making it the "largest creditor nation in history."

Further in the future, it is likely that other product-exporting Asian economies, particularly Hong Kong and Taiwan, will also participate in this Asian financial ascendency. By the mid-1980s, the Hong Kong and Shanghai Bank led all foreign banks in loans within the United States. Standard Charter Bank, tenth-largest foreign bank in the United States, once stood among London's proudest financial institutions. But in 1986 it fell under the control of three investors from former British colonial outposts: Hong Kong's Y. K. Pao, Singapore's Khoo Teck Puat and Australia's Robert Holmes à Court. As Peter Dutton, bank analyst with Wood, McKenizie and Co., put it: "Control of the bank has effectively gone to the East."

Another potential financial giant is just awakening in Taiwan. With thirty-seven years of strict foreign-exchange controls only now being gradually loosened, Taiwan, with its vast foreign-exchange reserves, could emerge as one of the world's most important sources of overflowing capital.

Ironically, this enormous financial accumulation grew in part out of a relative disdain for the importance of capital as an end in itself. In Korea, Taiwan and Japan, finance has served—often through government fiat—a role subordinate to the interests of industry. As one of the architects of the Meiji-era modernization put it:

> If we assign weights to these three factors with respect to their effectiveness (in building Japanese industry), the spirit should be assigned five parts, laws and regulations four, and capital no more than one part.

This attitude marked a radical departure from that which developed in the United States, Great Britain and other European industrialized nations. There the private banking system gradually imposed its basic world view—what Karl Marx called the "cash nexus"—upon the process of industrial development. In this spirit, Marx noted, "national one-sidedness and narrow-mindedness become more and more impossible." The power of capital now lent a "cosmopolitan character to production itself."

By the mid-nineteenth century this "cosmopolitan character" resulted in much of the capital, accumulated during Britain's decades-long reign as the supreme industrial power, deserting domestic industry for the higher returns to be gained by financing foreign ventures, notably in North America. Between 1870 and 1914, an astonishing 40 percent of Britain's savings were committed overseas. In the process, observes historian Martin Weiner, the City of London weakened the industrial infrastructure, nudging areas such as the north of England, south-west Scotland and the Midlands on the path to their present gruesome condition.

As a late industrializer, Japan, its leaders believed, could not afford a British-style "cosmopolitan" financial mind-set. From the beginning, Meiji government officials attempted to shepherd capital along lines deemed most appropriate for national development. Owing in part to such controls, Japan's government-backed financial system never developed the degree of dependence on foreigners that plagued China. Whereas China's railway loans forced that nation to use materials and equipment from Western nations, loans negotiated by Japan left open to domestic industry these great opportunities. When Japanese officials borrowed overseas, it was often only as a last resort, for such things as financing the successful war against Russia.

Long a debtor nation, Japan's balance of payments improved radically during World War I. With its European competitors preoccupied with destroying one another, Japan had a perfect opportunity to consolidate commercial gains, particularly in Asia. Between 1913 and 1919, Japan's foreign trade tripled, with the nation emerging after the war as a net creditor—a position it held until the Pacific War. Flush from this success, Japan underwent substantial financial liberalization, which flourished briefly before militarists seized control of the state and consolidated economic power in the mid-1930s.

The Asian societies that emerged from the devastation of the ensuing war—most particularly Hong Kong, Japan and its two former colonies, Taiwan and Korea—suffered from conditions even more drastic than those which confronted the Meiji reformers. Faced with postwar starvation, regimes imposed strict controls on scarce natural and capital resources. Communist control of the Chinese mainland, and later the Korean War, severed these societies from their major continental market, forcing them to adjust their economic strategy to deal with the advanced industrial nations of Europe and North America.

In Hong Kong, the capital shortage was solved largely by the Communists, who drove many wealthy Chinese to the Crown Colony. Every year from 1947 to 1955, displaced Chinese bourgeois brought into Hong Kong an additional $250 million in fresh capital. Although a modest sum compared with that poured into Europe during the Marshall Plan, these funds—and the entrepreneurial talent of many of their contributors—provided an early spark for Hong Kong's rapid industrialization. While foreign investments later would hasten the pace of development, the economy remained in large part self-financing, with four-fifths of all investment generated locally.

In its early years, the Nationalist regime on the former Japanese colony of Taiwan shared in this Communist-generated bonanza. Disposition of property left by the retreating Japanese provided some initial infrastructure. But unlike their brethren in Hong Kong, who eventually came to a mutually beneficial commercial understanding with the Communists, the Kuomintang regime on Taiwan found this inconceivable. Instead they turned to their stalwart allies from the United States, who not only provided a vast market, but in the early years even financed most of the capital goods imports necessary for mass industrialization.

At the same time, the Nationalists erected a classic mercantilist industrial policy, welcoming investment while placing high tariffs on foreign products except for those necessary for processing exports. These policies remained largely in place even into the late 1980s. Despite mounting trade surpluses with the United States, Taiwan maintained tariffs that averaged 25 percent of the retail price of the product and, in such areas of American strength as cigarettes and wine, slapped on stiff taxes, raising the cost three or more times higher than the domestic products.

How Japan Got Rich

But the most important developments in mercantilism were in Japan, once again with the Americans serving as unwitting nursemaids of their own ultimate competitors. Occupation authorities, concerned about the stability of the Japanese economy, set up strict financial controls to save scarce capital for rebuilding the shattered industrial infrastructure. To spur exports, they set the yen at a low rate of 360 to the dollar. "We wanted the Japanese to be able to export," recalls Tristan Beplat, who was in charge of money and banking for the occupation authorities. "We wanted them on our side politically. We figured that 90 percent of Japanese exports could sell at 300 exchange rate, even though some were profitable at 200. But we didn't want to be wrong on such matters."

American officials, however, thought that this would be a temporary situation. But the Japanese elite, who remembered how a radically devalued yen had helped spur imports during the Depression era of the 1930s, saw things differently. "There was a strong national consensus," recalls Michiya Matsukawa, a former top official of the Ministry of Finance and later senior advisor to Nikko Securities, " . . . that Japan would not be able to purchase food and raw materials to survive without strong and competitive manufacturing industries."

By the time Japanese such as Matsukawa were back in charge of the economy, a cheap yen and strict financial controls became essential elements of Japan's industrial strategy. And, to some extent, this approach was justified by the poor fundamentals of Japan's economy. Consigned by lack of resources to purchase virtually all its energy and much of its food abroad, Japan as late as 1957 imported twice as much as it exported. Under such circumstances, Japanese leaders felt compelled to adopt an "export or die" mentality. The fervent, even desperate nature of this drive occasionally provoked humorous comment from Americans and other foreigners. "The Japanese economy," noted *Look* in 1965, "is like a confectioner desperately eating his own chocolates on a raft, hoping that a passing ship will stop to purchase his surplus."

Yet what to Americans seemed an almost insane proclivity for overproduction turned out to be the perfect mercantilist business logic. Instead of heavily subsidizing "national champion" firms in the European style, the Japanese government placed trade barriers in front of the domestic market and then provided the conditions—such as cheap capital—for major companies to compete among themselves. The protected domestic market, not exports themselves, became the launching pad for conquering world markets. Even as late as 1985, Japan's exports accounted for 17 percent of its GNP, compared with 24 percent for France, 36 percent for West Germany and 30 percent for the United Kingdom.

The radio industry, one of the first taken over by the Japanese, illustrates how this system worked. Though the United States held the edge in radio technology in the 1950s and 1960s, American radios were banned in Japan while firms such as Matsushita and Sony—now established enough to access cheap capital—fought for control of the highly competitive domestic market. Gradually, with skilled application of transistor technology purchased in America, the Japanese products equalled those of overseas competition. As Japanese manufacturers took these products into the American market, domestic manufacturers pressured Congress for better access to Japan for American-made radios. In 1969, one American businessman in Japan recalled the maddening Japanese response:

They said one day, "you can make radios." But when you read the fine print, it turned out you couldn't bring in the parts. You couldn't even make a crystal set. Then came another round of liberalization and, by god, now you can bring in parts—for a crystal set.

By then the battle was all but over. An industry that could have been swamped by American or European manufacturers in the 1950s seized world leadership by the late 1960s. Sparked by such innovative newcomers as Sony, Japanese manufacturers, who had only 2 percent of the U.S. market in 1955, achieved 97 percent market dominance by 1971. Using similar tactics, Japanese firms soon successfully penetrated world markets in more sophisticated products such as stereo equipment, color television sets and, ultimately, high-technology electronics.

This approach, born of the destitution of the postwar years, was further reinforced by various *shokkus*, or external disruptions, such as the Nixon administration's forced revaluation of the yen in 1971, and the twin oil-price rises of the 1970s. In this atmosphere of periodically reinforced panic, Japanese corporations—and their banks—were urged to pour their resources into an ever-increasing drive for productivity and market share.

It was a remarkable mixture of traditional mercantilism and controlled competition.

Although capitalist in orientation and dominated by conservative social forces, the system erected in Japan contradicted much of Marx's analysis of capitalism. Rather than blindly following the logic of the "cash nexus," Japan's financiers accepted an honored, yet supporting role in achieving the national goals broadly agreed upon by the government and industry and at least assented to by labor. This coordinated consensual approach, notes Hisamitsu Uetani, chairman of Yamaichi Securities, made Japan in some senses "the most socialist country in the world."

In this "socialist" system, even investment bankers such as Uetani—bankers who in the United States or Europe tend to be unswerving advocates of the "cash nexus"—served largely as just another branch of the elite administration of the mercantilist system. Under the guidance of MITI and the Ministry of Finance, bankers directed the nation's precious capital (still under $5 billion in 1970) down through a carefully designed pyramid. Reflecting the mores of *keiretsu* dominance, small companies and individuals stood at the bottom of the pyramid, while large companies engaged in manufacturing activities gained priority status at the top. As a *Fortune* correspondent commented in 1965: "Big companies in Japan always have the money to pay up—that's what makes the establishment."

For those outside the industrial sphere, this system meant significant hardships. As late as 1964, for instance, a Japanese student going abroad could take out of the country a maximum of only $30. One Japanese scientist recalls arriving as a postdoctoral student in the United States for the first time in 1957 with several cameras, not for taking pictures, but to sell for living expenses.

In essence the students, like virtually all Japanese individuals, have sacrificed in order to finance the burgeoning export industries. Even top executives such as Uetani, while controlling enormous institutional wealth, receive salaries of only $400,000, a fraction of what their American counterparts might earn. This wealth is further diluted by the almost confiscatory income-tax rates, ranging up to the 88 percent imposed on the higher income brackets.

Under this oddly egalitarian system, even the top executives of Japan's most powerful companies lived modestly, particularly by the standards of their Western European, American and even Soviet counterparts. "Actually the CEOs in Communist countries enjoy a life-style much superior to ours," noted Yamaichi's Uetani. "You can see the cars, chauffeurs and special shops—the goods they enjoy. Compared to them we are very unfairly treated. Seriously speaking, it's almost impossible for me even to invite you to my home for dinner. We live in conditions that an American CEO will find quite beneath his status."

But Uetani's life-style seems regal indeed compared to that of the average Japanese who has been forced to cope with housing and with social and public services well below the standards of virtually every major industrial country. For instance, half of all Japanese families of four live in houses with less than 650 square feet, and 10 percent live in housing units of 400 square feet or less. Until the mid-1970s, credit cards were virtually nonexistent and consumer credit was largely the province of an estimated 50,000 *sarakin*, or "loan sharks," who by 1983 were loaning out nearly $5 billion at often ruinous rates as high as 60 percent annually.

Too cautious to take on such indebtedness, most Japanese have contented themselves with saving up for their purchases, receiving the meager interest paid at banks or the huge postal savings system. The whole Japanese economic system in fact has seemed to enforce high savings. Compared to most Europeans or Americans, the average Japanese *salariman*, or salaried worker, retires from his main employer at age fifty-five, five to ten years earlier than his American counterpart, forcing him to save for a potentially very long retirement. Perhaps more important is the price of buying a house, which now takes on average more than 7.5 times annual income, compared to 3 times more income in the United States. With no write-off for mortgage deductions and down payments averaging nearly 35 percent, it takes the average Japanese until age forty—ten years later than his American counterpart—to buy his first, usually very small, house.

Added to these economic pressures are intense social ones. Although democratic in form, the values of Japan's society are shaped by a sort of "mass self-hypnosis" fostered by the state through its influence over the media and strict control of the educational system. Saving money is not only a personal decision, but a societal obligation. This was particularly true in the 1960s and 1970s, when household savings approached more than one-fifth of disposable income. Although they are now spending a bit more, in 1985 Japanese were saving three times as much of their disposable income as were Americans.

As a precious "national resource," these savings were used to their full advantage. By the late 1970s, Japanese companies became highly leveraged—with debt-equity ratios averaging 3.5 to 1, compared to 1 to 1 in the United States—and accustomed to borrowing heavily to fund their growth. Since the bureaucrats at the Ministry of Finance and MITI controlled access to capital, executives found themselves obliged to adjust corporate goals to the "national interest." Banks, too, were heavily regulated, subjected to controls over interest rates and frequent examinations of loan portfolios. Every new branch went through a rigorous approval process. To make sure the money stayed at home, overseas loans were strictly limited well into the 1970s. Even as late as 1979, the Ministry of Finance stepped in to reduce Japanese banks' participation in a $600 million syndicated loan to the Korean Development Bank.

Many bankers chafed at this "baby-sitting," as one disgruntled financier put it, but gladly accepted the benefits of government protection. Under the iron fist of the Ministry of Finance, competition was sharply curtailed so that not one new bank has been created in Japan since 1955. Compared to over 14,000 banks in the United States, there are only 1,073 in Japan, with about thirteen elite "city banks" accounting for nearly 30 percent of all private loans.

Another major reason for "baby-sitting" the banks lay in the traditional Japanese fear of outside influence. During the capital-starved 1950s and into early 1960, plenty of money was to be had from foreign sources, mostly American. But in Japan the spectre of foreign domination raised in Servan-Schreiber's *The American Challenge* was exorcised by administrative curbs on foreign investment that by 1970 helped keep U.S. business investment in Japan at one-twentieth the level it was in Europe. Everything from silk and autos to semiconductors was protected from foreign investment. Responding to American criticism of this practice in 1969, Joji Arai, assistant manager of the Japan Productivity Center in Washington, explained bluntly: "Most Japanese businessmen don't want to make the same mistake the European businessmen did—turning over most of their businesses to American business."

One other tactic central to Japan's mercantilism was to keep the yen undervalued so that, despite steadily increasing trade surpluses, the value of the currency remained relatively low until the mid-1980s. At the same time, the massive accumulated savings and government credit priorities assured Japanese industrialists of cheap and abundant capital resources. Japan's semiconductor manufacturers, for instance, according to one UCLA study, enjoyed a cost of capital at least 20 percent less expensive than did their American competitors.

Inexpensive capital constituted an all-important weapon in Japan's assault on world markets. Between 1975 and 1985, gross fixed capital formation in Japan averaged 30.1 percent of GDP, compared to only 18.4 percent in the United States. Roughly during this same period, Japanese overall manufacturing annual fixed investment jumped from $4,000 to over $6,000 per employee, while that of the United States increased only from around $2,000 to roughly $2,800. Not surprising, Japan's manufacturing productivity per person almost tripled; by 1986, according to a study in the *New England Review*, it was comparable to that of the United States.

For over two decades these advantages, compounded by Japanese hard work and numerous American mistakes, resulted in soaring trade deficit. American business fumed, with Henry Ford II calling the Japanese tactics "stupid" and bound to incite protectionism. Yet at the negotiating table, the men from MITI were anything but stupid. While Japanese industrialists worked assiduously to conquer overseas markets, their helpmates in government treated their increasingly irate trading partners with an excruciating Asian version of the filibuster. The long-promised trade liberalization proceeded slowly, while Japan's exports flooded the world to such an extent that by 1977 the nation's trade surplus reached over $15 billion.

By the 1980s the cash-starved, uncompetitive Japan of the 1950s was a fading memory. With reform stalled by powerful pressure groups such as agricultural interests and low-tech industries, Japan's mercantilist corporations continued to devour the markets of the world, particularly those of the United States. Between 1970 and 1985, Japan increased its share of world manufacturing by over 15 percent, according to a 1987 study published by the Japan Economic Institute, while America's share dropped by 4 percent. Led by this surge in manufacturing and declining commodity prices, Japan in just five years between 1981 and 1985 saw its trade surplus explode almost tenfold to over $80 billion, with the surplus from the United States alone quadrupling to over $50 billion.

In the process, Japan became the most capital-rich nation of this epoch. Between 1981 and 1986 alone, Japan increased its net external holdings from $11 billion to $180 billion, while the United States became the world's largest debtor. By subordinating the "cosmopolitan" needs of finance to those of industry, Japan successfully overturned the century-old hegemony of Anglo-American finance. The Japanese are now—and will probably remain for decades to come—the ultimate shapers of the world's financial destiny.

"When I first joined the bank twenty-five years ago, we saw Bank of America or United California Bank [now First Interstate] as excellent. They were bigger than us. We sent people to them and I learned their methods. Now we are bigger and now I am confident we are more excellent than them," explains Tadashi Hasegawa, manager at a Los Angeles suburban branch of Dai-Ichi Kangyo Bank, by 1985 the world's largest bank. "Twenty years ago, American banks were like God," Hasegawa continued, his black eyes now flashing with pride. "Now they are only misleaders. We are the teachers now."

The Limits of Mercantilism

Many Americans are indeed ready to be taken to school by the Japanese. In one of the more prescriptive passages of William Ouchi's *M-Form Society*, the author suggests the adoption in America of many aspects of the Japanese financial system. Instead of the present rather haphazard system, with its over 14,000 banks and thousands of other financial institutions, Ouchi prefers the more closed system with its strong concentrations of banking assets and close equity ties between major banks and large corporations. With its heavy dose of regulation and coordination, this system, Ouchi argues, is simply "more efficient than ours."

Although arguably applicable in a developing country such as postwar Japan or, more recently, Taiwan and Korea, this model can prove destructive in an advanced industrial country. Even many Japanese—despite their country's phenomenal economic achievements and the accolades of their American admirers—now realize that the mercantilist system has become destructive to their nation's future. And they fear that unless radical changes are implemented soon, Japan may be about to begin its long descent from its current position of predominance.

"The challenge to the formula that has driven our country's growth, mass production and export is as profound as the challenge brought to our country from the Mongolian invasion or the coming of Commodore Perry's ships," observes Teruhiko Tsuji, a leading Japanese business consultant. "The strategy of large-scale exports has just about reached the end of the line."

This somewhat drastic viewpoint is more than merely a reaction to another *shokku* (shock) such as the oil crises of the 1970s, which were caused by unexpected forces external to Japan's economy. The problem addressed by Tsuji is more fundamental, a natural and inevitable result of Japan's heretofore successful mercantilist system.

In sum, mercantilism, through its relentless logic, is beginning to undercut Japan's success. Centered upon the fervent commitment to exports, ever-greater levels of productivity and expanding market share at virtually all cost, mercantilism has developed into a "beggar thy neighbor" trade policy. It earns megadollars, but in the process slows down the growth rates and wears out the patience of its prime customers. Adversarial trade, such as practiced by Japan, noted Peter Drucker, "is always self-defeating."

The self-defeating nature of this mercantilism is already clear. Widely regarded around the world as merely selfish and self-serving "economic animals," the Japanese have managed to supplant Americans as the most feared nation among executives and intellectuals from Paris to Peking. Besides the rising protectionism inside its prime market, the United States, as well as, in recent years, major European nations, has erected massive barriers to prevent the influx of Japanese cars and consumer electronics. Such fears—and protectionist retaliation—are also spreading to Japan's own backyard in East Asia. Like business people from the United States and Europe, Asians from such strong exporting locales as Hong Kong have until recently made little headway in Japan, blocked as they have been by complex product standards and other "nontariff" barriers.

In 1985, for example, Japan sold Hong Kong twelve times as much as it bought. Even Hong Kong's garments, renowned for quality the world over, and toys, of which the Crown Colony is the world's largest producer, barely penetrated Japan's tightly controlled retail marketplace. "You can't get anywhere with them. They won't even buy our toys," notes T. W. Wong, deputy director general from the Federation of Hong Kong Industries, one of the most pro–free-trade groups in Asia. "Their toy companies can be dying, living on subsidies, but they won't let us in."

With the dramatic strengthening of the yen, such imports were beginning to break through by the fall of 1987, albeit at a still slow pace. More significantly, key Asian nations—such as Taiwan, Korea, Singapore and Malaysia—are consciously seeking to break out of their traditional roles as receptacles for ever-greater shipments of goods made in Japan and now see themselves supplanting the Japanese in world markets.

Even before the 1985 yen *shokku*, Japanese firms increasingly worried about strong competition from Asian industrial upstarts such as South Korea, Taiwan and the People's Republic of China.

By 1986, this competition was causing major losses among Japan's flagship industries including steel, shipbuilding and electronic components. Particularly vulnerable were scores of smaller firms producing low-tech items for export, such as cutlery and dinnerware, suddenly forced to cope with 30 percent price rises against hard-driving Koreans, Taiwanese and others working in dollar-oriented currencies. And even as these mercantilist states challenge Japan in some of the more traditional industries, they themselves are being challenged by countries with even lower wages, such as Thailand or India. More recently, nations such as Taiwan and Korea have placed increasing emphasis on challenging even Japan's more sophisticated technology-based industries, such as computers and semiconductors.

As a result of this competition—and increasingly protectionist measures in the advanced industrial countries—economic growth rates in Japan already have fallen to 5 percent or less annually, and corporate operating profits have fallen as much as one-half since the salad days of the early 1970s. In 1985, exports boosted total sales of Japan's top corporations by 2.7 percent, but profits dropped by nearly 5 percent. In 1987, with the full effect of yen revaluation, profits of Japan's manufacturers were expected to drop further.

This lower growth and increasing challenge from abroad reveal some of the profound weaknesses in the much-praised Japanese industrial system. The mercantilist success of Japan has been based largely on a ''fast follower'' strategy. Rather than competing on the basis of innovation and creativity, Japanese firms usually preferred to buy the latest technology from abroad, an approach that worked when Japan's currency and labor rates were relatively cheap in comparison to those of Europe or the United States. But now Japanese costs approach or even exceed those of its advanced competitors. And with the rise of nations such as Taiwan, the one-time ''fast follower'' finds itself pursued by its own increasingly lethal competition.

The classic response of an advanced industrial state to competition from less developed nations has been innovation. But Japan's orientation to outside technology has hollowed out much of its native ability to think for itself. ''The technology of most products, the basic science which produced the technology and the very concept of most products Japan exports today—all find their roots in the West," admits Ichiro Yoshiyama, a managing director of Minolta Camera. "We import it, cultivate it, improve it and re-export it to the mother country, eventually controlling the market there."

Japan's dilemma then, Yoshiyama points out, is that its industrial machine often lacks the ability to develop new breakthrough technologies they can truly call their own. This has less to do with any native tendency toward conformity than with the perverse impacts of contemporary Japanese mercantilism. Under the conditions of "creative destruction" caused by the war and the Occupation reformers, Japan in the late 1940s and early 1950s ushered forth such remarkable native sons as Honda, Matsushita and Morita to provide an innovative spark to a then dormant economy. But the giant-dominated mercantilist system now works against the sort of "creative destruction" that is a precondition for such entrepreneurial upstarts.

In this sense, the much-admired "adjustment" policies and corporate stability of Japan are in reality signs of a profound structural weakness. A society facing a major industrial transition *should* be rife with the messy capitalist carnage caused by large-scale takeovers, mergers and spin-offs. But, instead, the structure of Japan's economy—characterized by giant conglomerates competing against each other with almost suicidal monomania—has remained largely intact. Yet where such competition in the past resulted in common profits, now the margins in many industries have shrunk to nothing. In 1981 and 1982, when Japanese firms first started exporting VTRs, they enjoyed gross margins averaging nearly 40 percent. Five years later those margins had disappeared almost entirely. Similar patterns also started to appear in semiconductors, silicon wafers, semiconductor equipment and cameras. As one Japanese economist commented: "We are in danger of going bankrupt with our surplus."

Faced with similar dilemmas, the American economy has managed to generate new growth companies and restructurings of larger firms as a source of innovation. But Japan's mercantilism has frozen the waters of its economy, preventing any such entrepreneurial upsurge. In fact, smaller companies—including the fledgling high-tech venture businesses—have been forced to bear the brunt of the yen revaluation as the *keiretsu* cut back orders and foreign customers seek other suppliers. "Small firms and venture businesses," observed one prominent Japanese business consultant, "are essentially being made to pay the price for the *zaibatsu*'s success overseas."

As its nation enters the 1990s, Japanese industry finds itself caught in a desperate vise: too expensive to compete with the lower cost NICs in mass manufacturing, while lacking the dynamic new growth companies—the economic *sokojikara*—capable of producing the necessary innovations and technological breakthroughs. "The whole system is breaking down," believes Hiroshi Katoh, a former official of an affiliate of the MITI and now a leading Japanese venture capitalist. "We just can't go out and get the growth we used to. The feeling is that Japan is in the beginnings of a decline. We need to find a new way."

The new way most likely to emerge resembles in many aspects the pattern first established by Britain in Marx's day. Unable or unwilling to invest in emerging new firms, the bulging coffers of the giant financial institutions and *keiretsu* are pouring into offshore investments, particularly in the United States where Japanese firms by 1987 already had more than $30 billion in plants, property and equipment. Today, large Japanese firms average about 4 percent of their total production overseas, compared to 15 to 20 percent for their American and European rivals. As the Japanese achieve an equivalent ratio by the year 2000, noted a recent MITI report, the move offshore will cost Japanese workers over 560,000 jobs.

This offshore trend reflects not merely a response to protectionism, but a bleak assessment among Japanese themselves of their own industrial future. A 1986 survey by the Economic Planning Agency, for instance, found 60 percent of the 1,600 companies listed on the Tokyo and Osaka exchanges—the cream of Japan's corporations—rated as "poor" prospects in their present lines of business. Not surprisingly, Japan's once-hefty rate of new manufacturing capital investment has started to drop, falling nearly 4.2 percent in 1986, while Korean capital investment jumped over 42 percent. In 1987, such expenditures, according to a survey by the Nippon Credit Bank, were expected to fall another 6.7 percent with an additional 4 percent drop projected for 1988. All this is certain to accelerate the decline of Japan's industrial plant, the world's most modern for more than a decade, which by the mid-1980s was aging more than that of the supposedly "de-industrializing" United States.

The shift away from domestic industry represents only one of the ways that Japan is now replicating the earlier bout of de-industrialization experienced in the United States. In a reprise of the financially driven strategies developed by American corporations in the 1960s and 1970s, Japanese companies increasingly focus their attention on the financial manipulation of stocks and other investments. The *zaitech* mania has even spread to such industrial heavyweights as Matsushita and Nippon Steel, which have opened financial subsidiaries in world money centers such as London. And at last one medium-size steel products firm, Hanwa Corporation, has transformed itself into one of the nation's leading foreign-exchange dealers, enjoying a turnover of between $300 million and $500 million daily from its trading office near the Tokyo Tsukiji Fishmarket. As one U.S. stockbroker explained: "They've taken the view that they were in commodities; what's finance but just another commodity?"

Such views might be common on Wall Street or in the City of London, but they represent a stark contradiction of the view of capital predominant in Japan since the Meiji era. And as Japan's Ministry of Finance, albeit reluctantly, further opens the nation's financial system, an increasing quantity of Japan's surplus cash is likely to find its way to other countries, particularly the United States.

Like their industrial customers, cash-rich Japanese financial institutions are shifting their assets overseas. In 1973, foreign loans accounted for a mere 6 percent of all Japanese lending; eleven years later, they accounted for better than one-fifth. Total outward purchases of bonds and securities overseas, largely insurance companies and banks, constituted only $80 million in 1984; the following year, due to deregulation, that total reached $520 billion, more than the total purchases made by American, British and Canadian investors combined. By 1986, Japan's banks for the first time boasted more foreign assets than their counterparts in the United States.

As Japan continues its financial liberalization, this foreign orientation should accelerate. In April 1986, for instance, Japan's insurance companies, which already held an estimated $31 billion in foreign securities, were allowed to increase the proportion of assets invested abroad from 10 to 20 percent. Japan's leading banks are following suit with Sumitomo, perhaps the most aggressive of the group, expected to raise its proportion of revenue from foreign operations from the current 22.7 to over 40 percent within a matter of years.

To some, Japan's emergence as a world financial power is the ultimate sign of its international economic hegemony. But many who helped create the industrial basis for that hegemony, such as Hiroshi Takeuchi, chief economist of the Long Term Credit Bank, see in Japan's new aura of luxury and worldwide financial clout the harbinger of an inevitable decline. ''Japan is the next America,'' predicts Takeuchi. ''We will follow the pattern of the United States and the United Kingdom. Go to the top and will go down. All within the next twenty years.''

A well-known economic nationalist, Takeuchi is particularly distressed by the shift of Japan's capital overseas to the United States. In Takeuchi's view, the United States, which accounted for a staggering 44 percent of Japan's direct overseas investment in 1985, still possesses the entrepreneurial dynamism, the resources, the *sokojikara* to reestablish its economic preeminence. By lavishing its current surpluses on America, he believes Japan's corporate elite, like the ''cosmopolitan'' British of the late nineteenth century, is simply handing over the keys of ascendency to its greatest competitor.

Given the enormous appeal of America, Takeuchi believes only Draconian measures—''a kind of Hitler regime''—can stop the long-term transfer of Japan's massive wealth to the United States. ''United States society is very strong, with all your immigration from other countries. You have the scale and the resources that we simply will never possess,'' the fifty-two-year-old economist noted resignedly. ''The Japanese role will be to assist the United States by exporting our money to rebuild your economy. This is the evidence that our economy is fundamentally weak. The money goes to America because you are fundamentally strong.''

Tairiku Power

Karl Marx observed over a century ago that ever since the Middle Ages, wealthy nations of one era often have provided the ''secret foundations'' for the emergence of the next epoch's leaders. Venice supplied much of the capital that underlay the emergence of Holland, which in turn financed the ascendency of England, its greatest rival. By the 1870s, America was benefiting from a similar pattern. ''A great deal of capital, which appears today in the United States without any birth certificate,'' Marx observed in *Das Kapital*, ''was yesterday in England. . . .''

Yet in a stunning reversal of Marx's dictum, the United States is not following the pattern of other capital-exporting empires (Venice, Holland and Great Britain), but now is attracting a new wave of overseas investment. In short, America continues to appeal to foreigners because of its ''open system,'' with its relative lack of controls on foreign business activity, its expanding population and its economic dynamism. Equally important, the United States attracts by its very physical expanse, its vast resources, its status as the world's richest and most developed continental power.

In the future this appeal will prove crucial to the nation's economic prospects. Although the bulk of U.S. investment capital from overseas still comes from the European continent, the financial and industrial ascendency of East Asia is already transforming that region into the key source of capital for the American economy. Whereas European capital, technology and markets dominated America's international business in its first two centuries, this role is likely to be taken by Asia in the Third Century.

This continental power, what the Japanese call *tairiku*, has particular appeal to people from small, densely populated and resource-poor places such as Japan, Taiwan, Hong Kong and Singapore. To them, the richness of the North American continent seems an almost unimaginably fertile base for economic development. "To put it in simplest terms, there are thousands of areas in the United States where you can build a hotel and do some marketing and you can develop it into a tourist area," explains Yumi Kobayashi of James Sagin and Associates, a Menlo Park, California, consulting firm that works with many large Japanese financial institutions. "There are no such unexploited areas in Japan, no unturned rocks."

Crammed onto their tiny island, and virtually devoid of resources, the Japanese spent much of the post-Meiji period attempting to achieve *tairiku* for themselves. Before the opening to the West, Japanese largely were content with their small, mountainous islands with their abundant water resources. But faced suddenly with competition from powers controlling vast territories—Imperial Russia, the United States, and the far-flung British Empire—the home islands, with their inadequate supplies of coal and iron ore, suddenly seemed a pathetic match.

This discrepancy between the miserable physical reality of the islands and the traditional concept of their land as "home of the Gods" consumed many Japanese, who felt their nation's destiny required a more expansive base for greatness. As Uchimura Kanzo, an early nationalist writer, said: "Grander tasks await the young Japan who has the best of Europe and the best of Asia at its command. At her touch the circuit is complete and the healthy fluid shall overflow the earth."

Virtually as soon as the nation developed its basic industrial and military infrastructure, this "healthy fluid" did overflow, first in 1895, after a brief war with China, into Taiwan, Korea, Sakhalin and a host of smaller Pacific islands. By 1920, Japan had doubled both its land mass and the population under its suzerainty, providing *Dai Nippon* with most of its coal and iron ore and much of its food.

Yet even these acquisitions failed to satisfy many Japanese military men and industrialists, who chafed under the limits of their young empire. "We feel suffocated," complained Yosuke Matsuoka, a leading Diet spokesman for the expansionists, early in 1931. "What we are seeking is that which is minimal for human beings. . . . We are seeking room that will let us breathe."

Within a matter of months the army made "room" by moving

into Manchuria, China's lightly defended but resource-rich northeastern province. This maneuver angered both the United States and the European powers, particularly Great Britain, who began cutting off Japanese access to its colonial markets. Limits or even embargoes on Japanese purchases of precious raw materials from such European colonies as Malaysia and Indonesia threatened to stop the machinery of the empire. Under the comprehensive title of *Construction of a New Order in East Asia*, the Imperial Navy in 1939 laid out the logic that would soon lead to war not only with the colonial powers, but ultimately with the United States as well.

Japan lacks some 38 important raw materials necessary for its further development as an industrial nation. Of these only coal, iron and salt can satisfactorily be obtained on the continent. Japan is still extremely short of cotton and wool. As for lumber, rubber and oil they are almost entirely unavailable at present. . . . It is seen therefore that continental expansion is not a problem confined to the continent itself but one that embraces the seas surrounding it.

With its defeat in World War II, Japan lost all reasonable hope of achieving *tairiku* status by force. Defeat cost Japan half its overseas territory, 43 percent of its national wealth and more than 30 percent of its industrial capacity, along with the vast majority of its energy reserves. Having suffered so grievous a loss, Japan's leaders have sought a more peaceable link to a continental market.

China, of course, represents the closest *tairiku* power, but it remains controlled by an unpredictable Communist bureaucracy that is fundamentally suspicious—with good historical reasons—of Japanese intentions. The Soviet Union has long been fundamentally hostile to Japanese ambitions and offers only narrow access to its potentially enormous market. Australia boasts many resources, but only few consumers. India's level of economic development is still primitive. Europe, like Japan, is resource poor. Its dwindling population, lack of economic dynamism and protectionist "closed system" limit its appeal.

In the eyes of the Japanese and most Asians, only America

has the ability to provide an acceptable surrogate *tairiku*. Living in a country so rich that the Japanese call it *bei-koku*, or rice country, Americans, in the words of Henry Adams, have always had "the continent stretched before [them] like an uncovered ore bed." Within its own borders, the United States contains thirty times Japan's arable land, 1,300 times the oil, 327 times the coal reserves and 170 times the reserves of iron ore. These differences explain how many Japanese, even with huge trade and current accounts surpluses, still regard the United States as something of a spoiled brat. "Our common perception," says Mikio Kato, a leading Japanese internationalist, "of American complaints is to see a rich person complaining. Americans have become too lazy. Yet the United States has all the resources it needs to revive."

Transpacific Integration

These "resources"—in terms of land, energy and people— have made America in essence the *tairiku* power of the Pacific, the ultimate focus of Asian ambitions, financial power and technological prowess. In a pattern with Japan that is in many ways similar to its nineteenth-century symbiosis with Europe, the United States is undergoing a process of what Japan scholar Kent Calder has labeled "transpacific integration," tying the economic fates of Asia and America inextricably together.

Owing largely to the strict capital controls imposed by the postwar governments in Japan and many other Asian nations, "transpacific integration" is most developed in terms of trade. Over the past few decades, the United States has emerged as the first- or second-largest trading partner of every significant Asian state, including Japan, Korea, the Philippines, Thailand and Singapore. It ranks third, after Japan and Hong Kong, in the commerce of China.

In this process, the United States has usurped much of the role once played by Europe in the Pacific economies. In 1960, Europeans accounted for nearly a quarter of the region's export market; by the early '80s, that share had dropped to a mere 15 percent. Similarly, Europe's share as a source of imports dropped from 22.1 percent in 1960 to little over 11 percent twenty years later. By 1986, not one European state ranked within the top three trading partners of virtually any East Asian state.

Nor do Asians expect Europe to play an important role in their economic future. Once their almost slavish imitators, the Japanese now sometimes refer to the Europeans as the *shayozoku*, or tribes of the setting sun. "From the Japanese perception, Europe has always been a teaching model," says Tadashi Yamamoto, director of the Japan Center for International Exchange. "But now that image is clouded. Lots of Japanese look down on Europeans and write them off."

Unable or unwilling to share in "transpacific integration," Europe seems to be moving toward its own separate economic destiny. The one-time ruler of continents now increasingly focuses its attention on its home redoubts as well as more geopolitically aligned states in Africa and the Middle East. In 1958, roughly one-third of European trade was among the continental countries. By 1985, that intraregional trade accounted for an absolute majority of Europe's commerce.

The experience of Australia illustrates the enormity of this decoupling of the European and Asia-Pacific economies. In the late 1950s, more than half of Australia's exports went to European countries, nearly one-third to Britain alone, while Asian trade accounted for no more than half as much. Today Asia and Pacific-facing North America account for over three-fifths of Australia's exports. Much the same pattern has occurred in Canada, which now does more business in the Pacific than with its traditional European markets.

In Southeast Asia, where European colonial ties were once strong, nations increasingly look overwhelmingly to the United States and Japan and other Pacific states for markets, products and investment. In other parts of the developing world, such as Brazil, Mexico, the Middle East and South Africa, Europe continues to be a major investor, but in Southeast Asia the Europeans contribute only 13 percent of the total. In terms of trade, Europe's position is even less important, accounting for roughly one-tenth. Thai foreign minister Dr. Chirayu Isarangkun points out: "If the trend continues, the trade pattern, even the cultural relationships between the two regions, would be slipping backwards."

Even in Hong Kong, founded by British capital and still flying the Union Jack, it has been the Americans, and more recently the Japanese, who have been the dominant investors. By 1984, Britain's share had dropped to a mere 6.7 percent, while the United States and Japan combined accounted for nearly three-quarters of total industrial investment. Americans employ nearly 40,000 people in the Crown Colony, and the 16,000 U.S. expatriates there in 1986 accounted for even more residents than the British. As James McGregor, chairman of the Hong Kong Chamber of Commerce, put it: "This may be a British colony, but it's an American town."

The pattern is particularly profound among the NICs and Southeast Asia. The United States absorbed 40 percent of Korea's exports and sank in more than half its foreign investment between January 1984 and June 1986. Taiwan, now eleventh of the world's leading trading nations, ahead of its ideological rival on the mainland, is the United States' fifth-largest trading partner, outdistancing the United Kingdom. Taiwan sends America half its exports as well as the largest portion of its foreign investment. Europe also constitutes only a tiny portion of direct foreign investment in Japan, the majority of which comes from the United States.

Perhaps the most glaring evidence of America's predominant status in East Asia can be seen in China. Although European states such as Great Britain and France had a decades-long head start in commercial ties with China, U.S. trade with China between 1977 and 1984 grew from $300 million to more than $7 billion, a total that exceeded the trade links of the entire European community. Between 1979 and 1985, Americans accounted for over 13 percent of all foreign investment in China, nearly 25 percent more than Japan and twice that of the entire European community.

In its future, China clearly aims to participate in "transpacific integration." In 1960, the vast majority of China's trade was with Soviet Bloc countries, with only 4 percent of imports coming from the Asia-Pacific region. By 1983, transpacific trade accounted for well over two-fifths of Chinese imports and well over half its total trade. Trade ties were growing rapidly with virtually all Asian countries, including one-time enemy South

Korea. As Tao Bingwei of the Chinese Institute of International Studies has said, "in the world economy, relations with the Pacific rank first for China."

With China still economically underdeveloped, the Sino-American relationship will remain oriented toward trade and outward investment. But among the already wealthy nations of Asia, the United States is beginning to reap the rewards of its status as the region's dominant *tairiku* power.

It should be stressed that this shift of Asian capital into the United States is still in its infancy. Japan's emergence as a financial superpower is remarkably recent. In 1981, Japan's net external assets stood at a mere $11 billion, but by 1985 they had swelled to $180 billion, surpassing the total accumulated by the OPEC nations in the 1970s.

Unless held up by political factors such as protectionism, it is likely much of this money will flow toward the United States. Between 1977 and 1984, Japan invested over $20 billion in North America, more than in its traditional market in nearby Asia and more than twice the figure for the entire European Economic Community. North America, which accounted for over one-third of all Japanese direct investment in 1980, took nearly 45 percent of the total five years later while increasing at a 30 percent rate from the previous year.

Indeed, as soon as the Ministry of Finance began to loosen its tight grip, Japan in the early 1980s emerged as the primary buyer of long-term treasury notes, accounting for over one-third of all such purchases in 1986. By 1986, the world's largest securities house, Nomura Securities, was handling an astounding $2 billion a day in treasury notes. At the same time Nomura has increased its participation in underwriting new issues for such corporations as Dow Chemical, Walt Disney Productions, Phillip Morris and IBM Credit Corporation. Reflecting Nomura's increasing "Americanization," the firm's New York operation—directed by two graduates of the Wharton School of Business—now gains three-quarters of its business by selling American stocks, a total reversal of the situation just a few years earlier when sales of Japanese stocks accounted for the bulk of the firm's business.

The other major securities houses—Daiwa, Yamaichi and

Nikko—have also aggressively moved into the American market. Since the early 1980s, most have doubled or tripled their staffs. "The U.S. is a very exciting market with huge growth potential," explains Akira Setogawa, president of Nikko Securities International. "In terms of creativeness, information, products and financial developments it's all here."

American stocks have also become extremely attractive to Japanese back home, particularly given the extremely high prices of their domestic issues. On the Tokyo Stock Exchange in 1986, for example, 70 percent of all listed foreign issues were American, while Japanese holdings of U.S. securities and government bonds jumped to over $60 billion, a threefold increase from just four years earlier. By that time 85 percent of all foreign bonds bought by Japanese were made in the USA. As one bond trader complained: "We have tracked gold, and we have been tracking oil. Now we have to track the Japanese mind-set."

Japan's mammoth commercial banks have also increased their U.S. penetration, with their assets in America more than doubling since 1981. Japanese now hold 45 percent of all foreign bank assets in the United States and made one-third of foreign banks' business loans—three times the amount of their nearest competitor.

But banking represents only one aspect of Japanese capital investment in the United States. Within the last decade hundreds of Japanese firms in a diversity of industries have set up shop in America, with Japan's share of direct investment in the United States increasing nearly fivefold between 1977 and 1984. During the same period, Europe's share, although still much larger, dropped by 7 percent. Particularly dramatic has been the upsurge in Japanese manufacturing investments, which expanded over 40 percent between 1983 and 1984, six times the rate of the European nations.

Today, virtually all parts of the nation, from the Deep South to the midwestern heartland, have benefited from new investment, plants and equipment from Asia. By the end of March 1985, Japanese firms were operating 400 factories in forty states and employing some 80,000 Americans. Another 652 Japanese companies were also engaged in joint ventures, three-quarters involving manufacturing activities. By 1987, Japanese business investment in Tennessee alone reached over $1 billion and provided over 10,000 jobs. Eager to share in this largesse, many states and even localities, including such small towns as Bartlesville, Oklahoma (population 36,000), have set up trade offices in Tokyo.

Without a major political upheaval on either side of the Pacific, the Asian search for *tairiku*-based growth should spark an ever-growing tide of investment. MITI predicts that Japanese investment in America will grow by an estimated 14.2 percent annually into the 1990s. Japanese auto production *within the United States* is expected to grow from roughly 500,000 cars in 1986 to three times that number by the end of the decade. Says Yoshitaka Sajima, vice-president of Mitsui and Company (USA): "The U.S. and Japan are not just trading with each other anymore—they've become part of each other."

Although still deeply in debt, Korea also is seeking ways to become "part" of the United States. By 1987, the rapidly industrializing nation had invested an estimated $200 million in plants and equipment in the United States, a figure expected to top $5 billion in the next decade, according to the Korean Economic Institute of America.

A similar symbiosis can also be seen in the escalating investments in the United States by other nations along the Pacific periphery. Most of the recent, dramatic moves by Australia's most aggressive millionaires—such as Rupert Murdoch, Robert Holmes à Court and Kerry Packer—have been not on a London stage, but in Hong Kong, Los Angeles or New York.

But by far the most significant financial source in the coming decade will be the cash-rich entrepreneurs of the Chinese diaspora. Like other Asians, the Chinese have a distinct American tilt to their investment preferences. In one survey of Chinese investors, conducted by SPS International Properties in Hong Kong, 77 percent of those polled named either the United States or Canada as their first choice of investment. Los Angeles, San Francisco, New York, Toronto and Vancouver dominated the list. Only 4 percent opted for the United Kingdom, Hong Kong's governing power. A poll of Singapore's five venture-capital firms found a similar proclivity: four out of five named the United States as their preferred locale of investment.

Investments from these "entrepreneurs on the run" can be expected to grow, particularly with the approach of the 1997 deadline for reunification with China. By 1986, outflows from Hong Kong were estimated at nearly HK $3 billion annually, with an estimated HK $500 million already invested in San Francisco, long the largest center of Chinese life in North America. "The presence of relatives in California is a big inducement to many individual investors," says John Loh, president of American Asian bank, located is San Francisco. "They are attracted by California's Asian enclaves."

Another key inducement is citizenship, which is leading many Hong Kong entrepreneurs to establish businesses in the United States. In July of 1986, one Los Angeles developer of minimalls raised nearly $5 million from Hong Kong investors interested in building businesses in his small shopping centers, something he believes represents just the beginning of a movement that will build as the date of the Communist takeover approaches. "There's going to be a tremendous shot of cash that's going to come between now and 1990, when most of my clients will get all their money out," he adds.

Even some of Hong Kong's largest manufacturers are planning to shift their capital—and even production—to the United States. Tony Cheung, chairman of the Koyoda Group and one of the Crown Colony's leading television manufacturers, in 1987 decided to establish a multimillion-dollar plant in Centerville, Iowa, where lower land costs and shipping rates now make the cost of production roughly equivalent to that in Hong Kong. Equally important, Cheung's move to the United States provides possible citizenship for a dozen middle- and upper-level managers eager to emigrate.

"If you have a lot of money, you can buy into Australia, England or Canada, but there's no future, no real jobs there," Cheung said over the din of a noisy Hong Kong restaurant. "But for our managers the best place to go is America, where there are markets for us and lots of opportunity. By putting the plant in Iowa we can give not only a good job, but a passport and a future."

Much of the same rationale is also turning Taiwan into a major source of new capital for the United States. Ever since the tattered remnants of the Kuomintang Army crossed the straits ahead of the victorious Communist troops in 1949, Taiwan has been something of an American protectorate. Now among Asia's wealthiest countries, tiny, crowded Taiwan naturally looks toward America, long its key market, as its *tairiku* power.

To date, much of Taiwan's investment pattern has been shrouded in mystery. As a mercantilist state, the country has only allowed a small amount of direct foreign investment, accounting for just $174 million between 1959 and 1984, the vast majority of it in the United States. But financial insiders believe that much of the island-nation's huge cash reserves also have been invested in short-term U.S. Treasury bills and in reserves hidden in San Francisco's Bank of Canton, an institution now *de facto* controlled by Taiwan's government.

In 1987, however, Taiwan finally liberalized its investment policy. Over time, notes Robert Packer, a lawyer in Taipei close to Taiwan's leading government and business figures, liberalization will inevitably provide yet another enormous source of capital for American economic development. "The Taiwan Chinese really only feel comfortable with the U.S.—the whole elite of the country has been educated here," Parker points out. "The professionals, the military, academic and business leaders are all comfortable with the U.S. This is the easiest place for them to do business."

And, indeed, even before liberalization of overseas investment many Taiwan entrepreneurs—in the classic pattern of Chinese "entrepreneurs on the run"—have been finding discreet means to quietly invest in the United States. Unlike those of the Japanese, these purchases have generally been small to medium in scale and are often designed not only for profit, but to provide the jobs and residency for family members. For instance, according to Cecil Chen, executive vice president of the San Francisco-based America California Bank, Taiwanese now own nearly two-thirds of all the independent motels in Los Angeles. "They are usually 30- or 40-unit motels," Chen notes. "Small enough for a family to run."

Nowhere has the impact of this largely under-the-table investment been more profound than in Monterey Park, a suburb east of downtown Los Angeles. Over the past decade an estimated $400 million in new capital, much of it from Taiwanese "entrepreneurs on the run," has flowed into the once-sleepy town, transforming it from a backwater into a modern complex of offices, shops and small industrial plants.

Anthony Chien, one of the leading financiers in Monterey Park, says many Taiwanese entrepreneurs see their island-nation as simply a place to make money, not for long-term investment. A native of Shanghai, Chien, a seventeen-year veteran with Citicorp, founded Monterey Park's Cal-Eastern Financial Services in 1986 to meet the demands of wealthy Taiwanese for American investments. "The government [on Taiwan] may not like it, but the reality is [that] all the money is coming to America," Chien claims. "They come here for the education, but the more they are exposed, they see that the possibilities in business are almost limitless. You don't see that horizon in Taiwan."

5

Winning in the Asian Era

Back in 1965, as Japan was well along in its drive to dominate the world's economy, Hisato Gotoh left his family's small farm on the southern island of Kyushu to seek his fortune. Without much in the way of financial resources or connections, he couldn't afford to enter college immediately and signed up instead as a technician for Oki Electric Corporation. During the next decade he worked faithfully for Oki while taking night classes at the Tokyo Science College.

As he earned his degree, Gotoh became increasingly fascinated with the infant microelectronics industry. It was almost an obsession, but one that was increasingly shared by the leaders of his company. By the early 1970s he had become an engineer and then a manager of a six-man team, working on the development of new, large-scale integration (LSI) semiconductors. He was, by his own description, very happy and loyal, an almost perfect company man.

Gotoh's world view changed forever in 1984, when he traveled to California's Silicon Valley. A visit to LSI Logic Corporation shattered his previous ideas about the adequacy of Oki's approach. "I was amazed by their level of technology and even more by their sense of business," the short, powerfully built engineer recalled. "Their software was better and faster. They really trained their customers. I was very impressed."

In comparison, Oki now seemed almost hopelessly stodgy and bureaucratic. Like most large Japanese electronics firms, Oki is part of a giant *keiretsu*, the Fuyo Group that includes such companies as Fuji Bank, Sapporo Breweries, Canon and Sharp Corporation. Even within Oki itself, different divisions produce over $2.4 billion worth of a staggering array of products, including telecommunications equipment, cellular telephones and computer peripherals. Within the context of these sprawling operations, LSI semiconductors constituted only a relatively minor operation, with much of its production going into the products from the other divisions.

To meet the competition, particularly from more focused, entrepreneurial American companies such as LSI Logic, Gotoh knew Oki had to change its way of business. The clubby world of related group companies, with its unspoken networks of hierarchy and obligation, did not translate well into the sort of highly customer-intensive relationship involved in designing advanced LSI circuits for American companies. "I told them we had to develop new kinds of customer relations outside the group and develop better software," he remembers. "I told them if I didn't see any changes in a year, I'd quit."

At first no one took Gotoh seriously. Few Japanese ever leave a job within a *keiretsu* and, in their minds, the largely self-educated Gotoh had done about as well as a Kyushu *onobori-san*, or country bumpkin, could expect. Since he earned his college degree after joining the company, many managers—particularly those from such elite schools as Keio, Waseda and Tokyo University—considered Gotoh an intellectual inferior, hardly the man to give new direction to the firm.

His wife was also against the idea of leaving. Pregnant with their first child, she clung desperately to the security provided by his job at Oki. But Hisato Gotoh could not be deterred. Unable to persuade his superiors to change their ways, he did the unthinkable: he changed jobs and joined the fledgling new Japanese subsidiary of LSI Logic. Sitting in his Tokyo office, Gotoh reflects:

All the big companies—Hitachi, Toshiba, Oki, Mitsubishi—are the same, very slow and bureaucratic. The problem is the guys at the top, whose attitudes were all formed long ago. They work everybody hard, but give you no freedom. You feel like a battery with all the energy drained.

There's no time to develop creativity. If they hope to be leaders in technology, they need some radical changes at the big companies. They'll have to kill off everyone over fifty and make all the guys in their forties *kacho, bucho*, even vice president. I just fear it may be too late for them to change.

Theory F

Ever since the publication of books such as Ezra Vogel's *Japan as Number One* and Bill Ouchi's *Theory Z*, Japanese management has been held up as a model that American corporations must emulate in order to survive. Japanese companies gain their strength, maintains Ouchi, because of an inherent "holistic concern for people" that motivates workers and managers alike to greater dedication. Vogel writes that "the Japanese have been in the forefront of making large organizations something people enjoy."

Yet for many Japanese executives, life in the *keiretsu* is anything but enjoyable. Rather than showing the benevolent, highly efficient economic instrument portrayed by Ouchi, Vogel and other admirers, a look under the kimono reveals a world where many Japanese managers see their own lives beset by institutional rigidity, murderous competition and, in recent years, rapidly diminishing expectations. Even Japan's much-admired low rate of employee turnover—about half the American rate during the first five years on the job—reflects not so much the intense organizational loyalty of the average *salariman* as his distinct lack of other alternatives.

A qualified American executive can easily sell his or her skills to another company up the street, or maybe even start his or her own business. But in Japan, where bigness denotes status and changing jobs suggests personal failure, such steps would seem nearly suicidal. Rather than the warm communal "family" cited by such books as *Theory Z*, Japan's corporate system functions increasingly from negative factors—such as lack of alternatives, increased competition and the glut of managers—that make Japanese managers, in the words of one executive, "prisoners of society." Michael Jablow, president of Nihon Teksel Corporation, a Tokyo-based electronics manufacturing and marketing firm, even had posited his own unconventional thesis about Japanese management. He calls it "Theory F." F stands for Fear.

"Theory Z-type theories don't talk about how the system actually works," maintains Jablow, a fifteen-year Tokyo resident and long-time student of the internal politics of Japan's major electronics corporations. "It is actually fear that moves those managers. There is no tolerance for failure. The penalty for failure is out, finished."

Intense competition, lack of options and a keen fear of the future, the essential elements of Theory F, long have characterized life in Japan. A nation virtually devoid of all resources except its remarkable and dedicated work force, Japan even since feudal times has felt a special need for structure and hierarchy. Only in exceptional times—most recently during the liberal reign of the American occupation forces after the war—have large numbers of Japanese individuals been able to break out of fairly well defined and prescribed societal niches.

It was during the occupation that the remnants of the prewar *zaibatsu*—the large corporate groupings which had dominated prewar Japan—strengthened such benefits as lifetime employment, strict seniority and other paternalistic measures, largely as a response to labor unrest. And as Japan's economy took off, with growth rates reaching double-digit levels throughout the 1960s and early 1970s, these reconstituted giants were able to create new positions of authority for the swelling ranks of the *salariman*. Impressed with both the successes of these firms and the seeming devotion of their employees, many foreigners began to wonder if Japan had somehow found the ideal system of corporate management.

But more recently, the conditions that engendered the "Japanese miracle" have begun to unravel. As growth has slowed, the progress of managers within the work force has as a result slowed measurably. For many other qualified Japanese managers the route to success seems so clogged as to be virtually impassable. "I am torn between two impulses," confesses Naruo Nakajima, a twenty-year veteran of Tokyo-based Bokusui Trading Corporation. "I want to work hard and be ambitious, but I realize the reward might not be there. As a result, I am like a bull without horns. My ambition and aggression have been taken away from me. I am trying to stay on the road toward the destination, but I fear I may get old before I get there.''

Even worse, just as diminishing growth is curtailing new opportunities for executives, Japanese companies are being inundated by maturing members of Japan's enormous baby-boom generation. Constituting roughly 30 percent of Japan's 120 million people, a large proportion of these baby boomers were trained for and expected high-level jobs. Between 1960 and 1970, the number of college students in Japan swelled by over 50 percent; today Japan ranks second only to the United States among the leading industrial powers in its percentage of adults with college degrees.

Caught between this demographic bulge and slower corporate growth, educational attainments—once considered a sure ticket to success—no longer guarantee steady promotion within the Theory F corporate structure. Nor will the situation soon improve. According to a projection in the ''2000'' Report issued by the Social Development Research Institute, the number of mature, college-educated executives expected to achieve the rank of *bucho*, or division manager, will drop from roughly two-thirds today to less than 17 percent by the end of this century.

''Foreign scholars like to emphasize the strength of the lifetime employment situation and the harmony of Japanese companies, but all that is changing now,'' notes Shin Watanabe, an expert on Japanese employment patterns and Tokyo-based researcher for Professor Ouchi. ''The demographics are putting the management pyramid on its head and disrupting the system. Theory Z explained the positive aspects of that system but maybe with the shrinking economy, the negative aspects will begin to assert themselves more.''

Although American executives also face some of these same demographic and economic pressures, the negative aspects are intensified by the peculiarly bifurcated structure that underlies Theory F management. For one thing, small and entrepreneurial businesses in Japan generally do not provide—as they often do in America—a viable escape valve for talented corporate managers. Although smaller enterprises constitute nearly 99 percent of all companies and employ 85 percent of all private-sector workers in Japan, their social status, pay scales, health and other benefits are low by comparison.

"Executives in the big companies tend to forget the rest of the world exists," notes Makiyo Mizobuchi, executive director of Recruit Jinzai Center Company, and one Japan's leading employment agencies. "He sees the company as everything. He ignores reality and works. Forgets his family. Loses his identity in the corporation."

This peculiarly Japanese monomania is in part a function of the limitations facing the *salariman* attempting to rise within their organizations. In comparison to the resilient American executive—who can still climb the corporate ladder at an advanced age—the Japanese executive's career seems, in Thomas Hobbes's phrase, "nasty, brutish and short." With retirement set at age fifty-five and early promotions slowed by the grindings of the seniority system, the Japanese executive at best has only fifteen years to gain power and position. He also knows that if he falls down in any way, there are hordes of often more technically qualified young executives bucking for the same promotions.

Burdened by these pressures, some older executives—particularly those passed over for promotion—feel themselves utterly trapped in an existence that is as meaningless as it is devoid of hope. Contrary to the notions promulgated by the popularizers of Japanese management, many Japanese executives, to paraphrase Thoreau, "live lives of quiet desperation." Expressing this sense of ennui, one *salariman* wrote:

> *My six month commuter pass will expire*
> *This single slip of paper purchased late last year*
> *Now worn by reflex motion*
> *Of hand to pocket as I took my place*
> *Numbly among the monotonous lines of working people*
> *Waiting to pass the gauntlet of ticket takers*
> *Day after day, morning and evening.*
> *Little did I know that to buy passage in six month*
>   *increments*
> *I paid out a half year of my life.*
> *Expired and useless*

In perhaps the most pathetic cases, older workers are simply put out to pasture, given functionless jobs until they are forced out at retirement age. These *madogiwa-zoku*, or window-side managers, were said to number well over 2 million in 1980 and can be seen in many Japanese corporate offices, reading newspapers at their empty desks, stoically wiling away the hours.

In such a situation it is not surprising that the old Japanese management system is breaking down. With the implicit promise of promotion now delayed, perhaps permanently, the traditional loyalty structure is breaking down, particularly among the young. A nation committed to the goal of catching up through hard work and industriousness is slowly becoming a nation of individuals, each pursuing his or her own personal gain. Even when young people enter a company they seem—as if worn out by the brutal competition of "examination hell"—to share little of the enthusiasm for work that characterized earlier generations of Japanese. One poll of Japanese from age twenty to twenty-five found that the percentage deriving pleasure from work dropped from 29 percent in 1970 to only 20 percent ten years later. A more recent survey revealed the shocking news that upwards of 20 percent of all younger workers lack any real commitment to their jobs. Increasing numbers of Japanese now consider the idea of jumping firms, or even of going to work for foreigners.

"All this loyalty stuff is basically garbage," believes twenty-seven-year-old Hideo Kikuchi, who in 1986 quit a job with the prestigious Mitsui and Company trading firm to join up with Baring Far East Securities, a British investment firm. "As I see it I am not interested in working for the company but for myself. I want good wages, good possessions and if I finish my work by six, I want to be able to go home."

Such attitudes represent a great opportunity for American business in Japan. With the breakdown of the old loyalty structures, a key source of Japanese success is being undermined. Equally important, the breakdown of the system allows American companies to follow the sort of "guerrilla tactics" employed by smaller Japanese firms who purposely accelerate their hiring programs during slow-downs among large firms.

With the growing independence of Japanese managers, and

the likelihood of a prolonged period of slow growth, American firms may well possess an unprecedented opportunity to hire top talent. In the past it would have been unthinkable for Keisuke Yawata, a twenty-eight-year veteran of NEC, to leave his firm. But with the chances of promotion reduced by problems at the electronics giant, Yawata recognized his options to be severely limited. He could accept appointment as head of a subsidiary, a traditional method of dealing with executives passed over for promotion, but Yawata knew that, contrary to the much bally-hooed notions about consensus decision-making, power within large Japanese corporations is exceedingly concentrated. "To go to a subsidiary is not considered a real promotion. It's really a sham," believes Yawata. "The NEC parent company is a very modern battleship. The executives at headquarters are on the bridge directing everyone. The rest of the company is down in the engine room."

So in 1985, when Yawata—then fifty-one—faced the option of such a "promotion," he chose instead to leave NEC alto-gether. Fortunately, unlike most Japanese executives, Yawata—one-time head of NEC's Mountain View, California, American subsidiary—had extensive contacts outside the home islands. Through his acquaintance with LSI Logic Corporation's presi-dent Wilfred Corrigan, he gained an appointment as president of Nihon LSI Logic, a Tokyo-based affiliate two-thirds owned by Corrigan's Milpitas, California, semiconductor firm. In join-ing LSI, Yawata—like a small but growing handful of expatriate Japanese executives—broke the bonds that tie by reaching out instead for the American way of business.

Although admittedly an unusual case, Yawata has found it less trouble than he suspected to attract the sort of younger ex-ecutives and engineers needed to staff his new operation. Unlike their older counterparts, these Japanese are too young to have experienced the grinding poverty of the immediate postwar pe-riod. Brought up on their country's spectacular success and ris-ing expectations, they find it more difficult than their fathers to adjust to the conditions created by Theory F management, their own huge numbers and the slowing down of the Japanese econ-omy.

"A lot of people want to leave because you can't use your

abilities in the big companies," notes Yawata's young protégé, Hisato Gotoh. "Even if the boss wants you to waste your time on irrelevant things, you have to do it. Nobody respects your talent or ability. People who know how to do things get too much work, while other people take it easy. It's very frustrating."

Back to the Roots

To succeed in the Asian era, the United States need not abandon entrepreneurialism, the source of its economic *sokojikara*, for the sterile model provided by Theory F corporations. A far more reliable guide to the American future lies in returning to the set of values—industrial, managerial and corporate—that characterized the great American companies of the past. "The only solution . . . to the problems jeopardizing America's future," observes Hajime Karatsu, technical advisor to Matsushita Communication Industrial Company, "is for American management to go back to its roots."

Rediscovering these "roots" is not a matter of technology, marketing skill or manufacturing power. Instead it is first and foremost a question of attitude, rooted in the soul of the entrepreneur, that sees the purpose of the corporation as intimately tied to its industrial mission, its customers and its employees. Great entrepreneurs, noted Joseph Schumpeter, are driven not by greed but by "a will to conquer," a "joy of creating, getting things done." Without such a spirit, America's great natural assets—its "open system," ethnic diversity and huge continental wealth—will prove insufficient for the great challenge of the Asian era.

Like Confucianism in Asia, it was a peculiar sense of a "calling" that took simple commerce and turned it into the dynamic force of modern capitalism. As Max Weber noted:

> The earning of more and more money . . . is thought of so purely as an end in itself that from the point of view of happiness of, or utility to the single individual, it seems entirely transcendental and absolutely irrational.

The epoch of America's economic ascendency was and will in the future be driven by entrepreneurs and organizations emboldened by such motivations. In explaining the continuing success of IBM, Thomas Watson, Jr., observed that it was the corporation's continuing adherence to "a set of beliefs" which propels its success.

But IBM's ability to perpetuate its sense of mission has become a rarity in American business. As founders died or deteriorated with age, most of the great organizations formed by them—such as Ford Motor Company and U.S. Steel—lost their sense of mission. Rising in their place was, in Pitirim Sorokin's phrase, a "managerial aristocracy" who has replaced the sense of mission with a bureaucratic mentality fundamentally opposed to the company-building ethos of a Thomas Watson, Henry Ford or Andrew Carnegie. By stripping away the "transcendental" element in business and replacing it with a blind adherence to the "cash nexus," the builders of the modern bureaucratic corporation, as Sorokin noted in 1941, unintentionally dealt "the first mortal blow" against the spirit of capitalism.

The deadening effects of this bureaucratization—the world in which the lawyer, accountant and stock analyst replaced the entrepreneur in the corporate driver's seat—were at first disguised by the predominant position of the United States after World War II. Only later, when integrated industrial challengers emerged first in Europe and then Asia, did the weaknesses of the "managerial aristocracy" become clear.

The conglomerate wave in the late 1950s and early in the 1960s showed the first full flowering of this new order. Conglomerates like Sperry Rand acquired profitable plants such as a library-furniture maker in Herkimer, New York; after two decades of solid profits, management decided to shut the plant down because it failed to meet the 22 percent return on equity demanded by corporate management. Such obsession with statistical returns—essentially substituting for industrialism a sort of financialism—eventually cut a path of devastation across the United States, particularly in the midwestern industrial belt. In 1969, another conglomerate, Lykes Corporation, bought the Youngstown Campbell Works. Management refused to refurbish the pre-World War I blast furnance, even as it milked the plant for cash in order to finance unrelated ventures. Eight years later the plant was closed.

This malady has not been limited solely to the conglomerates. When recession hit in the early 1970s, many of the nation's leading firms—including U.S. Steel, RCA and Shell Oil—promptly announced major reductions in research personnel. By 1972, an astounding 100,000 industrial scientists, engineers and technicians had been discharged. Such decisions do not only affect those suddenly unemployed; they also create disincentives for creative technologists throughout an organization. As Modesto Maidique and Robert Hayes have noted: "The best, most innovative people will leave an environment in which what they are doing is considered less important than meeting the financial community's current expectations."

By the mid-1970s, financialism had established a firm grip even on the largest of the classic industrial corporations, General Motors. Epitomized by the rise of chairman Frederick G. Donner, a former accountant, and his eventual successor, Roger Smith, GM became a pure expression of the "cash nexus." To Smith, Donner—who served as GM's chairman from 1958 to 1967—represented "a true financial genius . . . with a well-ordered, analytical mind" under whom "the corporation flourished . . . establishing new records in dollar sales, earnings, dividend payments and worldwide sales." Yet at the same time, for the corporation and its long-term mission (to be the dominant automobile manufacturer in the world), Donner proved to be a disaster. In his *Decline and Fall of the American Automobile Industry*, veteran auto journalist Brock Yates notes that it was under Donner that an increasingly finance-driven GM management began ignoring its engineers and production staff, cutting costs at the expense of quality, ignoring the emerging small-car market and, for the saving of $100 worth of parts, made the Corvair the menace described in Ralph Nader's *Unsafe At Any Speed*.

By the time Donner had retired, the legacy of Smith's hero was firmly embedded in the corporation. Once renowned for quality, GM now became synonymous with shoddy workmanship. In 1971, it was found that a fault with engine mounts forced GM cars to spin out of control; that year an astounding 6.7

million Chevrolets had to be recalled. Yet years afterward, the iron grip of financialism remained so strong that the manager of the company's Tarrytown, New York, plant—recognized for producing "the poorest quality cars" among all of GM's twenty-two U.S. assembly plants—received one of the highest bonuses in the company simply because his plant also had among the lowest production costs.

In contrast, the ascendent Asian industrialists reflected a dramatically different viewpoint. If industrial supremacy found its roots only in the "cash nexus," access to markets or technology, there would have been no logical explanation for Asia's success. What proved more lethal to American and European business people was the "transcendental element," this time rooted in a Confucian as opposed to a Protestant ethic.

In the Confucian world view, a leader seeks and wields power not for its own sake, but in a way informed by ethical principles. As the sage wrote:

> Wealth and honor are what every man desires. But if they have been obtained in violation of moral principles, they must not be kept. Poverty and humble stations are what every man dislikes. But if they can be avoided only in violation of moral principles, they must not be avoided. If a superior person departs from humanity [jen] how can he fulfil that name? A superior man never abandons humanity even for a lapse of a single meal. In moments of haste, he acts according to it. In times of difficulty or confusion, he acts according to it.

The centrality of such ideas can be seen in the career of such Japanese entrepreneurs as Soichiro Honda. When asked for the secrets of his success, Honda points not to technological superiority or marketing prowess, but to basic attitudes concerning his responsibility to customers, suppliers or employees. In Honda's view, financial return is important only so far as it advances those interests. "I always had a stronger desire for work itself than for money—the desire to explore something new that other people haven't done. I don't want to walk on a path that is already created by other people," he explained.

Honda's infatuation with creativity and serving his customers became the essence of his marketing strategy. Describing the evolution of the Super Cub, the little motorcycle that would first make his a household name in the United States, Honda explained:

> Our marketing people were told Americans would never buy motorcycles. Then we started thinking: "How can we modify a motorcycle in such a way that the Americans would buy them?" Then our thinking pattern went to: "Well, let's make some kind of motorcycle that can be carried in a car." Then you want to go fishing, you don't expect to find many fish in areas that are accessible by car. So you want to get off from the car and ride on a motorcycle to where you expect to catch many fish.

> I didn't even have money to conduct market research. I had to rely on intuition, believing that what I like must be liked by other people. . . . This is the kind of thinking that shattered the existing ideas about transportation.

Honda's approach to his employees followed a similar empathetic logic. At a time when American executives surrounded themselves in the trappings of luxury and privilege—what Lee Iacocca calls "the royal class"—Honda lived modestly and worked closely with his employees. At times he would even strip down to work at mechanical problems on the assembly line. And, he remarks pointedly, there have never been executive dining rooms at Honda Motor Corporation.

A story about the time several years ago when Honda and some employees were entertaining a customer at a Tokyo drinking establishment is revealing. When the customer accidentally dropped his dentures into an above-ground septic tank, everyone felt sorry for the man, but nobody wanted to retrieve the dentures. But Honda, already a man of stature in Japan, went in after the mouthpiece, arms first. "Nobody wanted to pick it up, not even the owner of the restaurant or the employees," Honda recalls with a slight grin. "I did it because . . . I wanted to show a good example."

Beyond Financialism

The central issue here is not so much a question of Eastern or Western values, but the attitude with which investors and managers approach their corporations. Many today simply see companies as vehicles of finance. Georges Doriot, in contrast, considered the firms he backed, such as a fledgling start-up called Digital Equipment Company, "his children." "When you have a child, you don't ask what return you expect," Doriot once explained. "Of course you have hopes—you hope your child will become president of the United States. But if a man is good and loyal and does not achieve a so-called good rate of return, I will stay with him. If I were a speculator, the question of return would apply. But I don't consider a speculator—by my definition—constructive. I am building men and companies."

As it turned out, Doriot's strategy of "building men and companies" paid off handsomely. An initial investment of $70,000 in Digital Equipment, for instance, ultimately was worth in excess of $350 million in stock. Other investments such as Cardis and Cooper Laboratories, all disciplined by Doriot's principles of ascetic management and total dedication, flourished during his lifetime.

Against the challenge of Confucian cultures, firms today must develop an ethos that unifies American entrepreneurialism with the sense of industrial commitment characteristic of many Asian companies. No longer can Americans rely solely on their technical or marketing brilliance; even in cutting-edge industries, the efficient implementation of the entire industrial process is the central imperative. "The Japanese and IBM create an environment where there is no tolerance for sloppy management," explains Compaq chairman and leading venture capitalist Ben Rosen. "In the old days you could get away with it because you were competing only with companies like yourself. Now the IBMs and the Japanese are in every field."

Unlike Silicon Valley *wunderkinder* such as Adam Osborne—who believed that IBM would soon "cease to be a significant force" in the small-business-computer market—the founding team at Compaq committed itself to the industrial challenge. With a combined thirty-three years at what venture capitalist

L. J. Sevin calls "TI University," the original entrepreneurial triumvirate saw that the coming battle with IBM—and the clones proliferating from Taiwan, Korea and Japan—required the presence of seasoned professionals. There were no shortcuts, no quick-fix solutions such as contracting out manufacturing to Asian firms or relying on financial gimmicks. At Compaq, financial considerations were important, but not to the exclusion of basic blocking and tackling in manufacturing and marketing. This integrated approach made it necessary to avoid the sort of egotism characteristic of many entrepreneurial companies. "We brought in people not to execute orders but [people] who could replace us," cofounder and president Rod Canion says.

The physical layout of Canion's office reflects his relative lack of egotism, in that the company supersedes any one individual. Most of his executive suite is eaten up by a large conference table. Canion's small personal office is placed discreetly on the side. Like Honda, Canion eschews such executive perks as private planes and private dining areas, choosing instead to spend his time visiting the factory floor and making sales calls, constantly gathering information.

Key to an integrated response to the challenge from Asia, as Jack Kuehler, executive vice president of IBM has noted, is control of the manufacturing process. Many American firms, such as AT&T, Sperry and Honeywell, have signed up for "joint ventures" that essentially concede manufacturing to their overseas partners. These arrangements are little more than a cloak for their own failures. IBM, on the other hand, has retained a strong manufacturing base, not only in the United States, but also in Japan, where it claims the largest installed base of mainframe computers. "We are not intimidated by our ability to compete as a manufacturer with anyone in the world," notes Kuehler. "We have the will, we have the desire and I believe our history has shown we can do it, and therefore we are doing it."

Like IBM, virtually all the firms that have survived the onslaughts of Japanese, Taiwanese and Korean competition in the computer industry—Digital Equipment, Tandem, Prime, AST Research, Tandy Corporation, Apple Computer—have committed themselves to extensive manufacturing improvements. They are fully aware that their competitors, such as NEC Corporation and Fujitsu, are so totally focused on the importance of manufacturing that they can build computer products in remote sites such as Massachusetts or Oregon and ship them back to Japan.

The successful focus on an integrated industrial strategy is crucial to success in the Asian era, whether in high-tech or, as shown by Nucor and other minimills, in traditional smokestack industries. Indeed, virtually all the rare American success stories of the 1980s—including Outboard Marine Company, A.T. Cross and Cummins Engine Corporation—have involved beating Asian competition through investment in continuous enhancement of the manufacturing process.

Few companies in America would seem easier prey for Asian competition than Stahl Speciality Company. Located in Kingsville, Missouri, a hamlet of 365 people an hour's drive from Kansas City, Stahl turns out aluminum castings—an industry that shrank by over one-third in the early 1980s. But Stahl survived by outperforming the Asian competition in the very areas in which they have so often gained ascendency. "Too many foundries have stayed still. People get killed by imports that way," founder Glenn Stahl explains. "The only way to do it is to invest in the latest machinery and have a higher level of technology than they do. That gives you the flexibility and the ability to diversify they can't compete with."

At a time when most American foundries have slashed capital spending, Stahl has been spending $2 million to $4 million annually—over 10 percent of sales—on new equipment. But he spends not just on machinery, but on his people, with a series of courses taught by professors at nearby Central Missouri State University. Combining high-tech equipment with well-trained people, Stahl has gained contracts from John Deere, Ford, Delco and IBM, by offering precision work not easily available from his competitors in Taiwan.

The one thing Stahl does not spend money on is himself. Like the classic entrepreneur described by Max Weber, Stahl epitomizes the "transcendental element" that lay behind the great American entrepreneurs of the nineteenth century and men such as Soichiro Honda today. Although his net worth is well in the millions, Stahl into his mid-seventies continued to live in a modest $40,000 one-story house. "I don't have the slightest inclination to drive a Cadillac or stay in Palm Springs," he explains. "I just enjoy seeing the company grow and challenging the employees."

Suicide Strategies

Perhaps no field of endeavor more illustrates the essential role of an integrated industrial strategy than consumer electronics. Once the dominant world player, the United States by the mid-1980s was suffering massive, double-digit-billion-dollar trade deficits, with foreign manufacturers accounting for virtually all such hot-selling new items as compact disc players and VCRs. As William Relyea, a leading industry analyst at New York's F. Eberstadt and Company, has commented: "Leadership in consumer electronics [manufacturing] has passed to Japan and it isn't coming back."

According to analysts such as Relyea, American companies seeking to sell consumer-electronics goods can find what they need by catching the next flight to Tokyo, Taipei or Seoul. Yet judging by the few American survivors in the industry, it seems more likely that the path to success lies in *not* relying on Asian manufacturers.

Tragically, this surrender of manufacturing was probably never as inevitable as Wall Street and other apologists for corporate America maintain, perhaps even during the era of the overvalued dollar. During the past three decades, for instance, Harmon International's various lines of American-made speakers—including JBL, Infinity and Harman-Kardon—have built a leading market share in the high-end and mid-range audio market. The company's Chatsworth, California, factory is not only among the largest and most efficient loudspeaker facilities in the world, but it ships as much as one-third of its total output overseas, with Japan providing the single largest foreign market.

Bose Corporation, a firm with a unique audio speaker system, for nearly a quarter of a century manufactured virtually its entire product line at its factory on a hilltop above Framingham, Massachussetts. While the American consumer-electronics industry has been largely written off by Wall Street analysts and most corporate executives, Bose emerged as a worldwide leader in high-end stereo speakers. When virtually every major American consumer-electronics firm shifted production to the Far East, or contracted manufacturing to Japanese firms, Bose kept plowing back 100 percent of its earnings into the company.

"We can only win by staying on the cutting edge of technology and that can't be done by just following short-run goals," says the lean and graying company founder Amar Bose, whose only compensation for his thirteen years of leadership has come in the form of salary. "No one ever won a chess game by betting on each move. Sometimes you have to move backward to get a step forward."

The successes of Bose and Harmon stand in stark contrast to those firms, large and small, which followed the conventional wisdom of the past few decades and contracted their manufacturing to Asian companies. This industrial debacle began in the 1960s with the rise of a new breed of financially oriented executives at the nation's consumer-electronics companies. Frustrated by low margins—sometimes reaching as low as 2 percent per unit—associated with products like television sets, these executives tended to shift production offshore, often contracting production to Japanese and other Asian producers.

This wholesale American withdrawal from the consumer-electronics battlefield provided a historic opportunity for the emerging leading electronics firms of Japan, Korea and other Pacific Rim nations. Some of the very firms that have been recipients of manufacturing contracts from American companies, such as Japan's Matsushita, have parlayed the cash generated in the process—as well as the expertise necessary to meet high-volume American orders—into a virtual industrial hegemony in the worldwide consumer-electronics marketplace. As Kiyoshi Suzaki, a former Toshiba engineer, now a consultant with Arthur Young and Company, puts it: "The skills involved in shrinking the number of components for automated production can be transferred from one product to another. You simply go up the learning curve."

The videotape recorder was a classic case of losing a market by conceding manufacturing. In the late 1960s, Ampex Corporation was among the world's leaders in videotape recorders.

Seeking to penetrate the growing Japanese market, the company entered a joint venture with Toshiba to jointly develop products in Japan. By 1970, Ron Ballintine, Ampex's head of development planning, was calling the joint venture—the majority owned by Toshiba—a "resounding success" that would lead to his firm's domination of Asia's videotape market.

The joint venture, which involved the licensing of original Ampex technology to Toshiba, did indeed prove a "resounding success," but not for Ballintine's company. Instead, Toshiba and other Japanese companies improved upon the technology, developing markets at home and abroad. By the early 1980s, Japanese producers controlled virtually the entire burgeoning videotape market, with only the Koreans providing any opposition. Even larger American electronics giants—which possessed the resources to develop and manufacture internally—have been reduced to marketing only Asian products.

In relinquishing high-volume consumer-electronics manufacturing, American companies surrendered markets they formerly dominated. A 1967 joint venture with Motorola helped launch Japan's Alps Electric Corporation into the car-stereo business; eleven years later Alps bought Motorola's stake and renamed the one-time Motorola subsidiary Alpine Electronics, which now supplies stereos to firms that include General Motors, Chrysler, BMW and Volvo. Alps also purchased UHF-tuner technology from General Instrument Corporation, a field in which the Japanese firm became a world leader by the mid-1980s.

Whereas a large company like Motorola could survive such a debacle, the offshore strategy virtually eliminated scores of smaller companies. Since the 1960s, Sherwood and Fisher, once leading audio firms, have become little more than wholly owned marketing subsidiaries of Japan-based manufacturers.

"When you forfeit designing for manufacturing, you usually end up losing it all," notes Sidney Harmon, a thirty-five-year industry veteran and president of Harmon International, with 1985 sales in excess of $200 million, one of the nation's few successful large audio-equipment manufacturers. "It's not like riding a bike. Once you fall off, you can't get back on."

Despite this grim history, much the same pattern has been repeated in newer fields like microelectronics and related industries. Like the consumer-electronics executives, American microelectronics entrepreneurs underestimated Asian talent and aspirations. Believing Asians would be content to remain mere contract manufacturers, American semiconductor firms in the late 1960s and early 1970s began the wholesale licensing of their designs to Japanese firms. Some firms, notes Arthur Jonishi, director of Kyocera Corporation, even surrendered their technology simply to gain access to Japanese markets through their Japanese partners. More often American firms, particularly those that were cash starved, used licensed technology to raise funds, technology that often came back to the American market in a somewhat improved form. Notes former NEC executive Keisuke Yawata: "If you sell technology on a one-time basis, it's gone."

In 1967 Varian Associates, then an acknowledged leader in the semiconductor-equipment industry, negotiated a joint venture with NEC Corporation that led to the formation of Anelva Corporation, a firm designed to bring Varian's technology to the Japanese market. But soon the Americans, thinking the Japanese market insignificant, gradually surrendered control of the joint venture to NEC.

Today that market is the largest in the world. Varian executives now look back at the joint venture, as one executive told the *San Jose Mercury News*, as little more than an attempt by Anelva and NEC to "steal" its chip-making know-how. But David Rubinfein, a former Varian executive who helped set up the Anelva venture, also ascribes much of the blame to the American company for underestimating both the significance of the Japanese market and the technological aptitude of their partner.

Despite this dismal record, many American firms—from mainframe manufacturer Amdahl to voice-data-product maker David Systems—have followed the suicide strategy, conceding manufacturing to leading Japanese firms. By the mid-1980s such manufacturing alliances became almost a fashion among young technology firms. Behind this lay a delusion that technological control could be maintained while surrendering manufacturing.

The case of LaPine Technologies illustrates the fantastical nature of this approach. When Anthony LaPine established the young California disc-drive firm, he celebrated the "strategic" nature of the partnership with Kyocera Corporation, a Japanese firm with over $1.5 billion in sales. While Kyocera would provide volume manufacturing, LaPine would retain its value-added through superior technology and marketing. Yet by the end of 1986, LaPine was himself removed from management, with all control now concentrated in Kyocera and Prudential Bache Trading.

A similar pattern of high-tech self-destruction has characterized partnerships with Singaporean, Korean and Taiwanese firms which, in line with the Japanese example, have been offering cash to small American high-tech firms in the form of licenses or direct equity investments, as a means of gaining technology, marketing expertise and getting contracts for volume manufacturing. By 1986, a host of American high-technology firms— including Advanced Matrix Corporation, Senior Systems Tech and the remnants of Osborne Computers—all fell under majority ownership by business interests from the Chinese diaspora. Korean *chaebol* have also been particularly active, establishing licensing agreements to equity positions in such high-tech companies as Zymos Corporation, Micron Technologies, Zytrex, Metheus and Tandon.

But if the names of the nations have changed, the results remain tragically similar. When Dr. Robert Harp founded southern California's Corona Data Systems in 1981, he came with a reputation as one of the nation's most brilliant microcomputer designers. The early Coronas lived up to that billing, in many minds equaling the quality of the early Compaqs. But there the similarities ended. Lacking both the capital and the industrial focus of the Texas firm, Corona came to rely increasingly on subcontract manufacturing from the Korean *chaebol* Daewoo.

Originally Daewoo provided only a small part of the value-added in the Corona machines. But as time went on, the aggressive Koreans—whose desire to dominate the microcomputer industry was no secret—pressed for a greater involvement. Their opportunity came in 1985 when the company, reeling from the slump in the microcomputer industry, took its first equity investment from the Korean firm. With a rapidly increasing level of Korean ownership came an almost total loss of manufacturing. Public perception that the company, now renamed Cordata, would soon be swallowed up by the Korean giant's own products was rejected by Corona's president Daniel Carter, who cited the presence of Daewoo chairman W. C. Kim on his board as proving the *chaebol*'s "fiduciary" responsibility for maintaining the integrity of the firm.

Within eighteen months, Carter and two other key executives were forced out and replaced by Hyo Bin Im, a long-time Daewoo executive brought in as the company's new CEO. When Daewoo started shipping large volumes of its own PCs into the country, Harp—still in a key technical post and retaining a minority equity interest in the firm—began to wonder about the *chaebol*'s true intentions, suggesting Daewoo might be using the losses at Cordata to offset earnings at some of the *chaebol*'s more successful operations. By 1987, according to Harp, Cordata's sales, $50 million two years earlier, had dropped to about half that, while its total debt to Daewoo soared to over $40 million.

The final confrontation came in the summer of 1987, when Daewoo officials decided to move the company's main offices from Newbury Park, a suburb north of Los Angeles, to the *chaebol*'s own facility in Compton, a city forty-five miles to the south. Though Daewoo officials claimed it was a cost-saving move, to Harp the relocation was tantamount to shutting down Cordata's American operation. Finally, in a steamy August board meeting, Harp exploded and allegedly punched Im and accused him of being dishonest in his intentions and responsible for the slow death of the firm.

"One thing about Orientals, they tend to lie a lot," Harp said after handing in his resignation. "They will tell you just a bald-faced lie. You know it's a lie, and they know it's a lie, but they think it's OK."

Making It Work

To a large extent, alliances with Asians may soon do for the term "joint venture" what Vidkun Quisling and Marshal Pétain did for "collaboration." This gruesome record, however, should not lead Americans to believe the problems stem from some inherent racial characteristic of Asian business. In their dealings with Asian companies, Americans such as Harp have often been prisoners of limited information, false conceptions about Asian motives and goals. With a naïveté they would rarely employ at home, Americans often stumble into alliances with firms whose ultimate goals involve usurping their partners' basic industrial mission.

Americans working in Asia must be aware of the deep-seated desire of firms there to move up the value-added scale. Before entering an agreement, for instance, they must make certain that their technology or customer base cannot be easily turned against them either by legal agreement or, preferably, by establishing common, mutually compatible objectives. U.S. firms also must understand the longer time frames in which many Asian companies operate; if an Asian partner thinks he can simply outlast his American counterpart, he will most often do so. And, finally, Americans must learn to reject the way of thinking that sees all Asians as essentially identical. Asian companies and their executives come in multitudinous forms, with some potentially excellent partners and others little more than rogues, with no qualms about exploiting unsuspecting American firms.

Fortunately, some American executives have learned these basic concepts and applied them effectively. Before setting up his highly successful venture in Japan, Bill Elder took a considered approach, interviewing ten different companies. He studiously avoided potential competitors such as NEC's Anelva subsidiary and settled on a recently formed division of the C. Itoh and Company trading firm. Although a multibillion-dollar concern, C. Itoh is not a manufacturer; its Data Systems Division, seeking to make a name as a distributor of high-tech equipment, was like a "small company" with interests parallel to those of its American partner.

To make sure Genus got the most of the bargain, Elder also worked assiduously to develop close ties—what the Japanese call a "wet relationship"—with the C. Itoh division leadership. He personally monitored all correspondence between his company and its Japanese partner; he also made numerous trips to Japan, meeting personally with C. Itoh's own network of small equipment vendors, who often do much of the actual direct selling. As Elder puts it: "We walked down the wedding aisle side by side, but I made sure I was leading."

As the Genus experience shows, not all Japanese companies have an "engulf and devour" mentality. But often American firms have found success by forging relationships with their smaller Japanese counterparts, who know all too well the dangers to corporate independence posed by *keiretsu* power. Such alliances often have the added virtue of providing a way to avoid the often vicious character of *keiretsu* politics. Large trading firms (*sogo shosha*) such as Mitsubishi and Sumitomo are linked to extensive groups of companies specializing in everything from banking and insurance to manufacturing and service. These connections, sometimes strengthened by financial cross-ownership, can hurt the prospects of selling a product to customers from rival groups.

"If you're doing business with Mitsubishi, it's tough to do business with the other groups they compete with," notes Steve Kwuse, vice president for marketing and sales at Cosmos Corporation, a Seattle-area software firm. To avoid getting caught in such internecine conflicts, Cosmos eschewed the *sogo shosha* route entirely and established a close relationship with Sun Grade Corporation, a subsidiary of Japanese Computer Science Company (JCS).

With sales last year in excess of $100 million, JCS proved an ideal partner for Cosmos. As one of Japan's leading software developers, JCS possessed the technical capabilities to adapt Cosmos's products—such as its Revelation database program—to Japanese hardware and language standards. The alliance with JCS also gives Cosmos, with U.S. sales last year of under $10 million, access to its network of 400 independent software dealers, whose reach extends into virtually every nook and cranny of the complex Japanese distribution system.

For JCS, the benefits of the alliance may even prove more crucial. While the yen's appreciation has driven up the cost of Japanese-made software, it has increased demands for software that enhances productivity. To Yasunori Tanaka, president of Sun Grade, this suggests an enormous potential market for re-packaged software from American firms. With Revelation sales alone expected to reach the million-dollar annual mark by the early 1990s, Tanaka believes total sales of adapted U.S. software could equal or even surpass the current total sales of JCS during the next decade.

Executing in Asia

When American merchants first started landing in Asia, they were renowned for their marketing savvy. In sharp contrast to their European competitors, the American traders—mostly New Englanders—tried to observe local customs and sensibilities. But in recent decades, particularly in Asia, the once-touted internationalism of the Yankee trader has become a rare commodity indeed. Deterred by protectionism, a huge domestic market and stronger cultural links to Europe, many American firms have neglected to adapt to the Asian style of business. Even as key new markets like China open up, American firms find themselves losing out to more determined Japanese competitors. For instance, a survey of 115 foreign firms in Beijing, carried out by British researcher Nigel Campbell, found that only one-fifth of American firms were willing to subsidize their operation for a decade in order to penetrate the Chinese market, compared to two-thirds of all Japanese firms surveyed.

In America's Third Century, when Asia represents the fastest growing and most lucrative market, attempts to apply methods appropriate to the "dry" transaction-oriented American and continental systems can prove disastrous. Among the nations of the Chinese-speaking world, often the most important element in a business deal is not the product or even the price, but *guanxi*, or the personal connection to the buyer. Even as new markets open up in China or Taiwan, American companies frequently are outflanked by Japanese firms who, although often objects of suspicion, often are more willing to dedicate the time needed for establishing close, personal relationships with potential customers.

Where Americans have succeeded in China, they have been willing to take this sort of committed approach. John Fluke Corporation first started doing business in the People's Republic in 1974. For the first seven years of operations, sales were little more than $250,000. Then in 1981, a Singapore-born employee named Roland Chua came up with the idea of setting up a joint venture in which the company would send "complete knock-down kits" to China to be assembled under Fluke's supervision and sold locally.

Although turned down at first, Chua was persistent, meeting repeatedly with officials at China's Ministry of Electronics. "The Chinese are not used to doing business by phone; it's still face to face," explained Tai Lee, another of Fluke's China marketeers. "Two or three sales calls a day are the most you can expect to accomplish." Over time, Chua's constant appearances developed enough *guanxi* to launch a large joint venture that by 1985 made China the company's largest foreign market.

With enough persistence, even smaller American companies have managed large sales in China. When Joe Wu left his native Canton back in 1945, the last thing he wanted to do was return to his Communist-controlled motherland. After receiving his undergraduate education at Purdue and his master's in engineering from Illinois Institute of Technology, Wu worked for General Electric and General Motors' Delco Electronics Division. In 1970 he set up his own company, TFT, a Santa Clara, California, manufacturer of sophisticated test and broadcast equipment for radios which last year achieved sales in excess of $5 million.

"I thought I'd be the least likely guy ever to come back here," says the fifty-two-year-old Wu, taking a break between negotiations with his Chinese partners. "But this country is changing. They really want the Chinese overseas capitalists to come help. Maybe they are realizing the Communism doesn't work."

But typically it was old-fashioned *guanxi*, not ideology or latent patriotism, that brought Joe Wu and TFT to China. TFT's entrance into China has its origins back in 1984, when Jiang Wen Zhao, economic advisor for the northern Chinese province of Hebei, contacted a brother-in-law living in the San Francisco Bay area about a local radio plant that needed the latest technology for the most modern test and measurement for FM broadcast, something just then being implemented at Chinese radio stations.

As it turned out, the brother-in-law, Lester Lee, president of

Recortec, a Sunnyvale, California, maker of recording equipment, knew Wu from the AAMA (Asian-American Manufacturers Association) and was aware that TFT manufactured exactly the sort of equipment needed by the Chinese factory. Lee promptly introduced Wu to Jiang, who then set up the meeting with Yang Zhen Sheng, director of Hebei's Zhang Jia Kou Number One Radio Factory.

But making the connection is but one part of doing business in China. For eighteen months since his initial contact with Yang, Wu shuttled back and forth to China, trying to cement the deal. Although the factory manager desperately wanted to purchase TFT's equipment, Wu ran into one frustration after another due in part to China's severe shortage of accoutrements necessary to modern business practice. Phones, for example, frequently don't work, even within Beijing; hotel accommodations, despite a spree of new construction, are often second-rate at best. In addition, business is often hampered by life-styles reminiscent of another epoch, such as long, two-to-three-hour lunch breaks and restaurants that close after eight in the evening.

But most debilitating of all, Wu had to shepherd his proposal through the vast Chinese Communist party bureaucracy which, despite all the publicity about China's move toward capitalism, still retains the final say on most every major economic decision. Owing largely to policy shifts within the party—a given risk of doing business in China—Wu ultimately had to accept only a $500,000 order, half the originally agreed sum.

"You have to totally reacclimate yourself to a different state of mind here. More than anything else, you have to concentrate on gaining their confidence, sitting down to eat with them, becoming friends," Wu said stoically in his run-down, out-of-the way Beijing hotel after completing his deal. "Decisions are made by committee and on a lot of levels. You have to make each person you meet feel involved and important. It sounds like a pain, and it cuts into your profits in the short run, but the potential is too great to let it get in your way."

Much the same mind-numbing negotiating tactics apply in other Asian locales. Eleven years ago, Dale Williams, vice president and general manager of Rockwell Semiconductor's Far East Operations, was in Seoul for a one-day meeting with a buyer, when the Koreans began using the familiar tactic of wearing down the other side. Aware that Williams was supposed to leave on a late-afternoon flight, the Koreans purposely slowed the discussion, covering the same points repeatedly.

Under such strains American business people frequently agree to terms that they later regret. But Williams, giving up on his flight, turned the tables, slowed the discussion even further and even suggested they all go to dinner. Now, Williams recalls, it was the turn for the Koreans "to get bored." Suddenly negotiations quickened and the deal was consummated that evening. By 1987, Williams and Rockwell enjoyed rapidly growing sales in Korea.

The growing presence in the United States of Asian firms also provides new opportunities for American companies to develop business in fields already under Asian domination. In the early 1980s, Brudi Corporation, a manufacturer of forklift attachments, depended almost entirely on sales to domestic forklift manufacturers. But company founder Ron Brudi realized that the once-potent American forklift makers were losing market share, with 40 percent of all domestic forklift sales going to overseas suppliers, mostly from Japan and Korea. This phenomenon became painfully clear when Hyster, just down the river in Portland, Oregon, closed its local manufacturing facility in 1983.

But instead of giving up in the face of tough Asian competition, Brudi turned the Pacific shift to his own advantage. First he improved his own operation, implementing a Japanese-style *kan-ban* system, which reduces inventory costs by having parts arrive "just in time" for manufacturing rather than languishing in the storeroom. He also hired Tom Jacka, a veteran of the Federal International Trade Administration, to bring Brudi's advanced attachment to the attention of the rapidly expanding manufacturers and shippers from Japan and Korea. By carefully nurturing ties to local subsidiaries of firms such as Toyota and Daewoo, Brudi also gained invaluable contacts with headquarters.

Owing to these moves, by 1985 Asian nations and their subsidiaries in the United States accounted for over 55 percent of Brudi sales which, in contrast to flat or declining sales for most

U.S. forklift makers, have more than doubled over the last five years. With a new agreement recently signed with Korean giant Daewoo to distribute Brudi products in Korea and the rapid expansion of Japanese facilities in the United States, Jacka expects his "Pacific connection" to play an increasingly important role in the future.

"You've got to get to the point where it doesn't matter if the manufacturers back east get in trouble," notes Jacka. "We see what's happening and that our future is to work with the Japanese and the Koreans. Our view is that the Asian market is our future."

A similar willingness to put time into developing Asian markets is helping other entrepreneurs in the Pacific Northwest. Long the mainstay of the region's economy, the lumber industry in the Northwest has been steadily losing its market share to producers in both Canada and the southeastern United States, with the Northwest's share of U.S. softwood lumber production dropping by more than one-fifth since the mid-1970s.

The results have been catastrophic for many small mill towns, where double-digit unemployment rates have persisted for over a decade. Since 1978, over 40,000 jobs—over a quarter of the region's lumber-related employment—have disappeared. Even long-time industry giant Georgia Pacific moved its headquarters out of the region to Atlanta, closer to its holdings in southeastern pine forests.

But not everyone is surrendering to the new pressures from outside. Reviving Thomas Jefferson's dream of a Pacific trade link, some local entrepreneurs have been able to more than offset losses in domestic markets with new and growing markets in Asia. Few have succeeded more than Vanport Manufacturing, a small lumber concern thirty miles outside of Portland. When Vanport's president Adolf Hertrich and three other investors bought an old mill for $64,000 in the Oregon hamlet of Boring, the town's name aptly described the prevailing business conditions. With the domestic market collapsing, annual sales were stuck at less than $3 million.

But Hertrich, an immigrant from the forestlands of Germany, saw a new future for Vanport in the Japanese market, which in the past has accounted for over half of all log exports from the

Northwest. Although dependent on imports for two-thirds of their raw logs, the Japanese long have been reluctant to buy finished lumber from American mills, whose processing they considered inferior.

To find his way into that lucrative market, Hertrich needed to convince the Japanese that he could meet their often-exacting quality standards. As in so many other areas from consumer appliances to vegetables, the Japanese are finicky customers. Similarly, they like their lumber cut to traditional specifications, with emphasis on aesthetics. "The Japanese didn't think our sawmills could do the right job. They didn't think a *gai-jin* [foreigner] could understand their system," recalls Hertrich. "But I saw no alternative but to adjust. We could go out of business or remodel our sawmill to meet their needs."

To accomplish this goal, Hertrich followed the path adopted by the Japanese in their commercial conquest of America. He traveled extensively throughout Japan, meeting with potential customers and inspecting the local lumber mills. "I took my camera and did a little spying," Hertrich admits readily. "They didn't take me very seriously since we were such a small company. It wasn't the kind of thing Weyerhaeuser would be doing."

As soon as Hertrich returned, he redesigned his mill, upgraded his equipment, installed the metric system and started teaching his foremen the complex Japanese lumber grading system. This system has no analogue in America. Instead of classifying lumber by thickness and length, the Japanese use five major grades based largely on such aesthetic factors as color and wood grain. To make matters even more complicated, different regions of Japan, such as the eastern Kanto Plain and the China-facing Kansai, employ somewhat different grading standards.

Soon Hertrich had his lumbermen thinking in Japanese, at least in terms of such grading standards as *tokuihi* and *hashima*. Although learning the new system thoroughly can take as long as two years, Vanport's foremen soon knew it well enough to impress their many Japanese customers. By 1986, at a time when many local mills lay idle, Vanport's 150 workers were laboring at double shifts while sales, 90 percent destined for Japan, reached over $30 million.

But what really made his point with the Japanese, Hertrich

believes, was the traditional Japanese teahouse that he erected with his own logs next to the mill. Inviting guests from Japan to drink or even stay overnight at the teahouse both provided an advertisement of Vanport's capabilities and revealed Hertrich's deep appreciation of Japanese folkways.

To Americans such tactics might seem peripheral, even silly. But to Japanese and other Asians—long victimized by the maddening sense of Western superiority—signs of respect for their culture can prove crucial. "The first thing you do when you make a deal with the Japanese is buy a flag," suggests Robert Berglass, president of DEP Corporation, a Los Angeles-based cosmetics firm. Berglass, whose firm boasted sales in excess of $20 million in 1986, unfurled a large Rising Sun flag. "When my partners come, I unfurl this thing and we've opened up 'Japan DEP,' " he says, holding up the flag. "It relaxes everyone. It seems so silly, but the meaning is there. We are in this together."

Indeed, just as a poor relationship with a Japanese partner can spell disaster, a close or "wet" one—such as DEP's with Ida Ryogokudo Company of Tokyo—can open doors all over Japan. Founded in 1918, Ida Ryogokudo has spent sixty-seven years expanding its network of cosmetics dealers, some of whom have been linked to the company since the days of its founder, Kohachiro Ida. "The loyalty of our customers is very strong," says executive vice president Hitoyuki Ida, older son of current company president Hideo Ida and grandson of the founder. "There is a personal commitment to our father and grandfather. That is a very valuable commitment in our opinion."

Like any good business relationship, the Ida-DEP connection is based on mutual interest. Ida was drawn to DEP's youth-oriented line of hair-styling products, shampoos and conditioners. Berglass, as president of a midsize company, needed distribution in Japan but lacked the resources to develop his own network. Through the Idas, Berglass went from *gai-jin* to insider—the ultimate path to success in Japan.

But what really made the relationship blossom—like most things in Asia—was the emphasis placed by both sides on developing a close personal relationship. Once a distribution agreement was signed, Berglass suggested that Japanese DEP representatives meet with him on a quarterly basis—once a year in Tokyo, twice at DEP's southern California headquarters, and once at a resort hotel in Hawaii. "The phone is fine, but it is the face-to-face meetings that make the difference," Berglass insists. "What we have wanted to achieve is the understanding that this company will do what we say and that we care what they do. That way, no one wants to break the chain of obligation."

Berglass's face in this chain of obligations—what the Japanese call *giri*—leads him to do many things many Americans would consider a waste of time. For instance, he changes the chemical mix and packaging of his products to meet Japanese tastes. And when Takao Ida, Hitoyuki's brother and director of Ida's international division, came to America, Berglass insisted that he stay at his house in Marina del Rey, sharing the family dinner and even the household chores. Today Berglass considers himself young Ida's "American father."

By 1984, this approach had boosted DEP's Japanese sales to over 7 percent of the company's worldwide revenues. But although the business connection has grown, the personal side remains the foundation of the relationship. "When we get together in Hawaii, we talk business one day, lie out on the beach the next day, do a lot of drinking and fun. It's a beautiful human communication," Hitoyuki Ida explains. "You see, we really like them, so we make every effort to help them. And it's not always the ideas you come up with at the meeting or on an agenda. Sometimes a sake party is the most important thing."

6

Making the World Nation

No one would mistake Harriet Nicholaus for a marketing genius. Back in 1983, Nicholaus, a Greenwich, Connecticut, housewife, concocted a home remedy in her kitchen—a muscle pain reliever made from pepper and water—in order to treat her choreographer husband's bursitis. When her husband and friends began raving about the product, it occurred to her that maybe she could sell some of the brew to the public.

But when it came to finding a market for her product, Nicholaus was in trouble. For nearly two years, her Muscle Medic languished on the shelves of Connecticut health-food stores. Then she discovered a market nonexistent in the homogeneous milieu of Greenwich. One of her distributors had placed Muscle Medic in some New York *bodegas*, small markets that cater to Hispanics. Unlike the health stores, the *bodegas* seemed able to move the product.

Since then, Nicholaus has become something of an expert on the Hispanic market. Shifting her operations to Miami, the nation's most heavily Hispanic major city, Nicholaus took her meager advertising budget and threw virtually all of it into the Spanish-language media. Although not fluent in Spanish, she taught herself enough to get on television and explain her product. However awkward her presentation, Hispanics seemed responsive to an Anglo woman attempting to sell them *mano a mano*. Almost immediately, Muscle Medic's sales skyrocketed. By the summer of 1986, she was selling more in Miami in a month than she had in the Northeast the whole previous year.

"When I got on and said in Spanish, 'You have nothing to lose but your pain,' it really caught on," recalls Nicholaus, who has subsequently moved with her family to Miami. "I use a very personal approach, like Frank Perdue and his chickens. I go on and say that I made this for them. They seem to appreciate that an Anglo woman would do that and in Spanish, too."

The Unfinished Country

Viewed from the perspective of international economics, Harriet Nicholaus's marketing coup may seem an event of minute importance. Yet her discovery of a new market among Hispanics parallels a broader revitalization of the American economy through the massive infusion of peoples from around the world. With their entrepreneurial energy, new purchasing power and links to virtually every nation, the new immigrants—perhaps even more than the nation's continental expanse and entrepreneurial vigor—represent the very essence of America's *sokojikara*.

At a time when most of the industrialized world seeks to fend off outsiders, America is taking in more legal immigrants than the rest of the world *combined*. This immigration, the greatest since the early decades of this century, is rapidly transforming American cultural, political and economic life. Whereas previous immigrant waves came predominately from Europe, today's new Americans hail largely from the nations of Asia and Latin America. During the first half of this decade, for instance, these immigrants accounted for 83 percent of the total, with Europeans accounting for a mere 11 percent of new Americans.

Through their explosive growth and tremendous energy, the new arrivals are transforming the United States from a European melting pot to a multiracial world nation. In this way American society is being prepared for the new era of non-Caucasian economic predominance.

No other major nation enjoys this social flexibility. Other countries may for a time imitate or even surpass American technology. They may enjoy brief periods of economic, political and cultural hegemony. But they are confined by the limits of their own peculiar social and economic systems. Immigration, however, notes Harvard sociologist Nathan Glazer, makes America "a permanently unfinished country." As Japan's Professor Fuji Kamiya notes:

> For older and weaker countries, it would have been fatal to have such internal conflict. Because it was so young, these conflicts actually turned into a stimulus. Amazingly, the U.S. continues to absorb new Mexicans and Vietnamese with equanimity. European civilization doesn't have that reserve; neither does a small vessel like Japan.

A brief look at population statistics reveals much about the enormity of this change. Once only a few drops in the national "melting pot," Hispanics and Asians together now represent nearly 10 percent of the American population. And these ethnic groups are growing at rates far above the national average. Since 1980, for instance, the Hispanic population swelled almost 30 percent to nearly 19 million, a rate of growth almost three times the national average. Recent changes in the immigration law, giving long-time resident illegal aliens the chance to opt for citizenship, could add another 2.5 million to 4 million Hispanics to the total population.

Even faster growing has been the Asian population, which jumped 142 percent between 1970 and 1980. Roughly 4 million strong, or 1.6 percent of the population, in 1985, the Asian population should double to 8 million by the year 2000, or 3 percent. Including black Americans, within thirty years non-Europeans will account for a full one-third of the population. And this trend will be felt far sooner in the five key states—California, Texas, Florida, New York, New Jersey and Illinois—which attract 70 percent of all immigrants. By 2010, California will become majority "minority" state.

With a rate of population growth seven times that of native whites, these new immigrants—and their progeny—will play an even greater role in the American future. By early in the next century Hispanics will easily replace blacks, the nation's largest nonwhite minority since the earliest European settlement, as the nation's biggest minority group. In the early part of the next century, Asians and Hispanics, according to the Washington-based Population Reference Bureau, could account for well over one-third of the nation's population.

The newly emerging post-European America already exists in many of the nation's largest cities, including New York, Chicago and Los Angeles. In Miami and San Antonio, Hispanics already constitute absolute majorities. San Francisco's Asians, less than 15 percent of the city's population in 1970, probably already outnumber the local Anglo population. And Los Angeles—once jokingly dubbed "the largest city in Iowa" for its predominately Nordic population—now boasts a hodgepodge of ethnic and racial minorities who together easily outnumber the European-descended residents of the nation's second-largest city.

Not all Americans regard this emerging world nation favorably. As large numbers of unfamiliar kinds of people rush into an area—often speaking a strange language, eating seemingly bizarre cuisine and following unusual customs—some feel themselves and the nation threatened. Some prominent national observers, such as columnist Neal Peirce, see in the large influx of Spanish-speakers the making of a "grim reality" that could "shred national unity" and spur in America the sort of divisive communalism characteristic of nations such as Belgium and Canada.

Former Colorado governor Richard Lamm even fears that the "unassimilated immigrants"—such as Asians and Hispanics—could even threaten the integrity of the majority culture. The very Miami which Harriet Nicholaus finds so exciting and profitable, Lamm finds particularly detestable, seeing in the Cuban, and later Haitian, upsurge the cause for increased drug traffic, political separatism and black race riots. In response, Lamm believes steps should be taken by "us natives" to follow the attempts of nations such as France, which try to protect their national cultures against "contamination" by American models.

Less elaborate arguments come from a wide cross-section of "native" American opinion. By 1982, one-third of all Americans felt that the new immigrants—Mexicans, Koreans, Vietnamese, Puerto Ricans and Cubans—were a "bad thing" for the country. Even in ethnically diverse California, half of all

Anglos and three-fifths of all blacks, according to a 1986 *Los Angeles Times* poll, felt that there were already "too many Mexicans" in the state. Hostility toward the growing Latin population is widespread among both blacks and whites in South Florida. A popular jest in Miami during the 1980s asked: "Will the last American to leave the city please lower the flag?"

With their rapid increase in population and growing economic significance, Asians have been particular targets of "native" fears. Hard-working Vietnamese fishermen have engendered the anger, and sometimes the violence, of Anglo competitors from northern California to the Texas Gulf Coast. Korean entrepreneurs opening stores in ghetto areas have been in sharp conflict with blacks in Los Angeles, New York and Washington, where in 1985 and 1986 eleven Korean-owned shops were firebombed.

Such fears about immigrants predated the founding of the Republic. Even so liberal a spirit as Benjamin Franklin rued the impact of growing numbers of Germans who flooded into his beloved Pennsylvania in the mid-eighteenth century, printing their own German-language newspapers and conducting church services in their native language. Denouncing these newcomers as "Palatine boors," Franklin asked: "Why should *Pennsylvania*, founded by the *English*, become a Colony of *Aliens*, who will shortly be so numerous as to Germanize us instead of our Anglifying them?"

Like most immigrant threats, the "German problem" quickly dissipated. Within Franklin's own lifetime, Pennsylvania's large German community quickly gained proficiency in English, joined the American revolutionary forces in large numbers and was well represented among the mourners at his funeral. Other minorities—including French Huguenots and Dutch in New York—also integrated rapidly into the new society, with persons of other than English descent constituting nearly one-third of the signers of the Declaration of Independence.

Anti-immigrant sentiments continued to fester, however, as large numbers of Irish Catholics began migrating to the new country. New England Federalists, in particular, worried about French Jacobins and Irish radicals who, they feared, might try to revolutionize the country. By the late eighteenth century, Federalists such as Harrison Gray Otis of Massachusetts were calling for a complete ban on immigration from Europe, most particularly the "hordes of wild Irishmen [and] the turbulent and disorderly of all parts of the world [who] come here with a view to disturb our tranquility. . . ."

For a brief time the Federalists succeeded in restricting immigration by passing laws to curb aliens' personal liberties and extending the naturalization process from five to fourteen years. These restrictions were quickly repealed after Jefferson took power in 1801, but the growing presence of Irish and other Catholics continued to serve as an irritant to "native" Protestant Americans.

One of the most virulent anti-Catholic spokesmen was Samuel F. B. Morse, inventor of the telegraph, whose 1835 book, *Dangers to Free Institutions of the United States through Foreign Immigration*, was built around the unlikely thesis that the Jesuits planned to use Catholic immigration as a prelude to overthrowing the government. Anti-Catholic passions—which historian Richard Hofstadter once described as "the pornography of the Puritans"—exploded in riots and church-burnings. In the 1840s, the nativist American Republic party, also known as the "Know-Nothings," briefly took control of the municipal governments in New York and Philadelphia, as well as several statehouses.

But perhaps the closest parallels to the contemporary situation occurred in the late nineteenth and early twentieth centuries, the period of peak European immigration. While racist pressures were sufficient to the stanch the flow of Asians, large numbers of eastern and southern Europeans flooded the nation's cities. The national elite of that time—now including many Germans and other non-English northern Europeans—were horrified by the new immigrants who they widely saw as a threat to national values and order. The Italians, for instance, were viewed as "the Chinese of Europe" and, in some southern states, were actually forced to attend all-black schools. In 1875, the authoritative *New York Times* declared that it was "perhaps hopeless to think of civilizing them, or keeping them in order, except by the arm of the law."

By the 1890s, the rise of Social Darwinism allowed the traditional nativism to dress up as scientific theory. According to what passed for anthropology, southern and eastern Europeans—as well as all peoples of color—were clearly deemed inferior to the "Nordic" racial stock represented by Anglo-Saxons, Scandinavians and Germans. In 1894, an Immigration Restriction League was founded by a handful of Harvard graduates and quickly gained important adherents like Senator Henry Cabot Lodge and historian John Fiske. Such feelings were deep-seated among the intellectual elite. After returning in 1907 from twenty-five years of self-imposed exile in Europe, Henry James complained about "this sense of dispossession" caused by the massive immigration of newcomers.

In the search for argument against immigration, the elite at times went to absurd lengths. Psychologist Henry Goddard in 1912 traveled to Ellis Island to test the mental level of the new immigrants. Not surprisingly, he found 87 percent of the Russians, 83 percent of the Jews, 80 percent of the Hungarians and 79 percent of all Italians "feeble minded," sometimes by simply looking at them.

The anti-immigrant hysteria reached its peak of intellectual respectability in 1919, with the publication of Madison Grant's *The Passing of a Great Race*. Grant, chairman of the New York Zoological Society and trustee of the American Museum of Natural History, saw the new immigration as a grave threat to the cultural, political and economic future of the nation. While considering successful attempts by Californians and Australians to turn back Asiatic immigration as an "absolutely justified determination to keep those lands as white man's countries," he feared that the "genius-producing classes of the community" in the United States—presumably Anglo-Saxon—were being usurped by newcomers of inferior stock.

"The new immigration contained a large and increasing number of the weak, the broken and the mentally crippled of all races drawn from the lowest stratum of the Mediterranean Basin and the Balkans, together with hordes of the submerged population of the Polish ghettos," Grant wrote gravely. "It is evident that in large parts of the country the native American will completely disappear."

Even as immigrants filled one out of every six places in the nation's World War I army, Grand and other opponents of immigration pushed vigorously for legislation to preserve the place of the "native" American. These ideas found legislative voice with the passage of new immigration acts in 1921 and 1924, which assigned quotas granting nearly four-fifths of all immigration to northern and western Europe; southern and eastern Europe, which in 1914 accounted for three-fifths of all immigration, received a mere 5 percent of the new quota.

By the late 1920s, the attempt to put an end to America's "unfinished story" appeared successful. While the new immigrants would, it was hoped, in time be transformed into pseudo-WASPs, the nation clearly had chosen—through its laws, educational system, and political and economic institutions—to identify itself, in Madison Grant's words, as "a racial colony" of northern Europe. As educator Gladys A. Wiggins observed:

> [Educators] have painted the ideal America and American partly through contrast and in comparison to other countries and people. The deepest identification has been made with certain European peoples; some of the Europeans plus the remainder of the world have remained outside the American pale. . . . If the immigrants came from Northern Europe, the movement into this country was commended. . . . Those who came after 1880 were often described as "waves," "swarms" or "hordes."

To many around the world, this freezing of the American "ideal" represented a profound disappointment. In 1916, Indian writer Rabindranath Tagore, coming from a land ruled by white colonialists and beset by communal dissensions, saw in the United States the epitome of anticolonialism and multiracialism. "America," he wrote, "was the only nation engaged in solving the problems of race intimacy. Its mission is to raise civilization by permitting all races entry and widening the ideal of humanity."

But when Tagore, by then recipient of the Nobel Prize for Literature, started to tour the United States in 1929, the racial attitudes and taunts he encountered in Los Angeles and elsewhere forced a quick cancellation. "Jesus," he wrote angrily, "could not get into America because, first of all, he would not have the necessary money, and secondly, he would be an Asiatic.''

The Immigrant Edge

It took nearly four decades to reverse the pattern of race discrimination. Despite attempts by congressmen representing the new immigrants and their progeny, ''native American'' spokesmen such as Nevada's Senator Patrick A. McCarran and North Carolina's Senator Sam Ervin fought bitterly to retain the essentially Anglo-Saxon concept of America. Although Hitler had discredited much of the old racialist theories, the new apologists of discrimination argued that preferences for ''readily assimilable'' groups such as northern Europeans would prevent the emergence of ''hard core indigestible blocs'' from other parts of the world.

Yet in reality these immigrants not only have proved ''digestible,'' but have played a central role in maintaining the nation's economic metabolism. By the 1980s, most of those groups characterized by Goddard as ''feeble minded''—Jews, Italians and Poles—enjoy per capita incomes well above that of the ''great race'' of Anglo-Saxons. The performance of nonwhite immigrants, including Chinese, Japanese and West Indians, also has exceeded that of ''native'' Americans.

Indeed, immigration—rather than a bane to development—has consistently spurred rapid economic growth. As early as 1791, Alexander Hamilton in his *Report on the Subject of Manufactures* saw in the ''disturbed state'' of Europe an ideal opportunity to import the ''requisite workmen'' needed for the building of American industry. In the late eighteenth and early nineteenth centuries, regions open to non-British immigration, such as Pennsylvania and Maryland, grew more quickly than did New England, which had a reputation for hostility to outsiders. By the 1850s, some states, such as Wisconsin, actually set up offices in New York to attract immigrants to their rapidly developing areas; after the Civil War, Iowa and Minnesota followed suit.

But it was New York itself that grew to epitomize the dynamic economic power of immigration. By the 1840s, two-thirds of all new immigrants passed through the growing eastern metropolis; by the 1860s, it greeted nearly three-quarters of all newcomers entering the country. By then, nearly one in four immigrants resided in New York State, two and a half times more than second-place Philadelphia. To some, then, the immigrant rush—as in Miami or Los Angeles today—was a harbinger of decline. "The man of old stock," complained Madison Grant, ". . . is to-day literally being driven off the streets of New York City by the swarms of Polish Jews."

Yet rather than destroying the city, immigrants—who along with their children accounted for two-thirds of New York's population in 1920—played a major role in turning the metropolis on the Hudson into the first true American "world city." Though New York had been basically a commercial center, Jewish and some Italian immigrants virtually created the city's garment sector in the 1870s, as both entrepreneurs and workers. Italians did most of the work on the city's expanding subway system, and, along with the Irish, were the workers on the hundreds of busy docks in New York Harbor. But it was not only as laborers or small-time entrepreneurs that the immigrants excelled. Within little over a decade, many of the "mental defectives" detected by Dr. Goddard, along with their progeny, entered the elite professions, with Jews alone accounting for more than half of New York's doctors and lawyers.

Immigrants also provided much of the muscle behind the rapid industrialization of the Great Lakes and Midwest, by 1910 supplying 70 percent of all the coal miners, two-thirds of the garment workers and half of the men employed in steel mills. In the Far West, Chinese and Japanese, despite a vicious pattern of persecution, helped build the railroads and lay the foundation for California's modern agriculture, digging the irrigation levees and introducing large-scale vegetable growing. The *London Times* described the anti-Asian hysteria among the turn-of-the-century California whites as a reaction against a "more efficient" civilization.

In the future, the ability of the United States to absorb new immigrants may prove an even greater economic asset. At a time when virtually every major advanced industrial country—from Western Europe to Japan—is entering what French demographer

Gerard-François Dumont describes as "a demographic winter," immigration keeps America's population relatively young and growing. The average Hispanic, for instance, is twenty-three years old, eight years younger than the average for the rest of the population. Without the influx of these and other newcomers, America's population, like that of its competitors, would age more rapidly and actually begin shrinking by 2020.

The role of immigrants in supplying a large working population is particularly crucial. Owing to a lack of new immigration and falling birthrate, Japan's elderly by the turn of the century should constitute nearly one-quarter of its population, almost twice the percentage in the United States. By early in the next century the financial burdens of this demography are expected to become almost unbearable, according to OECD projections, with nearly two in five West Germans and Japanese collecting pensions, while in the United States, that percentage, due largely to immigration, should remain at no more than one in four. Notes Bryant Robey of Hawaii's East West Institute:

> In the next few decades . . . our economy may need new immigrants—legal or illegal—more than they need jobs. As the number of entry-level workers declines—a result of the baby bust—labor shortages for many industries will start. If businesses cannot find enough people in the United States to fill unskilled and entry-level positions then these businesses may have to invest overseas to find affordable workers.

> . . . The country may need the contributions of as many workers as it can to make the baby boom generation comfortable in its old age.

Even now, immigrants are having a massive impact on major regional economies. Like the Northeast and Midwest in the late nineteenth and early twentieth centuries, states such as California, New York, Illinois, New Jersey, Florida and Texas—which together account for 70 percent of all the new immigration—have benefited tremendously from the presence of the newcomers. A 1985 Rand Corporation study contradicts the popular perception that immigrants place an undue burden on social services, finding that only 5 percent of Mexican immigrants receive public assistance, compared to 10 percent for the general adult population. With rates of labor participation higher than among European immigrants and natives, Asian and Hispanic immigrants in many more cases are bringing back the work ethic that has been eroded among so many long-time residents in the United States. As one Labor Department specialist put it: "You see exhortations all the time to hire the handicapped, minorities, women. But did you ever see an ad campaign to hire an immigrant? Apparently there is no need."

This dynamic has been particularly crucial in the manufacturing sector. The large infusion of Vietnamese and Chinese, for instance, has been essential for the staffing of high-technology manufacturing plants in the Silicon Valley, where over 10,000 Chinese-surnamed engineers now work. Leading Silicon Valley companies—such as electronics subcontractor Solectron and Circadian, a producer of microprocessor-controlled medical instruments—offer English classes and other educational programs to attract highly prized immigrant talent and energy.

Asians are prominent as well throughout southern California, home both to one out of every eight foreign-born Americans and to the nation's largest concentration of high-technology industries. "Without the movement of Asians, particularly Vietnamese," notes Robert Kelley, president of the Southern California Technology Executives Network, an association of 170 local technology firms, "there would not have been the sort of explosion you had in places like Orange County."

The impact has also been strong in the growth of more traditional industries. During the 1970s, garment manufacturing, an industry hard hit by Asian and other Third World competition, expanded in two parts of the country—New York City and Los Angeles, both among the most expensive areas in the nation, but blessed with large numbers of Asian and Hispanic immigrants. Phillip Martin, an economist at the University of California at Davis, notes: "An outside observer would say that's crazy. But the answer is that in both places you've got all those immigrant workers available."

Hispanic immigrants already play a crucial role in the garment, leather, textile, furniture and lumber industries in southern California, all of which grew by over 50 percent during the 1970s, while these same industries declined in the rest of the country. Rather than taking jobs from "native" Americans, note Rand researchers Kevin P. McCarthy and R. Burciaga Valdez, the massive influx of Mexicans into California actually boosted employment. As Richard Rothstein, manager of the Amalgamated Clothing and Textile Workers Union in Los Angeles, put it: "Prohibiting employment of immigrants, the only workers willing to labor in minimum or near-minimum garment jobs, will only accelerate the destruction of domestic industry."

But perhaps the most spectacular economic benefits come from the immigrants' own entrepreneurial energy. Although underrepresented in the boardrooms of the Fortune 500, immigrants cut a huge swath through America's entrepreneurial Third Century economy. Virtually all the ethnic groups decried by early twentieth-century racists—Japanese, Chinese, East Indians, Jews, Greeks, Arabs—have pursued the American entrepreneurial dream, measured by business establishments per capita, with far more vigor than have the "native" sons.

West Indians, for instance, constitute a vibrant entrepreneurial presence far outweighing their numbers. As early as 1900, West Indians owned 20 percent of Manhattan's black enterprises, more than twice their percentage in the population. Through rotating credit networks, known as *susus*, West Indians have pooled capital among several families that was then used to launch new enterprises. Virtues like thrift and hard work were part of the basic West Indian ethos. *Oakland Tribune* publisher Bob Maynard recalls how the "Barbadian network" helped his father build a successful small trucking company in New York, a company whose profits provided Maynard with his ticket to a highly successful career in journalism. "There's something about the immigrant experience that's different," notes Maynard. "It's like the Chinese. There's a communal business spirit. That's something outside the experience of most Afro-Americans."

Like Maynard, the sons and daughters of these immigrants later played a disproportionate role in the professional and political life of black America. Groups such as Jamaicans enjoyed a rate of self-employment and income above that of blacks native to the United States, but by the second generation, these groups surpass the average income levels of whites as well. In Hartford, Connecticut, a relatively small community of 25,000 West Indians own an estimated 20 percent of real estate in the North End, an area they have helped turn around with their groceries, bakeries and restaurants. "West Indians love to own things, to be part of something," observes Vincent Cockett, one of the city's early West Indian settlers. "It's part of our culture."

Entrepreneurialism is also an increasing part of Hispanic immigrant "culture." In the decade between 1977 and 1987, the number of Hispanic-owned businesses increased by more than a third, with gross revenues of nearly $20 billion, a figure expected to rise to over $25 billion in 1990.

This sort of aggressively entrepreneurial behavior is particularly evident in Florida's Dade County, where Hispanics now outnumber whites and Cuban Americans have helped transform a sleepy resort area into a dynamic entrepreneurial center. Like other immigrants, Cubans have started small, opening tiny *bodegas* and shops. Between 1960 and 1980, the Hispanics increased their share of Dade County gas stations from barely one-tenth to almost half.

By the mid-1980s, Cubans in South Florida have created over 25,000 businesses, enjoying the highest rates of self-employment and per capita income of Hispanics anywhere in North America. Developing what amounts to their own economy, complete with restaurants, accounting and law firms, and advertising agencies, they also pioneered the city's fast-growing garment business, now third after New York and Los Angeles, and they run more large-scale Hispanic-owned businesses than any of the longer-established Hispanic communities in the nation. Cubans and other Hispanics over the last twenty years also have established twenty-nine banks in southern Florida, accounting for some 40 percent of the total market. One Cuban-owned bank alone, Miami's Republic National, has grown over the past twenty years from a few million in assets to over $900 million.

By most accounts, the immigrant-engineered transformation of Miami's economy is just beginning. Already the 1980s have seen an influx of over 50,000 Haitian refugees, who are displaying many of the same entrepreneurial characteristics. "In ten years, you'll see people eating Haitian food over in Coral Gables," predicts Tony Villamil, a Cuban refugee who is now vice president and chief economist at Southeast Bank. "Those who risk their lives in boats are your more entrepreneurial-type people. They are making their impact felt, just like the Cubans did."

Much the same process is taking place in Los Angeles. Always a city of transplants, Los Angeles by the late 1980s has become the ultimate Third Century American town, with the highest proportion of recent immigrants—over two-thirds from Asia and Latin America—of any city in the country. As did immigrants in New York in America's second century, the new immigrants—by their hard work and entrepreneurial energy— are laying the foundation for the Los Angeles area's emergence by the year 2000, according to Department of Commerce projections, as the nation's leading region in terms of population, employment and income generation.

One reason for Los Angeles' popularity as the launchpoint for ambitious immigrants is its rapidly expanding industrial sector. Long derided as "Tinsel Town," Los Angeles is now the nation's premier manufacturing center, with nearly 900,000 factory jobs. Hispanics, who make up roughly half the city's manufacturing workers, also are increasingly moving into ownership of small industrial concerns. By the mid-1980s, an estimated one-fourth of the city's Hispanic-owned businesses were in manufacturing. These industrial firms enjoyed the highest rate of sales growth among all Hispanic businesses, according to a 1985 Price Waterhouse survey.

Many other ethnic businesses are in the retail field, including a large number devoted to serving their own people; between 1982 and 1986, for instance, the city's Mexican American Grocers Association increased its membership from 260 to 860. Perhaps the most prolific entrepreneurs have been the Koreans, who flocked into Los Angeles during the 1970s. Like the Cubans with their banks, or the West Indians' *susus*, the Koreans financed many of their own businesses through *kye*, an informal credit association made up of money pooled among immigrants. By the mid-1980s, Koreans boasted the highest self-employment rate of any immigrant group and a rate of business ownership nearly 50 percent above the national average. With over 7,000 businesses in southern California, one-quarter of all the Korean-owned businesses nationwide, these entrepreneurs were widely credited by local financial institutions with reviving a huge and decayed section west of the city's downtown and transforming it into a bustling commercial district.

The benefits derived from these and other ethnic groups have been dramatic. With once-decayed areas now clearly recovering, even such conservative bastions as First Interstate Bank have established new branches in inner-city areas. Explaining the new policy, John Popovich, First Interstate's director of public affairs, explains how immigrants have radically altered the economic realities not only in Koreatown, but throughout the sprawling Los Angeles basin:

> It's not social responsibility—this is a great base of future business for us.

> Five or six years ago we were adjusting to no growth. But immigration has changed everything. New arrivals here are astounded by the opportunities; they look at the opportunities with fresh eyes. To ignore that ethnic market, whether consumer or entrepreneurial, is to fly in the face of data and the future of this town. Anyone who ignores it does so at his own peril.

Marketing to the World Nation

In the country's Third Century, new Americans represent a massive growth market right at home. Although many white entrepreneurs tend to ignore these consumers, those willing to market nonwhite America have before them a customer base that by 1986 boasted nearly $170 billion in purchasing power, larger than the gross domestic product of all but a dozen countries in the world. By the year 2000, according to estimates by *Inc.* magazine, that number is expected to explode, in 1985 dollars, to over $650 billion—nearly equivalent to the entire 1985 gross domestic product of West Germany.

This growing wealth stems from the tremendous economic dynamism of immigrants. Rather than mere "huddled masses," the new immigrants are outperforming the "natives," according to a 1980 study for the Senate Commission on Immigration and Refugee Policy, which found that most immigrant families within ten years of arrival earn more than native-born Americans. Asian Americans, for instance, already claim among the highest per capita incomes in the nation. Constituting a mere $30 billion in 1980, the total income of Asian Americans is expected to double by 1990.

Perhaps less nationally recognized than Asian affluence is the growing consumer wealth of the nation's Hispanics. Contrary to the common perception of Hispanics' low position on the economic ladder, their total purchasing power, slightly less than $54 billion in 1980, stands at over $134 billion today; according to the Miami-based Strategy Research Corporation, it could top $172 billion by 1990.

In many cities—including San Antonio, Miami and San Francisco—the economic potential of the new America is already evident. The Los Angeles Hispanic community already constitutes a larger market than that of *all* metropolitan Saint Louis. Observes Ed Escobedo, a Los Angeles business consultant and Hispanic marketing expert, "People have to start realizing that these new immigrants have a lot of buying power. Instead of thinking of them as undocumented aliens, maybe it's time to start thinking of them as undocumented consumers."

Selling to this new America requires entrepreneurs to adopt new techniques and attitudes. Strategies that worked in the past often do not apply when dealing with the ascendent non-European ethnic groups. "Every new group that comes in is different," notes San Francisco auto dealer Ron Greenspan, who built his business largely by serving the city's growing Asian community. "You must adjust yourself to each reality. It's an empathy thing. You need a heat-seeking missile these days. You just don't use the same old conventional artillery."

For Greenspan, the son of a Jewish traveling salesman from Cleveland, "the heat-seeking missile" means tailoring his advertising and sales pitches to Asian tastes, understanding the dynamics of Asian families and gaining the ability to reach them through media in their native languages. In other regional markets—such as Miami, New York, Chicago, San Antonio or Los Angeles—marketing the new America translates into Spanish and to appealing to such differing Hispanics as Cubans, Mexicans and Puerto Ricans.

This new reality first arrived at the Mars Market in the Los Angeles suburb of El Monte back in the late 1960s. Like many of the communities in the San Gabriel Valley east of downtown LA, El Monte was changing rapidly from predominately white to mostly Hispanic. The market's owner, however, wasn't willing to change his business to suit the new consumers.

"The guy simply wanted no Mexican trade," recalls Mark Roth, who finally purchased the failing market in 1969 for a mere $72,000. "He didn't carry the products they wanted and sold only the most expensive cuts of meat. He just wanted to cater to the so-called elite of El Monte and was starving to death."

But where the old owner saw a mere rabble, Mark Roth spotted opportunity. A former manager at the local Safeco thrift chain, he knew that the Hispanics were constituting an ever-greater portion of the Los Angeles consumer market. If other Anglo-owned markets, most of them larger chain operations, chose to ignore the swelling Hispanic population, Roth reasoned he would find his niche by catering to them.

Although he spoke little Spanish and came from the Midwest, Roth was uniquely prepared for marketing to newcomers. His own family experience told him that one didn't have to be Hispanic to sell to them. His father, Adam Roth, had also been a grocer back home in Bellfield, North Dakota, and 80 percent of his customers were recent immigrants from the Ukraine.

Victims of the brutal agricultural collectivization drive initiated by Soviet dictator Joseph Stalin in the late 1920s, these often penniless Ukrainians migrated to North Dakota in search of a better future. Like Hispanics and Asians today, the Ukrainians often were looked down upon by many of Bellfield's 800 residents, most of whom were, like Roth, of Germanic descent. "The Ukrainian was considered a lowlife," Roth recalls, who started working at the family store at age six. "We didn't think they had brains. You didn't even think of going out with Ukrainian girls. The German immigrant everyone accepted, but no one thought the Ukrainian would fit in."

One place these new immigrants could fit in, however, was at Adam Roth's Southside Mercantile Company. To attract Ukrainians and Poles to the store, he imported sauces and foodstuffs traditional to eastern European cuisine. Where products weren't available, he made them himself, offering such things as fresh-made *kielbasa*, a favorite Polish-style sausage. The elder Roth also taught himself Ukrainian to communicate with his new customers. "My father always said that the new arrival was the best customer," Roth points out in his cramped office above the shop floor. "They are settling down and need pots and pans. These are people on the way up. Back home today they dominate the whole area."

Like the Ukrainians in the '30s, Mexican immigrants have many characteristics appealing to a grocer. For one thing, their families are larger than those of Caucasians. In California, for instance, Hispanic families average 4.11 persons per household, compared to 3.11 for Caucasians. Not surprisingly, then, the average Hispanic shopper in Los Angeles, according to a study conducted by the Von's supermarket chain, spends on average $20 more per week on food than his or her Anglo counterpart.

To appeal to these customers, however, Roth radically changed the Mars Market's marketing strategy. For one thing, he immediately hired Spanish-speaking employees, something his predecessor failed to do. Today nearly two-thirds of the thirty-one employees at Mars Market are Spanish speaking. He also keyed in on the strong family orientation of Hispanics, seeking to attract weekend trade by creating a warm, fiestalike atmosphere at the store. In his first week after taking over the store he brought in Ray Walston—star of the then-popular "My Favorite Martian" TV show—as a celebrity guest. A Mexican *mariachi* band provided music. Roth admits losing some old-time Anglo customers who objected to the new Mexican orientation. But sales doubled from the previous week. Not surprisingly, such fiestas are now a regular feature at Mars Market.

Roth's marketing drive, however, went well beyond mere theatrics. He stocked his vegetable section with cactus leaves, hot chiles and other Mexican-style spices. In the meat department he aggressively marketed such cuts as the ground chuck and neck bones used in many traditional Mexican dishes. Within two years, sales volume doubled yet again.

Later, Roth added still more features for his Hispanic customers, who now constitute over two-thirds of his total market. For instance, he included a *tortilleria*—a machine for baking fresh tortillas. More recently, other, larger markets—such as Von's in Los Angeles, HEB in San Antonio and Fiesta Stores in Houston—have adopted many of the same techniques. Their reasons, like Roth's, center on tapping a vast potential market, a new nation of consumers developing within the nation. ''When we started this, people asked us 'Why are you catering to those wetbacks?' '' Roth said, standing proudly in front of his large tortilla press. ''The payoff is that we have built credibility with these people over all these years. It will help keep us in business.''

Mark Roth's experience in El Monte reflects the more traditional side of marketing to immigrants. Merchants in New York during the turn of the century—selling goods to the waves of Italian, Irish and Russian immigrants—would appreciate and easily understand the goings on at Mars Market. But today's immigrant wave also includes many relatively affluent and well-educated individuals. In the 1950s, for instance, half of all Hispanics failed to finish high school; by the 1970s, that rate had fallen to one-fifth, or near the national average. By the year 2000, according to a study by Ogilvy and Mather, ''the majority of Hispanics will live in the suburbs, firmly ensconced in the middle class—both economically and occupationally.''

Besides a market for such things as produce and household items, this new American middle class represents a growth market for ''big ticket'' items such as automobiles and homes. This is particularly evident in Miami, where Hispanics now comprise 56 percent of the total city population, and have developed a local economy that by 1983 reached roughly $6 billion. Their median income has risen from 80 percent of the national average in 1980 to roughly 84 percent currently.

Faced with this Cuban economic juggernaut, many Anglo

entrepreneurs simply gave up or moved elsewhere. But Miami car dealer Richard Goldberg had a different idea. Six years ago he *moved* his family's Toyota dealership out of Miami's heavily Jewish and black north side and plunked it into the midst of a heavily Hispanic section across town. In a city now less than one-fifth Anglo, to stay in "white Miami" seemed to Goldberg like swimming against the tide of history.

"We came here because it was a growing area, not because it was Hispanic," the blond, balding Goldberg points out. "We just wanted to go where there would be the most people with the bucks to buy Toyotas."

Once in the Cuban community, Goldberg went out and hired a contingent of bilingual salespeople—a majority of Hispanics in Miami speak little or no English—to make sure there would be no communications problem. Now nearly all of Expressway Toyota's 150 employees, including much of his top sales staff, are Hispanic. Today Goldberg claims to own over 50 percent of the Hispanic market for Toyotas. Within just six years, Expressway's total sales have mushroomed to $75 million, a fourfold increase, turning the dealership from the 350th largest to the 38th largest out of 1,060 Toyota dealers nationwide.

But it is the Asian American who represents the ultimate example of this new upwardly mobile immigrant. Nearly 44 percent of all adult Asian immigrants, for instance, hold college degrees, compared with only 16 percent of the general adult population. Already some Asian groups—notably Japanese, Chinese and Filipinos—enjoy income levels above those of whites. Asians in southern California, according to a *Los Angeles Times* survey, purchase more men's suits, televisions, shoes and furniture than the average consumer in the region.

In many ways, selling to Asian Americans reflects many of the same principles important in marketing across the Pacific. Perhaps the classic case can be seen in Monterey Park, America's first majority Asian city. A mere decade ago Monterey Park was a sleepy, all-white suburb on the eastern fringe of Los Angeles. Local business people, many reared in the area, gathered—like a scene in a Norman Rockwell painting—at the Monterey Park drugstore to gossip in an atmosphere of easy congeniality.

Since then, Monterey Park has developed along lines that

normally would fulfill the wildest fantasies of local economic boosters. Spurred by a massive influx of well-educated, affluent Asians, the town's population since 1970 has risen by more than one-fifth. Chinese money created the scores of new commercial corridors—glistening with new office buildings, shops and restaurants. Commercial space that rented for $5 a square foot back in the 1970s now goes for as much as $45.

Yet if prosperity has come to Monterey Park, few of the old-line business establishments are still around to enjoy it. Rather than welcoming the Asians, many of the city's Anglo businesses refused to accept the new reality. Some sold out to Chinese interests. Others tried to hold on to a shrinking Anglo customer base and went bankrupt.

But not all of Monterey Park's businesses refused to adjust to the new reality. In 1980, Kelly Sands took over his family-owned Bezaire Electric Company. Long a leading electric contractor in the area, Bezaire by 1979 had fallen on hard times. Annual sales were only $300,000. Even worse, virtually all the developers and major contractors who had worked with Sands's father and grandfather had either gone out of business or left town.

But Sands, a college dropout in his early twenties, noticed the rising number of Chinese developers around town. Rather than disdain these often well-heeled new players, he courted them, hiring a staff of young, aggressive Asian managers to help communicate with prospective customers. He also adjusted his own hours to accommodate the demands of his work-oriented Asian customers, often meeting them at local Chinese restaurants late in the evening.

As a result of his efforts, today Sands is one of the few Anglo entrepreneurs to cash in on Monterey Park's new demography. Sands estimates Bezaire gets more than half the area's Chinese-related contractor business—accounting for four-fifths of his total clientele. His biggest project right now, for instance, is a massive new Buddhist temple going up several miles east of town.

"I think it's all in the mind-set," believes Sands, whose sales last year grew by nearly one-third to $3.7 million. "If the expanding market had been French or Japanese we would have done just as well. Either you adjust your mind-set to reality or you better get out of the way.''

Fighting off the Saracens

Perhaps most important of all, then, the immigration process offers a tremendous opportunity for Americans such as Kelly Sands to adjust to the realities of the post-European world. By marketing to Asians and Hispanics within the United States, by being exposed to their languages and cultures, American business people can themselves become more multicultural in their world view, and in the process jettison much of the baggage of prejudice.

This process—which earlier changed American attitudes toward Jews, Poles and others from outside northern Europe—is only now beginning to create a new and tolerant spirit. At this date it is still absurd to assert, as does George Gilder, that racism in America is not widespread and is the product of a "false liberal hypothesis." Yet it is also undeniable that there has been real, fundamental progress. "The growth in tolerance toward people of different religions and races," noted a 1979 Gallup survey, was among the "most dramatic trends" of over forty years of polling. In just two decades, according to a Harris survey, the number of Americans believing blacks are less ambitious has dropped from almost two out of three persons to only one in four.

This process is particularly remarkable when compared to the experience of Europe over the past decade. While the United States was trying to bring some order and fairness to its immigration policy, Europeans were simply slamming the door shut, and, in some cases, trying to remove those already in their countries. The deep-seated European fear of Asia and the Third World has been made palpable by the presence of some 16 million nonwhite immigrants throughout the continent. Rather than adopt the American model of absorption and intermingling of races, Europeans seem determined to resist any attempt to alter—despite their rapidly aging population—the continent's racial makeup. "You can't use the model of Europeans gaining acceptance in America—three generations and then assimilation—as applicable to these people,'' notes John Rex of the University of Warwick in England, an authority on European immigration. ''There is a much stronger sense of racism here than in America.''

This pattern is clearest in European attitudes toward the relatively small numbers of nonwhites in their midst. An estimated 1.5 million North Africans, for example, is clearly too numerous for many Frenchmen. Even the French Communist party, despite its traditional internationalist rhetoric, has organized demonstrations against influxes of people from North and West Africa, which they maintain threaten the employment of native-born French workers.

But the Communists have certainly not been alone on the anti-immigrant bandwagon. Running almost exclusively on a platform against these immigrants, Jean-Marie LePen's far-right National Front party won 10 percent of the French vote in March 1986. The victor in that election, conservative Jacques Chirac, promised for his part to ''preserve the identity of our national community'' by tightening visa and citizenship requirements. In the presidential election two years later, LePen's racist appeal attracted some 14 percent of the total vote.

Similar patterns have developed in West Germany, home to an estimated 1.4 million Turkish workers. In an attempt to learn about their conditions, West German journalist Guenter Wallraff disguised himself as a Turkish menial worker for two years. In his 1985 best-seller *At the Very Bottom*, Walraff wrote that Turks in Germany are ''abused, insulted, threatened and enslaved'' and live under conditions that seem ''a piece of apartheid.'' Certainly these immigrants, some of whom have been in Germany for over two decades, are not becoming new Germans in the manner of America's Hispanic, Asian and other immigrants. Despite their sometimes long sojourns in Germany, for instance, only 5,400 had become citizens by the summer of 1986.

In the United Kingdom, once the proud center of a vast multiracial empire, the presence of about 2 million non-Europeans—a minority of no more than 5 percent—now living in Britain, has led to a rapid growth in racial hostility. A 1986 poll found that 90 percent of all Britons agreed that their country discriminated against nonwhites and more than a third favored measures to encourage immigrants to go home. A government report the following year, called "Living in Terror," found that one in four blacks and Asians in East London had been victims of racial harassment over the previous twelve months. "There's a rather nasty mood at the moment," notes Michael Barnes, director of the United Kingdom Immigrants Advisory Service. "It's more respectable now, particularly among the middle class, to make racist remarks."

As a response to this public sentiment, Prime Minister Margaret Thatcher has placed tough limits on new immigration from nonwhite Commonwealth countries. "People are really rather afraid that this country might be rather swamped by people with a different culture," explained Mrs. Thatcher. "If you want good race relations, you've got to allay people's fear of numbers."

This alien malaise also characterizes much of the European approach to the increasing ascendency of the nonwhite world. As concerned as they are about nonwhites already in their nation, some Europeans also view the swelling populations of Third World nations such as India as a direct threat to what French author Jean Raspail describes as "our Western way of life." In his controversial book *Camp of the Saints*, Raspail depicts the eventual takeover of southern France, and eventually all Europe and America, by surging nonwhite humanity:

> Yes, the Third World had started to overflow its banks, and the West was its sewer. Perched on the shoulders of strapping young boys, first to land were the monsters, the grotesque little beggars of Calcutta. . . . And the monsters snuffled and sniffed at the sand, mouthed it by the hand, struck it with their fists to make sure it was real, and, convinced it was, sprang somersaults over their horrid, twisted limbs. Yes, the country would suit them fine. No question.

Europe's growing sense of racial unease also has been directed against the more prosperous nations of the nonwhite world. Although Europe's imports account for a far smaller percentage than America's, Europeans have tended to be quicker at raising the spectre of the *peril jaune*. "While U.S. businessmen are merely angry," commented *Time* during one of the innumerable Japan-EEC trade disputes, "the attitude in Europe borders on hysteria."

This "hysteria," notes Australian scholar Jenny Corbett, first expressed itself in the 1930s, when Japan's penetration of traditional captive Asian markets raised "frantic outcries" from European producers. Although Japan barely accounted for 4 percent of world trade at the time, Britain and other European nations set particularly tough tariffs against the Asian island-nation. This pattern of hostility, believes Professor R. P. Dore of the Institute of Development Studies at the University of Sussex, has at its core the "curious racially tinged tensions of Anglo-Japanese relations."

Europeans have also long feared that the United States' longstanding Asian connections must someday tear them from what Madison Grant described as their "racial colony." Even before the Second World War, noted one American historian, there was apprehension that "the closer the cooperation" between the United States and Japan "the greater the opposition of Britain and the European nations to America's ambitions." Throughout World War II, European powers were terrified that America would concentrate its resources on Asia rather than on Europe and, once the war was over, force them to surrender their Asian colonial empires.

More recently, as the Asian and American economies have become more intertwined, Europe has displayed a growing desire to seek a separate economic and political destiny. Although they have allowed some Asian economic penetration, often at the urging of the United States, the pattern of protectionism against Asian nations, particularly Japan, has been far harsher than in the United States. America's Atlantic-oriented postwar leaders may have helped conceive the European Common Market as an expression of New Deal idealism and free trade, but many Europeans have seen the market as a means, in the words of German economist Gustav Schmoller, to "save not only the political independence of these states, but Europe's higher ancient culture itself."

In economic terms, saving his "higher ancient culture" has often expressed itself in attempts to stem the Asian tide. Today even modest Japanese attempts to invest in Europe, as *Forbes* magazine put it, ''seem to stir xenophobia'' about the repatriation of profits and the spectre of ''working for them.'' This anti-Japanese hysteria reached its apogee when, in 1982, France created a huge bureaucratic bottleneck by forcing all Japanese VTRs through a tiny station in Poitiers, the town where Charles Martel won his historic battle against the Moors in 732. In the European press there was a clear tendency to substitute the Japanese for ''Arabs and Moors.'' Shocked by the ferocity of this racially tinged attack, Hitachi's French subsidiary felt compelled to take out an ad proclaiming ''We are not Saracens.''

The Limits of Insularity

Ironically, the Japanese—themselves the prime target of such racial attacks—are also prisoners of homogeneity. Like the Europeans, many Japanese, including former Prime Minister Yasuhiro Nakasone, have had a difficult time understanding the advantages that derive from the sort of racial diversity now flourishing in the United States. Indeed, Nakasone has maintained that racial cohesion remains a central advantage of Japan's economic and political system. ''The Japanese,'' Nakasone insisted in 1983, ''have been doing well for 2,000 years because there are no foreign races.''

Although this homogeneity may have served Japan well in the past, some Japanese are beginning to realize it may now pose one of its most severe problems. As racism has colored European responses to Japan, the extreme ethnocentrism of the Japanese has prevented them from developing political, cultural and social skills appropriate to their great economic power. Even with its global financial and industrial reach, Japan today remains, in Frank Gibney's term, a ''nation village,'' a country that functions with the strong but narrow kinship loyalties characteristic of a small hamlet. As Norio Ouchi, chief executive director of the Japan Trade Center in New York, put it:

If everyone of the [120 million] Japanese has a chance to trace each family line to its origin I'm sure we will find most of us related to one another in some way. And I'm sure this is why, even though we are total strangers, we feel quite close to one another and rarely approach another Japanese with the pre-conceived sense of distrust which appears commonplace among peoples with ethnically and culturally such different backgrounds.

However comforting this village mentality is to the Japanese, the reverse side of it is a profound lack of empathy or under-standing for outsiders. Inward-looking, confident of their place in the internal national hierarchy, many in Japan's business and government elite often seem incapable of comprehending the growing worldwide hostility toward Japan.

This sense of exclusivity has been central to the development of the modern Japanese state. Although Japan sent cultural mis-sions to China as early as the seventh century, and borrowed heavily from neighboring Korea, the national ethos has been largely constructed around a sense of racial uniqueness, a feel-ing particularly pronounced during the three centuries of virtual isolation from outside contact under the Tokugawa shogunate.

Often narcissistic, bordering on the obsessive, this attitude was understandably exacerbated by the spectre of European im-perialism which, by the early nineteenth century, had reduced even the great Chinese empire to a state of semicolonial vassal-age. In order to fight off what they saw as the debilitating effects of Western influence, the Meiji reformers and their successors continued to reinforce Japan's sense of uniqueness and cultural superiority. In command of wide powers over information—the Meiji constitution did not guarantee basic human rights—they did not uproot the feudalistic tradition of obedience among the Japanese people.

As Japan began to enjoy successes on the Asian mainland, this nationalism quickly developed into a sense of racial suprem-acy. Japanese leaders, noted one American diplomat in the early 1900s, objected not so much to exclusion of their emigrants as to being classified in world councils "below Hungarians, Ital-ians, Syrians, Polish Jews and degraded nondescripts from all parts of Europe and western Asia."

Sensitivities were particularly pronounced when comparisons were made with other East Asian nations, even those to whom

Japan owed a huge cultural debt. Although cloaked in the garments of pan-Asian nationalism, Japan's expansionist leaders sought to impose a clear hierarchy on their new Asian order, with the Yamato race clearly in control. As historian John W. Dower has noted, Japanese war posters stressed the whiteness and erect bearing of their soldiers, contrasted with the images of short, round-faced and yellow Chinese. Even before the war, theorists of expansionism, such as Ishiwara Kanji, one of the plotters of the Manchurian invasion, saw a clear division of labor in the new Asian order:

> The four races of Japan, China, Korea, and Manchuria will share a common prosperity through a division of responsibilities: Japanese, political leadership and large industry; Chinese, labor and small industry; Koreans, rice; and Manchus, animal husbandry.

These other Asians, although originally sympathetic to Japanese anti-imperialist rhetoric, predictably proved unwilling to accept their designated "responsibilities" during the war. Even Japan's staunchest Asian allies found themselves subjected to insults by occupying troops, who routinely slapped them and insisted they bow toward Tokyo, learn Japanese and celebrate Japan's national holidays. "The brutality, arrogance and racial pretensions of the Japanese militarists in Burma," later wrote Ba Maw, one of the leading collaborationists, "remain among the deepest Burmese memories of the war years; for a great many people in Southeast Asia, these are all they can remember of the war."

Even defeat failed to snuff out this strong ethnocentrism. As Japan began to recover and emerge as a world economic power, the old, obsessive patterns reasserted themselves. Looking for the sources of their success, Japanese became obsessed with the cult of *nihonjinron*, or the study of their own uniqueness. "After the war we grew up with a negative image of ourselves," noted Tetsuya Chikushi, senior staff writer for the *Asahi Journal*, "but now that Japan is an economic superpower, masochism has turned to narcissism."

As in the prewar period, this "narcissism" has retained a

strong racial character. Although many Japanese have recently gained new respect for Korean successes in industry and trade, Japanese still express their contempt toward the 600,000 Korean residents on the home islands. Even today, Koreans are often discriminated against in employment and denied citizenship despite generations of residence in Japan. Korean suffering is somehow considered less important than that of Japanese. It took years of agitation by local Koreans, for instance, to gain permission to build a small monument for the estimated 20,000 of their brethren who died at Hiroshima.

The nation's new economic status—particularly in contrast to the relative poverty and underdevelopment of the rest of Asia— also reinforced Japanese arrogance and superiority toward other Asians. "Please tell me," one high-level government official asked a reporter from *Look* in 1965, "what we have in common with the Indonesians, Cambodians or any of these Afro-Asian nations. Perhaps we all share some basic 'Asian' way of looking at things, but I have yet to find it."

Yet as Asia has developed, these attitudes have hurt Japan's status. Although its powerful economic system is widely admired—and often emulated—by other Asians, Japan's ethnocentrism and predatory trading practices have hampered its ability to become the leader of non-Communist Asia. Even Malaysian prime minister Mahathir Mohammad, architect of that nation's pro-Japanese "look East" policies, more recently has announced that other Asian nations are no longer willing to be "hewers of wood and drawers of water" for the region's economic superpower.

The behavior of Japanese companies and business people in these countries has often been particularly offensive. With their own schools, shops and even golf clubs, Japanese businessmen—like the "ugly Americans" of the previous generation— have tended to remain separate from the world around them. As a former Japanese diplomat observed: "The Japanese harbor an inferiority complex toward Europeans and Americans, while they tend to treat Asians with a superiority complex. That is why the average Japanese . . . often betrays arrogance and disdain."

Yet Japan's Asian neighbors are changing and Japan may come

to regret its ethnocentric behavior. Former colonies such as Korea and Taiwan, once seen as mere suppliers of rice and cheap labor for *Dai Nippon*, have developed industries in direct competition with Japan's. Frustrated by persistent trade deficits and fearful of dependence on its former colonial masters, Korea in 1986 even set up an Import Diversification Program, with the stated purpose of replacing Japanese suppliers with Americans. Taiwan, anxious to maintain its lucrative trade relations with the United States and suffering massive deficits with Japan, has also initiated a similar program.

Perhaps nowhere have their insensitivities hurt the Japanese more than in China. Although perhaps the most promising long-term market for Japan after the United States, the Tokyo traders already have succeeded in deeply alienating many of the billion potential new customers. Japan's refusal to acknowledge its wartime atrocities has done little to heal old wounds; a 1985 visit by Prime Minister Nakasone to a shrine for Japanese soldiers killed during the war engendered large, government-sanctioned student demonstrations. And in the weeks that followed, Chinese television, which is under strict Communist Party control, showed a miniseries about Chinese resistance to the wartime occupation which painted the Japanese as brutal, treacherous and utterly contemptuous.

But beyond memories of past abuses, many Chinese also resent Japan for more contemporary economic reasons. In China, as well as in much of the rest of Asia, Japanese firms are widely accused of the crudest economic imperialism, by muscling into markets with a juggernaut of Japanese-made consumer products. By 1985 Japan had gained 26 percent of all China's trade, producing in characteristic mercantilist fashion a massive $9 billion trade surplus. In the process, China's highly prized foreign-exchange reserves dropped from $16 billion in September 1984 to $11 billion the following year.

Part of the problem with Japanese trade, Chinese officials claim, is that, unlike American or European firms, Japanese companies have traditionally been reluctant to share technology. Instead, they sell completed products or set up assembly plants with "black box" technology. The Chinese assemble parts made in Japan with technology that they never learn to master. "The goal seems to be to keep us backward and buying," notes Zeng Xiao Ming, manager-engineer at Beijing's Chang Feng Industry Corporation. "There isn't a lot of thought about mutual benefit."

By late 1985, the Communist party expressed its displeasure by placing tough new restrictions on purchases of consumer goods, such as cars and television sets, which have provided the bulk of Japanese sales. Like their Korean and Taiwanese counterparts, Chinese officials have been clearly seeking to cut their dependence on Japan, turning instead for vital technology and machinery to other suppliers, notably the United States and Europe. In 1986, China fired Japanese contractors, who had built the first stage of the giant Paoshang Iron and Steel Works, for refusing to transfer basic technology, and replaced them with a team from West Germany's Siemens. Through these and other actions, by early 1987 Japanese sales to China were dropping at a 14 percent annual rate.

Japan's relentless ethnocentrism has also bedeviled its relations with the United States and its European trading partners. Although ancient race antipathies toward Asians have played their part in creating friction, so too has the perception that Japanese business is fundamentally incapable of building mutually beneficial relationships. In contrast to American or European companies, most large Japanese companies—with the exception of such firms as Honda, NEC Corp., Sony and Kyocera—have been notably slow about transferring their production facilities, much less their technological resources, to their overseas markets. Such an approach, notes IBM senior vice president Alan Krowe, has served to damage Japan's long-term prospects:

> You cannot exploit a nation very long, and I think the Japanese are finding that out. If the Japanese continue to pursue their current policy of producing in Japan and exporting to the United States, what is going to happen will be an extension of what has happened in the past—either it's a quota on automobiles, or a trade embargo. It cannot sustain itself.

This approach is often particularly maddening to American executives working for Japanese companies. John Rehfeld, a top official of Toshiba's computer division, helped engineer that company's successful drive into the lap-top computer industry. As U.S. sales began to grow, Rehfeld, in the American internationalist tradition, "begged" his superiors in Tokyo to start manufacturing some of the computers in the United States. Yet even as sales rose to an annual rate in excess of $500 million, Rehfeld could not gain acceptance for his proposals. Although top management supported the concept of building a factory near the computer division's Irvine, California, headquarters, the company's Japan-based factory managers strongly opposed the plan. As one top Toshiba executive later admitted: "They [the factory managers] told us they didn't believe American workers could build as good a product. It was basic racism and that was that."

Ultimately, Toshiba paid for its insularity. Within six months, imports of the company's computer products were virtually banned, as a result of a semiconductor trade dispute and an incident involving the illegal sale of hardware by another Toshiba division to the Soviet Union. By the summer of 1987, Rehfeld had won his fight: Toshiba announced it would open a manufacturing facility in California.

Like Rehfeld, many Japanese increasingly realize the self-destructive nature of their insularity and are seeking to change it. But the villager mentality—with its desire to keep outsiders away—continues to dominate corporate policy. "Toshiba worries about competition from Hitachi. Hitachi worries about competing with Matsushita. That's all they think about," explains Takashi Hosomi, a retired Finance Ministry official who now heads Nippon Life Insurance Company's Economic Research Institute. "They haven't the faintest idea of the impact they have on the United States."

Not only are Japanese oblivious to foreigners' sensibilities, but they often convince themselves that the barriers between them can never disappear. The irony of such attitudes in a trading country was noted in a special advisory committee convened by MITI in 1985:

> For the Japanese, accepting or even recognizing the diverse ethnic view of the world's people is not quite second nature. . . . In a country like Japan—which is both literally and

figuratively ''insular'' as evidenced by the high degree of commonly shared information—the recognition of ethical diversity may take time. However, Japan's successful internationalization depends on its success in recognizing and comprehending the diverse nature of other cultures.

To a large extent, the call for ''internationalization'' is still all talk and little action, a *tatamae*, or public face, offered up for the foreigners. But when expressing their *honne*, or true, inner feelings, sometimes even the most sophisticated Japanese reveals the deeply defensive villager mentality. Like the small-town mayor who fears that the big-city reporter may learn all the local dirty secrets, many Japanese still fear foreigners learning about Japan. When John Rehfeld started studying Japanese, the response of his superiors was largely negative; while American firms often pay foreigners to learn English, Rehfeld financed his own Japanese lessons. Similarly, one top official of the Japan Electrical Industry Association, a powerful lobbying group which has sought to mollify protectionist sentiment in the United States, expressed reservations about growing American interest in the inner workings of the nation. ''Better,'' he told one fellow Japanese, ''that Americans know little about Japan.''

Indeed, for all the recent talk about internationalization, Japan's ascendency may well founder upon the limits of its villager mentality. Instinctively insular, Japanese continue to look at the world with the mind of a small, developing country. Desperate for explanations of world hostility toward them, Japanese have often reacted with defensiveness, blaming their problems on others' jealousy of their success. One particularly absurd example was a spate in 1986 and 1987 of best-selling books blaming a Jewish conspiracy for growing anti-Japanese sentiments. One writer, Masami Uno, charged that Jews—whose role in giant American corporations has generally been small—were in control of such American companies as General Motors, IBM, Exxon and even Ford, a firm founded by one of the twentieth century's most fervent anti-Semites and still largely controlled by his descendants. As one leading internationalist, former MITI official Naohiro Amaya, puts it: ''Japanese are geniuses in the factory and morons outside.''

The Blessings of Diversity

In sharp contrast to both Europe and Japan, the United States is blessed by a diversity perhaps unprecedented in world history. Although many have traditionally regarded the Chinatowns, the Hispanic barrios and the Little Italys of America as sociological sore spots, in reality these communities—with their special family and cultural ties—represent some of the nation's greatest assets in the emerging world economy.

When Satsuma Mukeada first landed in Seattle in 1908, he was welcomed by a group of white ruffians who threw rocks at him and other arriving Japanese. Undeterred, Mukeada settled in the still-small cow town of Los Angeles, a city whose atmosphere of benign neglect was vastly preferable to the rabid anti-Asian sentiment prevalent elsewhere on the coast. In the heart of downtown, Mukeada and a handful of others developed a tiny Japanese colony into the bustling Little Tokyo section which, with its temples, gambling joints and *nomiyas*, or sake houses, would soon emerge as a cultural center of Japanese life on the U.S. mainland.

Like their counterparts in the Pacific Northwest and elsewhere, the *issei*, or first generation, of Los Angeles mostly labored as shopkeepers, fishermen, truck farmers and gardeners. They lived modestly, although far better than their relatives in Japan. "We never dreamed of Beverly Hills," recalled John Fujikawa, who grew up on a fifteen-acre farm south of the city. "We knew we were second-class citizens."

This second-class status became all too real with the outbreak of war. The removal to the relocation camps cost Japanese Americans close to $400 million and devastated virtually the entire ethnic economy. But after the war a new American-born generation, the *nisei*, started rebuilding. Many went to school and developed skills. Today Japanese Americans are among the wealthiest ethnic groups in Los Angeles, producing their own prominent lawyers, judges, school administrators and even a Rose Bowl Parade queen.

By the early 1960s, the success of these Japanese in Los Angeles began to have consequences that would ultimately reshape the metropolis. As Japanese companies first started moving across the Pacific, they gravitated to Los Angeles, which by then accounted for 30 percent of all Japanese on the U.S. mainland. The 1960 decision to locate Honda of America's headquarters in the Los Angeles suburb of Gardena was based largely on the "comfort" of locating amidst a large Japanese American community. "You had the stores, the shops, you could get sushi here and get away speaking Japanese," recalls Willie Tokishi, a Honda vice president and himself a native of Hawaii.

This mounting Japanese presence has transformed the one-time "Tinsel Town" into what could well be the nation's most important city in its Third Century. Dominated by the growth of Japanese and other Asian commerce, Los Angeles's international trade volume between 1972 and 1982 increased over 500 percent, more than twice the rate of New York. The adjacent harbors of Los Angeles and Long Beach, whose expansions were largely financed by Japanese firms, now constitute the nation's single largest port in dollar value of cargo handled. A vast complex of Japanese-owned manufacturing plants—concentrated in everything from consumer electronics and computers to automobile parts—has helped transform the area into the largest industrial center in North America. From 1972 to 1982, manufacturing employment in Los Angeles jumped by 18.5 percent, while dropping by a similar figure in both Chicago and New York.

Perhaps most striking of all has been the city's emergence as a leading banking center. Until the 1970s and except for its savings and loans, Los Angeles was considered a financial backwater, second in the West to long-dominant San Francisco. But when the Japanese banks began their move into the United States, five of the twelve largest established their U.S. retail banking subsidiaries in Los Angeles instead of New York, the nation's premier financial center.

"They went there for the same reason they went to Pearl Harbor," jokes Richard Hanson, publisher of the Tokyo-based *Japan Financial Report*. "It was close and easy to reach. And there were a lot of Japanese there. It was the place they were most at ease."

The expansion of Japanese banking and business activity transformed Los Angeles into a major financial center. In control of five of the state's top banks, the Japanese now hold well over 13 percent of the area's banking market, a figure expected to reach 30 percent within the next twenty years, according to a top official at First Interstate Bank, the city's second-largest bank. Aided by this growing presence, total deposits in Los Angeles banks and thrift organizations grew by 60 percent between 1980 and 1985, while New York's deposits actually declined. By 1986, Los Angeles had passed both Chicago and San Francisco as the nation's second-largest banking center.

"We are becoming a financial center and what did it was trade," observes Richard Kjeldsen, international economist with Security Pacific Bank, the city's largest U.S.-owned financial institution. "The force leading this was the Japanese. They have played a huge role in helping make Los Angeles a financial center."

Although on a far smaller scale, the influx of Hispanics into the United States is also expanding America's economic internationalization. Many of Mexico's leading industrialists have been shifting large amounts of capital into Hispanic-oriented American cities such as San Antonio and San Diego, where according to a 1987 Merrill Lynch study, twenty-eight newly arrived families injected an additional $126 million in liquid and fixed assets into the local economy. Similarly, hundreds of millions of dollars from Mexico are flooding banks in San Antonio, according to local banking sources. "People just come into the office, open suitcases and there it is," notes a top official at San Antonio's Broadway Bank. "We are becoming the real financial center of northern Mexico."

Much the same process has been taking place for over a quarter of a century in Miami. The massive influx of Cubans and other Hispanics has helped turn Miami from a sleepy resort center into, as the late Jaime Roldos, former president of Ecuador, put it, "the capital of Latin America." Bolstered by flight capital from South America and sprinkled with some not inconsiderable drug money, the city has emerged as a major international banking and trade center. Much of Latin America's middle class does its shopping in Miami's Spanish-language shopping malls, with the annual total of Latin American visitors jumping nearly eightfold to over 2.4 million between 1973 and 1982.

This Latin connection, now responsible for the bulk of Florida's $23 billion international trade in 1985, is likely to become more important for many reasons. Mexico and Venezuela, for example, possess among the largest excess-energy capacities outside the Middle East. By the year 2000, this mingling of cultures and currencies, according to the *Harvard Business Review*, will set up Miami as a "global city" along with such long-established world centers as Paris.

Of significance, perhaps further in the future, will be the ethnic ties of American blacks to both Africa and the Caribbean. Unlike Japan and Europe, the United States boasts a large—and growing—black entrepreneurial and professional class. Although only now beginning to make their impact felt, these American black-owned companies doing business in Africa and the Caribbean, meanwhile, have more than tripled in number to 300 since the early 1980s. One of these entrepreneurs, New York businessman Walter Long, has built a growing import-export business, trading African oil for over $14 million worth of American goods in 1985, up from $6 million in 1982.

Thomas Farrington, a former RCA engineer who has won extensive payroll-automation contracts in the Cameroons, notes that many African and Caribbean countries are anxious to establish business ties "with people they weren't colonized by." French firms, which dominate in most of their former colonies, generally staff their overseas projects with their own countrymen. Farrington instead hires predominately Cameroonians, with whom his blackness helps win invitations, rarely extended to white executives, to the homes of officials. "Africa is a new market and it's a market in which the color of [my] skin might be a positive, not a negative," explains Farrington, who has won a $15 million contract to set up computer networks in the central African state of Cameroon.

But perhaps nowhere is this "ethnic connection" more potentially important than among America's one-million-strong Chinese community. More than other immigrants, Chinese Americans tend to retain their strong cultural, emotional and family ties to the mainland. Although usually themselves the most passionate of capitalists, overseas Chinese have long felt an extraordinary commitment to the development of their people. Much of the money for the 1911 Chinese Revolution, in fact, came from the Chinatowns of New York and San Francisco, where the revolution's first currency was printed.

Today, Chinese Americans are playing a role in another revolution, one that involves the transformation of mainland China into a major industrialized country. Though once Chinese Americans were denigrated for their mercantile disposition, since the mid-1970s the Chinese government-controlled press has lavished attention on the spectacular accomplishments of these overseas students, scientists, musicians and academics. And when Chinese American astronaut Taylor Wang, for instance, flew on the Space Shuttle in May 1985, the *Liberation Daily*—the official Communist party newspaper in Shanghai, China's largest city—hailed him as "the first descendant of the yellow emperor to travel in space." In a message directed to the United States, Prime Minister Zhao Ziyang said: "The Chinese nation shares your pride."

But pride is not the only thing the Chinese derive from their far-flung diaspora. Aware of their growing financial and technological power, the mainland Chinese since the late 1970s have promoted economic ties with its overseas cousins, allowing them—as officially designated "Chinese with American citizenship"—far wider latitude in terms of both travel within China and scope of business operations. The government has gone out of its way to woo investment from Chinese-American entrepreneurs such as Wang Laboratories founder An Wang, who is something of a folk hero among the People's Republic's technologists. Close networking relations have also been established with the Asian American Manufacturers Association, a Silicon Valley grouping of 70 mostly Chinese-run companies, several of which have already established joint ventures inside the People's Republic.

One reason for this special consideration, government functionaries explain, is their belief that members of their race's far-flung diaspora will prove more considerate of their nation's long-term needs than other "foreigners," most notably the Japanese. "Chinese people are enormously proud of what Chinese Americans have done. We feel a special bond of understanding and sympathy with them," says top Beijing science official Tang

Junde. "We know that, no matter what the problems, they are committed to China."

Ironically, many of those now being courted are exiles from the current regime. Henry Hwang immigrated to southern California from China shortly after the Communist takeover. At first Hwang struggled as an accountant, largely serving local Chinese-owned businesses. Later he formed his own small Far East National Bank on the fringes of Los Angeles's Chinatown. Today his bank boasts assets of over $100 million, and Hwang now travels regularly to the People's Republic to put together multimillion-dollar deals for firms back in his adopted land. Like many immigrants, Hwang considers his Chinese connection not only in his own interest, but an asset for American business as well. As Hwang explains: "Chinese Americans are very passionate about this country and when I go to China it is as a Yankee trader to bring business back for America. We want America to be number one in China and with our special relationship we can get it there."

One use of this "special relationship" has been to turn Chinese against their now-dominant Japanese suppliers. Many Chinese like Hwang share painful memories of the brutal fourteen-year occupation of the mainland by Japan. "When we come to China, we are shocked to find all those Japanese goods," says Hwang, whose earliest boyhood memories include having to bow before Japanese soldiers guarding bridges in Shanghai. "We tell them they are crazy doing business with Japan instead of America. The Japanese killed millions of Chinese in the war and now they want to dominate them economically. I think we are beginning to convince them."

Taking advantage of the Japanese unwillingness to share technology, Chinese such as Hwang are beginning to parlay the growing anti-Japanese sentiment into a major American opportunity. Although tiny by the standards of most major American—not to mention Japanese—financial institutions, Hwang's Far East National Bank by 1986 had been named lead bank on a $150 million shopping and office complex for the headquarters of China's chain of Friendship Stores, a massive new hotel and cultural center in Shanghai and a multimillion-dollar contract to supply electronic education training facilities for Chinese schools.

As more Chinese entrepreneurs leave Hong Kong, Taiwan and other locales for the United States, the benefits of this connection for American businesses will grow. In the dark days after the collapse of his father's Japanese enterprise, Wing Chung lived with his grandparents in a tiny apartment in Hong Kong, sharing a bed with two of his brothers. But by 1958, the family's finances had sufficiently improved to send him to the University of California at Berkeley, where he received a degree in mathematical statistics. He went on to earn a master's degree from Columbia University and an IBM Watson Fellowship.

Before Wing's arrival at Berkeley, the Chungs had little to do with America. But Americanization proceeded quickly. Eschewing the family business, Wing joined Hoffman LaRoche, the pharmaceutical giant, married a Chinese woman from an upper-class Beijing family and settled down to a comfortable life in suburban New Jersey.

When he finally succumbed to K. S.'s blandishments and joined the family business, Wing brought with him many American ideas. One key concept was to move the family away from the commodity-trading business and into more technology-intensive fields. In 1978, Wing convinced the family to invest $50,000 in Action Computer Enterprises, a fledgling microcomputer firm in Pasadena, California. The first sales of the company's product were for use in the family's Thai tobacco-growing operations. Later, using K. S.'s carefully cultivated local connections, Action also started selling computers to government agencies and banks in Thailand.

But Wing soon focused attention on the newly opened Chinese market. Although virtually every major computer manufacturer in the world was assaulting this seemingly bottomless market, tiny Action flourished in China. By 1984, operating with a staff of twenty-five sales and service personnel in Hong Kong, Action was enjoying sales in China accounting for nearly one-third of its total $5 million in revenues.

More recently, the Chungs have expanded their American connection, with several family members—including K. S.'s heir apparent, Wing—taking U.S. citizenship while the offspring of even the distant Bangkok branch of the family are shuffled off to American schools. Even the family's unofficial newspaper, the *Chungs' Times*, is printed on a Macintosh in Wing's son Ivan's bedroom in suburban Claremont, California.

At the same time, the family's business operations have also grown in the United States, including a silk-importing business in Los Angeles and a planned garment factory. Perhaps more important, however, is a newly established computer operation known as Universal Digital Computer Corporation (UDC). Run from a small suburban office in La Mirada, California, UDC sold roughly $5 million worth of high-technology equipment in its first year of operation. By 1987, the company had won a contract to distribute Convergent Technologies' powerful new microcomputers in China.

It proved an auspicious arrangement, both for the Silicon Valley manufacturer and the Chungs. Using connections cultivated during the years with Action, UDC president Victor Chung, a former Red Guard rescued by the family in the mid-1970s, followed his grandfather's business methods, networking carefully deep into the Communist Party bureaucracy. These connections reaped over $4 million worth of sales in 1987, including a key contract with the Industrial and Commercial Bank of China, which controls more than half of the retail banking trade in the People's Republic.

"We've been building our reputation with the Chinese Administration of Technology Industries for years," observes the thirty-two-year-old Victor, now a model capitalist in a freshly pressed blue suit and white shirt. "We may be a small family business with limited resources and no [proprietary] product, but we have the connections. That gives us an excellent chance."

In the years ahead the Chungs—like many of the Chinese diaspora—plan on expanding their role as conduits between Asia and the United States. Like British mechanics, German scientists, Jewish scholars and Japanese farmers of the past, the Chinese trader now is adding new assets to the nation's economic wealth.

"We will always have our links back there. China must be the future market for us, and Hong Kong a key base of operations," Wing Chung said over lunch at a Los Angeles restaurant. "But for us, for the kids, for the family, the real base—our home—will be here in America. Of all possible worlds, this is the best choice."

7

Empires of the Mind

In its Third Century, the American Republic retains many characteristics that can assure continued world preeminence. Yet in a world that is rapidly changing, marked by the emergence of dynamic new economic forces, particularly in Asia, even the strongest advantages may not prove enough. To succeed in its Third Century, American business can no longer rely merely on the objective conditions, the unique combination of physical resources, ethnic diversity and the "open system" that propelled its ascendency during the last century.

We are entering a new era in which technological, scientific and cultural innovation will become ever more important components of economic success. As Winston Churchill once observed: "The new empires are the empires of the mind." Today, economic—and hence political power—depends less on external factors, such as control of natural resources or supplies of cheap labor, and more upon the creativity of a society's citizenry. The estimated contribution of technological progress to economic growth in Japan, according to a study by Japan's Science and Technology Agency, grew from only 20 percent in the mid-1950s to roughly 65 percent by the early 1980s. In another key sphere of the "empire of the mind," mass culture in the 1980s has become one of the world's fastest-growing industries and now accounts for the second-largest export surplus for the United States.

In the race to build "an empire of the mind"—perhaps the most crucial contest in America's Third Century—both the nation and its business institutions must adapt to new and radically different realities. A sweeping reevaluation of values, concerning everything from racial attitudes to management systems, must be undertaken or the race will indeed be lost to other countries, most probably in Asia. Although they lack many of America's assets, and its *sokojikara*, these nations today appear to possess a greater will to adapt to the new conditions of competition. To succeed against such competitors, American business must not only comprehend change, but inculcate the desire to act upon the new realizations. We must, as Nietzsche put it, "transform the belief 'it is thus and thus' into the will 'it *shall become* thus and thus.' "

New Fundamentals of America's Third Century

1. **The center of the world's economy is shifting from the European-Atlantic basin to the Asia-Pacific basin.** "Human happiness," the Greek historian Herodotus once wrote, "never continues long in one stay." For over four centuries, the nations bordering the Atlantic dominated the world's science, culture and economy. Now that dominion is ending, and American business must adapt to that change or risk casting its fate with the diminishing Atlantic economies.

To date, Americans have been slow to adjust to this change. Reflecting the European biases of our nation's second century, U.S. firms have generally underestimated the technological and overall economic strengths of Asia. Equally damaging, they have also tended to write Asia off as a potential market, preferring instead to do business exclusively at home or in more familiar European markets.

This seems particularly true for the small and midsize companies that now represent the most dynamic force in the U.S. economy. A 1987 *Inc.* magazine subscriber survey of small and midsize firms found a large majority had little interest in overseas markets. Equally disturbing, among those expressing interest in foreign sales, the United Kingdom—a nation with only limited economic growth potential—emerged as by far the most favored locale for overseas expansion, almost twice as popular as Japan, the world's second-largest capitalist marketplace and for over twenty years the top purchaser of American products after Canada. Companies also showed a marked preference for France, Germany, Italy and other slow-growth European countries over China, Korea, Hong Kong, Singapore and Taiwan—countries which represent the most rapidly expanding economies and markets in the world.

Yet despite American preferences, the Asian ascendency will only accelerate in the future, as Europe's working-age population begins to age and even decline. By early in the next century, according to projections by the *Economist*, Taiwan and Singapore will boast per capita incomes above those of Great Britain. At the same time in China, the active, working population is expected to soar to well over 700 million, representing in absolute terms the world's most rapidly expanding consumer market. Growth rates of the economically active populations in other developing countries, such as Pakistan, India and Thailand, are expected to be even higher.

In their reluctance to do business overseas, or to choose Asia as a preferred base of operations, American firms display instincts they would rarely show at home. Ignoring Asia for Europe, for instance, makes as much business sense as neglecting areas such as Los Angeles, Phoenix or Orlando—all with rapid population, industrial and financial growth—in favor of concentrating on those sections of the nation, such as parts of the industrial Midwest and Plains states, that have been losing both jobs and population.

By ignoring the new growth markets, American business could well be conceding vast fields of opportunity to other nations, most notably Japan. With 80 percent of the world's population and only 20 to 30 percent of GNP, these Third World nations, according to a special 1986 University of Tokyo report, are likely to continue benefiting from the expanding ''vertical division of labor among nations'' that has seen the developing world's share of manufactured goods soar nearly 80 percent since the mid-1970s. With this industrial growth serving as a base, these countries should begin to develop into key commercial markets for advanced nations such as the United States.

2. **The rising numbers and impact of new Americans, particularly from Asia and Latin America, are changing the United States from a European offshoot to a multiracial "world nation."** The shift of economic power from the European nations to the non-European has its parallel *within* the United States. Like Asia and the Third World in international markets, the rapidly expanding Hispanic and Asian communities in America represent the fast-growth opportunity for domestic commerce. Rather than being burdened by their immigrants, regions such as southern and northern California, South Florida, greater New York and Texas are all likely to experience unprecedented entrepreneurial activity and market growth, thanks to the impact of the new Americans. By 1982, for instance, Hispanic- and Asian-owned businesses in California *alone* accounted for over $10 billion in sales.

In the future this ethnic stimulus is likely to increase because America's appeal will remain strong throughout the developing world. One poll of Latin Americans showed one-third wanted to emigrate, 90 percent of them to the United States. A similar percentage of Vietnamese refugees expressed a corresponding preference, while a poll by a South Korean newspaper revealed nearly half of that vital nation's populace wished to find new homes in America.

This trend could not come at a better time for American business. Like its European cousins, white America is aging rapidly; the economically active segment of the population is increasingly burdened by a large mass of retirees requiring massive support for their housing, food and medical needs. In contrast, the nation's Asian and Hispanic populations remain young and vigorous. By the twenty-first century, nearly two in five Americans under the age of eighteen will be black, Hispanic or Asian, up from roughly one in four in 1980.

The new non-European America constitutes not only tomorrow's customer base, but increasingly a most crucial portion of the nation's work force. Nearly all the most rapidly expanding manufacturing areas—from California and Texas to Florida—rely heavily on immigrant labor. Equally important, these groups account for a growing percentage of the nation's skilled work force. By 1984, nonwhites accounted for over 40 percent of all entering freshmen at the University of California at Berkeley, a majority of them Chinese, while, across the continent, Asians accounted for 10 percent of all new entrants at Harvard University.

But recruiting this new ethnic brain power will not be enough. American business, accustomed to stereotypical views of non-whites, must learn how to better utilize the skills of the new Americans. Asian Americans, for instance, are well known for their technical skills, but are often overlooked for key management and sales positions. Asians, for instance, fill nearly half of the technical staff at Intel Corporation, but "very few," according to Albert Yu, a corporate vice president, are in top management positions.

As these Asians acculturate more into American society, Yu believes, American managers should take advantage of their potential for leadership in management and marketing, particularly given the growing technological importance of Asia. "Americans think just because they have a slight accent, Asians can only be workhorses," complains Silicon Valley electronics entrepreneur David Lam, former president of the Asian American Manufacturers Association. "They haven't realized that some of us can be racehorses."

3. **In the battle to regain the economic initiative, America's best weapon lies in exploiting its wealth of entrepreneurial, smaller organizations.** Over the past decade, conventional wisdom among liberals and conservatives alike has held that only large corporations can effectively compete against giant foreign organizations such as Japan's *keiretsu* groups or Korea's *chaebol*. Yet in reality it has been those areas dominated by corporate giants—notably in such mass-production-oriented products as automobiles, steel and consumer electronics—that have fallen most readily to Asian competition. The economic forces most resistant to overseas challenge, in contrast, have been those young, entrepreneurial firms with new technologies, unique products and market strategies. These firms span a wide range of activities from personal computers and software to biotechnology, fast foods, medical equipment and steel minimills.

While many American political, academic and business leaders seek to emulate the tightly ordered economic systems such as those of Japan and some European countries, people in those and other nations see in America's entrepreneurial system the harbinger of the economic future. Faced with rapidly tightening product-development cycles, growing competition from other Asian nations and the burgeoning of niche markets, Japan—according to a 1986 MITI report—must move away from a reliance on "the organization man" and toward individuals displaying such entrepreneurial characteristics as "adventurousness and strong individualist leadership." Similar realizations have also sparked a radical decentralization and privatization of economic activities in China and, more recently, even within that paragon of bureaucratic centralism, the Soviet Union. "What is happening in China is vitally important for us," noted one top Soviet official. "We now look at their reforms as if it were our own personal business."

In the coming economic competition, the edge will belong to those nations and organizations strong enough to nurture individual initiative, creativity and quick decision-making. With the explosion of entrepreneurial vitality in the last decade, the United States—which provided the role model for the mass-production methods and giant organizations of the past—could again forge the next great economic paradigm. Similarly, this trend will also likely increase the importance of the highly entrepreneurial family networks within the Chinese diaspora. Dominated by fast-moving and highly flexible small firms, Taiwan and Hong Kong—not Japan and Korea—may provide the key Asian role models and the most potent competitors in the coming decades.

As the advantages of entrepreneurial firms become more apparent, they naturally will generate change *within* large organizations in both the United States and Asia. One startling indication of this trend has been the growing tendency toward the breakdown of large corporate units, leading to a threefold surge in leveraged buyouts between 1980 and 1986. Other large firms—such as Campbell Soups, NCR Corporation and IBM—are attempting to meet the entrepreneurial challenge by setting up independent business units and other measures for organizational decentralization. Similarly, many large Japanese corporations, such as Toshiba, C. Itoh, NEC Corp. and Nippon Steel, have sought to "entrepreneurialize" by buying promising venture businesses or by setting up quasi-independent corporate units. Korea's government leaders have also recently placed more emphasis on developing a strong entrepreneurial sector, as have the once almost totally multinational-oriented rulers of Singapore.

Although significant, such attempts, notes Silicon Valley venture capitalist Don Valentine—who played a major role in the founding of such firms as Tandem Computers, Apple and Cypress Semiconductor—are not likely to duplicate the dynamism characteristic of self-generated entrepreneurial organizations, whether in America or overseas: "Big corporations flap their lips a lot about all the great things they are going to do, but basically they are obedient people. When you run a big company, it's like running anything else that's big—a church or an army: the key ingredient is obedience. Anything big requires people performing and acting in conventional, predictable ways—within the rules. Entrepreneurism is by comparison the role of the nonconventional person who's going to do it differently. And in a big corporation, he's just a flat-out pain in the ass."

4. **Despite the recent celebration of an emerging "postindustrial economy," manufacturing will remain a critical element in determining the economic winners and losers in the Third Century.** Entrepreneurial creativity is important, but without manufacturing few product-oriented companies can hope to retain preeminence for long. Nor over time can a prosperous American economy. Service exports, according to estimates by the U.S. Office of Technology Assessment report, will likely never amount to more than one-quarter of the value of all exports in the foreseeable future.

Inattention to the unglamorous but vital realities of manufacturing, together with an overvalued dollar, has played a crucial role in the devastation of many of America's consumer-electronics firms, the erosion of its once-dominant automobile industry and the disappearance of once-promising independent high-tech firms such as Corona Data Systems. In contrast, those American companies that have done best in resisting Asian competition—ranging from giants such as Digital Equipment Corp., Ford Motor Co. and Hewlett-Packard to entrepreneurial upstarts like Nucor, Apple Computer, Compaq, and Cypress Semiconductor—have combined technological and marketing strength with strong emphasis on the industrial process. "It is clear," says Intel Corporation founder and chief executive Gordon Moore, "that we have to be pretty darn close to the Japanese from a manufacturing standpoint to compete. We used to do our cost reduction by jumping to the new technology. But that approach is no longer sufficient."

Such changing attitudes toward manufacturing could spark an American industrial renaissance, not only in high technology but across the industrial spectrum. Aided by the lower-priced dollar, even once-dismissed fields like consumer electronics and even so-called smokestack industries such as steel and metal fabrication could gain the upper hand against overseas competitors. One 1987 study by MIT's David Birch showed that of all new businesses, nine of the ten most likely fields for high growth were in manufacturing, ranging from building electronic components and communications products to such mundane activities as basic steel, pharmaceuticals and plastic products.

One key technique for improving production will be to turn the tables on the Japanese and other Asians by *importing* their industrial expertise to the United States. Firms as diverse as Textron, 3M, Brunswick and Cummins Engine have all implemented the Japanese *kanban* manufacturing systems, resulting in labor-cost savings of up to 30 percent. Some companies such as Borg-Warner and Fireplace Manufacturing (a small industrial company in Santa Ana, California), have recruited top Japanese industrial experts such as Kio Suzaki, a one-time engineer with Toshiba. At Fireplace Manufacturing, for instance, Suzaki in three years used proven Japanese methods to cut scrap by 60 percent, increase worker productivity by 30 percent, cut inventory by one-third and improve product quality so much that sales increased threefold. "The future for manufacturing in America is very good, if American managers are willing to take the time and effort," believes Suzaki, who has published widely on the topic in English, French and Japanese.

5. To meet the Asian challenge, American business must evolve a new set of ethics and approaches toward manage-

ment. New machinery and methods can improve performance only so much. More important, believes Suzaki, is the issue of motivating workers and managers. Although often ignored for the lures of financialism and instant ego-gratification, such knowledge is commonplace in Asia. As Soichiro Honda once explained: "The most important thing in the world is not gold or diamonds, but humans."

To date, American business has largely produced two equally lethal archetypes: the sprawling corporate bureaucracy, characterized by remote-control management and financialism, and ego-driven, individualistic entrepreneurism. In both cases managers have often treated themselves royally while shortchanging their companies, employees and investors. "Industrial companies around the world are in trouble because their executives draw big salaries, even if they are driving their companies into the ground," notes Formosa Plastics founder Y. C. Wang, who has taken over troubled U.S. plants of such American giants as Manville Corporation.

But out of the difficulties of the last decade a new breed of company has emerged, one that combines the entrepreneurial spirit of America with the humanistic approach and long-term perspective characteristic of many Asian firms. Although risk-oriented and quick to exploit new markets, these companies often function not under the domination of one person, but as "smart teams" that share responsibility among top management while granting greater autonomy for assembly-line workers.

This new form of organization is most evident among younger companies, many of which never developed the inbred sense of superiority toward Asian ideas and methods characteristic of older generations of American managers. Among the most prominent of these "crossover companies"—firms making the transition to America's Third Century reality—are Compaq Computers and Conner Peripherals (a leading Silicon Valley disc-drive maker), both of which stress long-term development and teamwork within the organization. In many cases, crossover companies are themselves led by Asia-born executives who, attracted by America's entrepreneurial climate, also seek to inculate home-bred Confucian principles into their organizations. At firms such as Sigma Designs, a computer firm run by Vietnamese refugees, top executives provide role models by keeping corporate perquisites low and investing all profits for the long-term health of the firm. "We are devoted to surviving, no matter what," explains Binh Trinh, the company's vice president for finance. "Salaries are fixed expenses. High salaries don't give you much flexibility. We don't want to lose the ability to react to adversity."

Central to the success of such crossover companies is the realization that American business can learn much from Asian models, while still retaining the entrepreneurial culture that lures so many to these shores. Jim Pinto, an Indian-born engineer who in 1972 founded San Diego-based Action Instruments, synthesizes these principles by sharing 80 percent ownership of the company with his employees while reinvesting virtually all profits in new production, research and development. Pinto even works without a secretary. "I guess I'm a bit of a new hybrid," says the fifty-year-old Pinto, whose measurement and instrumentation firm has been among the fastest growing in the industry. "My body was made in India, my science learned in England and my management philosophy comes largely from the Japanese, but I'm putting it all together in California."

The Virtues of Openness

Such a synthesis of Asian and American values could play a crucial role in the renaissance of the nation's economic vitality. Yet many in America's intellectual, political and economic elite often chose to ignore, or seem threatened by, these new and unfamiliar influences. Preferring instead to retreat toward a rigidly Eurocentric view of America, they seek to identify the nation's future with European models of economic and political adjustment, such as those developed in West Germany and France.

Sometimes this Eurocentric approach reflects a traditional, yet still deep-seated, fear of Asian civilization. Echoing the heralds of the "yellow peril" of decades past, novelist Gore Vidal has warned that, through the combined force of technically advanced Japan and China, "the long feared Asiatic colossus takes its turn as world leader." To Vidal, such an ascendency means "an end to empire"; in the future, he argues, the nation's "only way out" from total subordination to Asia is through an alliance with our fellow Europeans, particularly the Soviets. Together, Vidal says, such a liaison would provide "an opportunity to survive, economically, in a highly centralized Asiatic world."

In many other cases this retreat from reality stems not so much from blatantly anti-Asian or pro-European sentiments as from a deep-seated American cultural conservatism. Like their predecessors in the 1920s, who recoiled against the growing cosmopolitan character of that time, today's fundamentalists seek a return to a bygone, largely imaginary America of small towns and farms. With its stress on traditional small-town virtues and belief in America as a "Christian" (read "white Protestant") nation, fundamentalism seeks to reduce the influence of anything outside its narrow interpretation of the national experience.

Yet unfortunately such narrowness is not confined to the traditional "Know-Nothings" of the religious right. Rejection of the new influences has also become fashionable among a large portion of the intelligentsia, as laid out most notably in the writings of University of Chicago's Allan Bloom. In his best-selling *The Closing of the American Mind,* Bloom—while rightly lambasting the appalling ignorance of history and culture on the part of many students—casts much of the blame for this lamentable situation on the principles of "cultural relativism" and "openness." Among his special targets are those who, seeking to redress the Eurocentric biases of the past, teach that Euro-American culture must be viewed in relative terms, not as necessarily superior to those of Asia and the Third World. This "relativism," Bloom argues, breeds a lack of proper respect for "our virtue" as a nation, as if lifting Americans out of their traditional ignorance about the East somehow diminishes the importance of our own culture. For this reason, Bloom and his supporters, such as Nobel Prize-winning author Saul Bellow, attack the tendency in some major schools to include instruction in Asian and other non-European cultures in the basic curriculum as "demogogic" and reflective of the "unrestrained and thoughtless pursuit of openness.'' Writes Bloom: ''. . . openness has driven out the local deities, leaving only a speechless, meaningless country.''

However elegantly argued, such notions ignore the new, developing realities facing American society, both at home and abroad. If the United States is to remain a great nation, the ''openness'' to new influences so offensive to Bloom may indeed prove its greatest virtue. In the quest to become a true world nation—and assure its cultural, technological, economic and political leadership—the United States must break away from its European roots and begin treating Asian history and culture equally with those of the West.

Such a tendency toward openness has long been the key to the establishment of powerful hegemonic nations and empires. Oswald Spengler traced the rise of great political power to the emergence of cosmopolitan ''world cities,'' centers of international culture and commerce, from the days of the Greek city-states to Alexandria and Rome. Indeed, the very idea of ''*cosmopolis*,'' as historian Michael Grant points out, has its origins in the Hellenistic cities created or nurtured by Alexander, who built his short-lived yet enormous empire upon a deeply cosmopolitan vision. Writes Grant:

[Alexander] was evidently more interested in transcending race by the creation of a mixed elite and ruling class: while God is the father of all human beings, he is reputed to have said, it is the noblest and best whom he makes especially his own.

Perhaps the most spectacular early expression of this Alexandrian spirit—and precursor of the ideal of a ''world nation''—was the Roman Empire. Although crafted by Italians, the empire's truest genius lay in its ability to co-opt and integrate the many peoples under its tutelage. Rather than insisting that its subjects adopt ''Roman'' ideals, the empire required fundamentally only obedience. This openness helped make imperial cities such as Alexandria, Antioch and Rome itself truly cosmopolitan centers, populated and deeply influenced by such diverse groups as Syrians, Greeks and Jews. Indeed, many of the more prominent of these minorities, although themselves not Romans, were proud to boast the citizenship of Rome and served as willing supports for the imperial system.

The importance of openness in building and maintaining an empire characterized not only Western history, but Asian as well. During the flourishing Tang, Sung and Ming dynasties, China welcomed new commercial, artistic and intellectual influences from Persians, Indians, Arabs and Jews. In the centuries preceding the Manchu conquest, China—particularly in coastal cities such as Canton and Foochow (now Fuzhou)—developed an exceedingly cosmopolitan and aggressive trading civilization. Similarly, before the Tokugawa shogunate restricted contact with foreigners, Japan too displayed a similar "openness," enjoying significant commercial and intellectual ties with China, Korea and, briefly, Portugal.

But it was Europe, in the aftermath of the Middle Ages, that employed openness to outside influences to achieve world hegemony. As both Japan and China focused inward—with China even moving its capital from cosmopolitan Nanking (Janjing) to the isolated, barren reaches of Beijing—traders from peripheral European states such as Portugal, England and Spain moved outward in search of the riches of the East. Equally important, China's bureaucratic centralism, seeking to retain control at all costs, stifled entrepreneurialism and random innovation as threats to order. In Europe, as historians Nathan Rosenberg and L. E. Birdzell have pointed out, the proliferation of diverse states and weaker political control allowed for both greater individual autonomy and experimentation.

The continent's great awakening took place most dramatically in those places—Spain, Portugal and the city-states of Italy, such as Venice—most open to the influences of technically more advanced civilizations, most notably the Arab and Jewish civilizations. Like Alexandria and Rome before them, Venice and Amsterdam, and later London, became quintessentially cosmopolitan centers of commerce. Where religious, racial and political intolerance ruled, such as in Russia and eventually Spain, entrepreneurial and technological development became stymied. As the great historian of early modern Europe, Fernand Braudel, notes: " . . . the miracle of toleration was to be found wherever the community of trade convened."

But it was in America that the blessings of openness have been, and continue to be, most manifest. From its earliest days, the nation has been remarkably diverse, drawing immigrants from throughout Europe. By transcending the boundaries of European ethnic and religious prejudice, noted the late eighteenth-century French observer J. H. Crevecour, a new, distinct kind of nation was being born, one that defied narrower traditional concepts of nationality. "Here," wrote Crevecour, "individuals of all nations are melted into a new race of men, whose labors and posterity will one day cause great changes in the world."

The emergence of this "new race of men" has stood at the foundation of America's "world cities." The emergence of great world commercial centers in the United States followed closely the incorporation of new ethnic groups. Such a receptivity, or at least tolerance, of newcomers and their ideas helped place Philadelphia, and later New York, ahead of Boston, with its more restrictive social order. Indeed, by incorporating the vast diversity of Europe, New York emerged as the nation's premier "world city," a development Oswald Spengler characterized as "the most pregnant event of the nineteenth century." Today that same pattern reappears in new emerging "world cities" such as Los Angeles, San Francisco and Miami, where America's "new race of men" increasingly reflects the nation's growing tilt toward Asia and the emerging countries of the Third World.

The American virtue of openness has rested not only upon tolerance of diversity, but on the freedom granted to both enterprise and capital, whatever the source. While many see in the current upsurge in foreign investment an unprecedented threat to national sovereignty, openness to overseas financing has long been characteristic of American economic development. From colonial times, the United States—except for several decades following each of the great World Wars—has been a consistent importer of capital. Rather than viewing such infusions as a threat, Americans should study the logic of Alexander Hamilton, the first secretary of the Treasury, who observed in 1791:

Instead of being viewed as a rival . . . [foreign capital] . . . ought to be considered as a most valuable luxury, conducing to put in motion a greater quantity of productive labor and a greater proportion of useful enterprises, than could exist without it.

While overdependency on foreign capital could, in the long run, pose some dangers, the enormous influx of foreign capital into the United States during the 1980s was not so much a harbinger of national decline—as claimed by some—as it was a reaffirmation of the nation's status as, in Max Weber's phrase, "the area of optimal economic opportunities." In a world increasingly dominated by socialist, welfare state and mercantilist economies, America's "open system" will likely continue to attract foreign capital from both Asia and Europe. As Arthur Furer, president of Nestlé of Switzerland, explains: "We believe free economies have a much better future than planned ones. The U.S. seems likely to continue along the path of economic freedom, while Europe risks going in a more socialist direction."

Given the trade and budgetary deficits left behind by the Reagan administration, Americans in the coming decades will do well to retain their openness to foreign capital. But the long-term solutions, and basic strengths, of American openness lie not solely with capital, but with those human resources essential to establishing an "empire of the mind." It is in this respect that immigration, in addition to capital flows, is a vital component for America's resurgence in its Third Century.

Reliance on foreign intelligence and skill, like the reliance on foreign capital, is nothing new for the American Republic. From the earliest days, the federal and state governments consciously promoted the importation of skilled craftsmen fleeing what Hamilton described as "the disturbed state" of Europe, most particularly Great Britain. Yet America's lack of native science remained a persistent problem; the United States, noted de Tocqueville in the 1830s, possessed "good workmen, but very few inventors." Like the Japanese, Koreans and Taiwanese of contemporary times, the Americans, using imported craftsmen and designs, proved ideal imitators, often to the outrage of European industrialists.

Even as the nation began to develop into a major industrial power, it remained sorely dependent on European technology, leading some to question the country's ability to ever catch up with the more innovative industries of Great Britain and, later, Germany. As the *New York Times* glumly asked in 1860: "American science: is there such a thing?" Indeed, it was only decades later, with the full-scale transfer of European intelligence to the United States as a consequence of fascism in Europe, that the United States consolidated its position as a first-rate scientific power. What the Inquisition had done for Amsterdam and London, Adolf Hitler and Benito Mussolini now did for the United States, with Germany alone sending America nearly twenty scientists who were then or would become Nobel laureates.

Even today, the United States still gains much from its European scientific connection. Attracted by the higher living standards, intellectual freedom and entrepreneurial opportunity of the United States, European scientists and technical experts continue to enrich America's intellectual resources. Despite consistent efforts by European countries to halt this "brain drain," American scientific predominance has grown, evidenced by the nation's winning nearly three times as many Nobel Prizes in science as have Germany, France and the United Kingdom combined. The situation is particularly acute in Britain, Europe's leader in the basic sciences; the number of British-born scientists residing in the United States at the time of their election to the prestigious Royal Society has tripled since the early 1960s. As a 1987 European Commission report observes: "America is the hub of the European research community, about which its [scientific] disciplines rotate like planets around a sun."

In the Third Century, Asia will probably replace Europe as the leading source of new American technological and scientific power. By the late 1980s, Asian countries accounted for eight of the ten top nations sending students—totaling well over 140,000—to American universities. The Asian predominance in the technology and science field is particularly marked, with Asians accounting for some 70 percent of all foreign engineering doctoral students. Many of these students choose to stay after graduation, including well over 5,000 Koreans and many more Chinese, including over 10,000 in northern California's Silicon Valley alone.

Indeed, while Americans cringe at the looming technological power of Asia, many nations there—particularly Taiwan and Korea—have initiated programs offering special incentives to slow this erosion of precious human capital. But America's openness, its field of opportunity, usually provides too attractive an allure. Taiwan, for instance, has sent nearly 100,000 students to the United States for graduate degrees, and of the 10,000 who earned Ph.Ds, as many as four out of five of them, including several eventual Nobel Prize winners, have remained in America.

Even Japan's oft-cited drive for technological supremacy faces severe disadvantages in competition against America's scientific "empire of the mind." Much has been written, for instance, about Japan's so-called Technolopolis Strategy, the building of planned science parks that are seen as part of that nation's scheme, as one writer put it, for "control of the 21st Century." But as usual, brick and mortar—and the best-laid plans of bureaucrats—have been only marginally effective. "No one talks about it anymore," admitted one well-placed MITI official.

Moreover, despite its proficiency in applied science, Japan continues to lag behind in most basic research. Part of the problem may be the bureaucratic and seniority-oriented system under which science is organized in Japan. For this reason Japan has had considerable difficulty holding on to some of its own best talent, with many of its top scientists, including at least two Nobel laureates, now residing permanently in the United States. And perhaps even more important, Japan, owing to its insularity and crowded conditions, lacks America's facility for attracting top scientific talent from other countries. After touring several American laboratories, one stunned top Marubeni Corporation executive remarked: "In one laboratory, all the researchers were Chinese. Japanese society can never draw on such resources."

But perhaps nowhere is the American "empire of the mind" more powerful than in its culture. As in science, America's beginnings as a cultural power were inauspicious; for most of its first century, with the exception of Herman Melville and a handful of others, American culture seemed a pale imitation of the great European tradition. One depressed American literatus, Sydney Smith, complained in 1820: "In the four corners of the globe, who reads an American book, or goes to an American play, or looks at an American picture?"

One reason for this may have been that for many decades American artists and writers flocked to Europe and even on return wrote in styles reflecting European tastes. John O. Sullivan, writing in the nationalist *Democratic Review* in the late 1830s, wondered why American writers were forever "bending the knee to foreign idolatry, false tastes, false doctrines, false principles?" In their craving after Europe, however, American writers were simply responding to the prejudices of their publishers. When *Harper's* in the 1840s started to publish a library of novels, no more than ten of the first six hundred were from American authors.

Slowly, however, unique American voices began to break away from the grip of European culture. As early as 1837, Ralph Waldo Emerson declared that America's "day of dependence, our long apprenticeship to the learnings of other lands" was drawing to a close. Emerson lived long enough to see his own vision of a truly American culture flourish in the writings of the poet Walt Whitman. A man of monumental openness, Whitman, in contrast to the Anglophile literary elite of his day, saw in the wildness, vast expanse and political drama of America ample inspiration for the most daring literary expression. Equally important, Whitman—unlike many of the Europhiles of Boston or southern literary circles—exulted in the influence of the new immigrants who flocked to cities such as Brooklyn, where he lived and wrote:

> *These States are the amplest poem,*
> *Here is not merely a nation but*
> *a teeming Nation of nations.*

It would be at least half a century, however, until American culture could truly capture the promise of Whitman's message. Seeking to keep the nation on a purely Anglo-Saxon keel, political leaders such as Theodore Roosevelt railed against "hyphenated Americanism," which could threaten this narrow concept of the national character. Ethnic minorities in the public schools were expected to suppress their identities and conform to WASP models. "The immigrants," observes professor James Banks of the University of Washington, "were best instructed in how to repulse themselves; millions of people were taught to be ashamed of their own faces, their color, their family names, their parents and grandparents and their class patterns, histories and life outlooks."

Similarly, American writers and artists were often instructed to reject their own country and follow instead the European fashions and attitudes. Not surprisingly, many artists even felt compelled to go the mother continent to practice their craft. In perhaps the most famous instance of this tendency, the "lost generation" of the 1920s flocked to France and Italy for inspiration and recognition, reflecting widespread perception that after nearly a century and a half, the Republic remained a cultural backwater.

Yet even as Europe retained its reputation for intellectual supremacy, original American culture began to be felt in every corner of the globe. The breakthroughs, characteristically, were not from the imitators of Europe, but from the periphery of Whitman's "nation of nations." Jazz, the product of black America, became the nation's first great cultural export, by the 1920s informing the music, fashions and life-styles of millions, from Paris and London to Shanghai.

Equally important, as in the sciences, was the role played in the crisis of the 1930s, which sent much of the flower of European thought and culture—Bertolt Brecht, Thomas Mann, Paul Tillich, Hannah Arendt—to the United States. For the first time, the United States emerged as the world's premier cultural center and forum for experimentation. As the noted German social scientist and émigré Franz Neumman observed, even England, the other major haven for Hitler's victims, was "too homogeneous and solid" and opportunities there "too narrow" for displaced German and other European intellectuals. America, he argued, was where "a clean break—psychological, social and economic—had to be made, and a new life started."

Yet while educated Europeans were turning American universities and New York salons into world-class intellectual centers, in Los Angeles—far from the center of national power—a motley collection of parvenus, including many American-born Jews, Italians, Greeks and a plethora of recent European immigrants, laid the foundation for America's emergence as the center for the nascent motion picture industry.

Although they usually stayed close to classic American or European motifs, the Hollywood creators, reflecting their own diversity, forged a culture that, for the first time in history, reached the hearts of virtually every national and racial group. By the 1930s, Hollywood's "long arm," noted Leo Rosten, reached the consciousness of cities from Bombay to Oslo to Hong Kong. Boston intellectuals and New York society matrons might parrot British pronunciations, but street kids in Wallsey, a suburb of Liverpool, picked up slang from films about Chiago gangsters.

Today, American movies—joined by the music and television industries—are an overwhelming force in world culture. By 1975, the American film industry, which accounted for only 5 percent of world production, claimed one-third of all film imports and half the cash receipts. More recently, with the decline of the once-strong Italian and other European film industries, the American predominance has been growing. In television, domination is even more complete, with U.S. firms accounting for 60 percent of all programs exported. By 1986, American entertainment exports, according to *Forbes* magazine, posted a $4.9 billion international surplus, representing the nation's second-largest export category, behind aircraft but ahead of computers, soybeans and coal.

Central to this hegemony lies the peculiar genius of modern American culture, which, rather than adhering to past forms, remains open to new influences. Increasingly liberated from reliance on Anglo-Saxon motifs, American culture now reflects the nation's growing heterogeneity. The worldwide popularity of such black American stars as Michael Jackson and Bill Cosby, particularly in Japan, are testaments to the increasingly multiracial character of the American "empire of the mind." Perhaps more on the cultural edge is the music produced by Latino artists—such as California's Los Lobos or the Tejano bands of south Texas—that, by synthesizing traditional Hispanic music with American rock, are producing a new and unique sound. Also promising has been the rapid evolution of a young, San Francisco-based Asian film industry that already has produced such excellent Chinese-oriented films as *A Great Wall* and *Dim Sum*.

Such new cultural forms undoubtedly will offend many who regard America as a fundamentally European and Atlantic-oriented civilization. Threatened, too, will be traditional perceptions of what American culture is and where it is made. In its Third Century, American culture may no longer be based predominately on European themes. Its motifs may be as much Latin or Asian as traditional Anglo-American, and its artistic center may as likely be Los Angeles or Miami as New York. As Mexican-American playwright Louis Valdez, whose work has been rejected on Broadway but eagerly accepted in California, points out:

> New York has its face turned towards England and Europe in general, and its ass towards California. And it doesn't like to be, shall we say, sodomized. New York refuses to look at the real world. . . . New York should be a lot smarter than it is. It's so varied, yet so provincial. It has an outmoded, backward point of view.

Although difficult for some to accept, the sort of post-European American culture epitomized by writers such as Valdez is already gaining acceptance around the world. In fashion, in life-style, in the world of ideas and new trends, it is California—the most multiethnic, Pacific-oriented region of the nation—that now presents the face of American culture abroad. Indeed, across the industrialized world, particularly Japan, the attitudes and life-styles of the younger generation reflect not so much the influence of traditional Anglo-America but, as Kenichi Ohmae puts it, "the Californianization of the Free World."

The New American Mission

"There is nothing more difficult to plan," noted Niccolò Machiavelli in *The Prince*, "more doubtful of success, nor more dangerous to manage than the creation of a new system." Yet in its Third Century, the United States must attempt something every bit as ambitious: a drastic reorientation of its long-entrenched systems and ways of thought.

Ever since becoming a hegemonic world power after World War II, the United States has defined itself, and has been defined, in terms of the defense of "Western civilization" against the menace of "the East," represented by first the Soviet Union and, later, the People's Republic of China. Although liberals and conservatives could disagree upon the means employed, virtually all responsible opinion agreed upon the essential wisdom of this mission. All other considerations—including the interests of America's own industrial base—were secondary to halting this "Eastern" tide.

In this struggle, the central focus of American policy was the defense of Western Europe. Since Europe was the prime focus of American investment, trade and cultural interests, European concerns naturally overshadowed all others in the world. Although Asia certainly presented an important field of rivalry with the Soviets, the assumption remained that, in the words of historian Gaddis Smith, "If the conflict was lost in Europe, all was lost."

During the early part of the postwar era—the times Henry Luce saw as the beginnings of the "American Century"—it was assumed that the United States, as the unquestioned premier economic and military power, could, in Luce's words, "exert upon the world the full impact of our influence." Often it seemed that no defense commitment, or trade concession, was too great a burden for maintaining defense of "the West." Even today these priorities and attitudes remain deeply in place. In 1986, for instance, the United States allocated an estimated $134 billion for *conventional* defense of Europe, nearly half again as much as the Europeans spent on their own accord and three times the American expenditure in Asia.

Perhaps appropriate in their time, such commitments, and

the attitudes underlying them, make little sense in an era of huge budget deficits and rapid integration of the American economy with Asia. Europe no longer represents the nation's predominant center of American economic interest, and thus is does not warrant such an enormous commitment of national resources. At the same time the ideological underpinnings behind these grotesque expenditures—fanatical, single-minded opposition to Communism—seem feeble at a time when American policymakers look upon the People's Republic of China as a *de facto* political ally, and Gorbachev's reforms could at least ameliorate the traditional terror inspired by the Soviet state.

Nor does this view of the American mission fit readily with changing attitudes in Europe itself. Although no longer a hegemonic world power, Western Europe has developed into a mature, largely self-sustaining economic force. Bereft of their overseas empires, Europeans today seek to retain their importance by pooling their resources under the umbrella of European Economic Community. The primacy of the Atlantic alliance is falling before a new pan-European vision that intrinsically deemphasizes ties with the United States.

Indeed, a totally integrated European economy, scheduled for 1992, would likely turn into what Italian Socialist leader Pietro Nenni once called "a colossal cartel," one that, as the *Economist* noted in 1986, would likely take on a distinctly "mercantilist flavour." Seeking to protect itself against the much-feared technological hegemony of the United States and Japan, Europeans have already begun excluding American and Japanese companies from joint-research projects in both high technology and defense. "European economic union," says a concerned Jacques Maisonrouge, France's former minister for industry, "could create a new form of Euro-nationalism."

Under the sway of this "Euro-nationalism," this new and powerful economic force probably will deemphasize its postwar dependence on America for both markets and security. With the United States shifting toward greater reliance on Asian trade and its own home markets stagnating, the obvious field for European expansion in the next century is likely to be in the vast and resource-rich territories of the Soviet Union and its Eastern Europe satrapies. This trend, pronounced before the rise of Gorbachev, can only accelerate as further *glasnost* and *perestroika* and put a more social-democratic gloss on the Soviet socialist reality.

Sharing many of the same European racial, cultural and political roots, encouraged by force of geographic contiguity, Western Europe and the Soviet Bloc seemed destined to share an increasingly common destiny. This "gigantic restructuring" of the postwar world alliance, notes geohistorian Immanuel Wallerstein, can already be seen in growing commercial links between key Western European nations and the Soviet Bloc. By 1985, for instance, European trade with the USSR had reached well over $25 billion annually, over three times the *combined* Soviet commerce with Japan and the United States. And by the end of the 1980s, West Germany, whose banks provided the bulk of financing for the trans-Siberian gas pipeline, could be importing about 30 percent of its natural gas from the Soviet Union. The USSR is also the largest supplier of uranium to France, a nation dependent on nuclear fuel for much of its electricity-generating capacity.

Paralleling developments in Europe is the growing integration of the Pacific Basin economies. Once a backwater to be defended against Communist encroachment, the nations along the shores of the Pacific are no longer subsets of European realities. Even Australia—which once banned Asian immigration and looked almost exclusively toward Europe—now counts Asians as its fastest-growing group of new immigrants and looks north, not west, for its economic sustenance.

The rapid integration and development of the Pacific economy in coming years will likely speed the growth of the less-developed parts of the region. As Singapore, Taiwan and Korea progress up the value-added scale, entrepreneurs are likely to shift more labor-intensive production to the less developed nations such as Thailand, China and perhaps India. In the process, Asians will look increasingly not toward Europe, their one-time imperialist tormentors, but toward each other for trade, capital, technology and culture.

In the emerging Asia-oriented economic order, Japan inevitably will move further beyond its postwar role as a mere instrument of American policy. If Japan can push beyond the boundaries of its insularity and begin opening itself up to other Asian economies, it possesses the potential to develop into the dominant financial, technological and even cultural center of the region. This effort will founder, however, if attempts are made to remilitarize or somehow establish a worldwide hegemony—what could be called the "Japan as Number One" syndrome. Lacking the necessary military power, such an aggressive effort would inevitably falter against the resentments of other Asian nations as well as the superior resources of continental nations such as the United States and China.

For its future destiny, Japan must reach beyond its traditional nationalism. Rather than seek domination, Japan, as the most advanced Asiatic nation, could fulfill a vision of its future that has been dear to some native intellectuals since early in this century. Japan's destiny, wrote two young scholars in the 1920s, is to be a nation where "centuries of human achievements in Europe and Asia may be harmoniously weaved together for the realization of a more perfect fabric of civilization."

To weave this "more perfect fabric," Japanese companies must transcend the narrow confines of racial nationalism. Some firms, such as Honda Motor Corporation, have already achieved this, becoming truly international companies with production, design and research facilities spread across the globe. With its enormous financial and technological power, a Japan following the Honda model could play a central and positive role in the emerging economic world order. Rather than a universally feared economic predator, Japan could emerge, as suggested by Berkeley's Chalmers Johnson and former MITI vice-minister Naohiro Amaya, as the new "Venice of the East," taking on the role of supreme financier, dealmaker and marketplace played by that great Italian city of the early Renaissance.

To some Americans, the emergence of a truly international Japan, particularly as a preeminent financial power, is the ultimate harbinger of American decline. Although this need *not* happen, the United States will indeed decline if it fails to recognize that the nation's primary interest in the years ahead lies with Asia and the Third World.

An era of American history—created during two centuries of intense interface with Europe—is coming to an end. Yet this reality represents new and unprecedented opportunities for the United States. As the dominant "empire of the mind," the well-spring of international science and culture, and the first "world nation," the United States is ideally suited to serve as the focal point of a new, multiracial, Pacific-centered economic order. Far more than any other nation, the United States can best fulfill the vision prophesied in 1893 by Ernest Fenollosa, one of America's first experts in oriental art and later a professor at Tokyo University, of a new world culture combining the riches of Asia, Europe and America:

> It is not that the West will from its own point of view tolerate the East, nor the East the West; not even that the West shall try to understand the East from the Eastern point of view—but that both, planting their faith in the divine destinies of man, shall with co-operation aim at a new world-type, rich in those million possibilities of thought and achievement that exclusion blindly stifles.

Adopting such a central role, however, does not mean that the United States should deny its fundamental, historical values. By extending the nation's mission to the whole of mankind, in fact, the United States for the first time could begin to fulfill the greatest aspirations of its founders. Unlike many of America's intellectual and political leaders today, the leading lights of the early Republic saw its destiny as something greater than a mere national enterprise or simply the outcome of westward expansion of European civilization. In the words of John Adams, America represented "the opening of a grand scheme" for "the emancipation of the slavish part of mankind."

This sense of mission sustained the United States throughout much of its early history. At a time when most Europeans saw the world outside the continent as a candidate for domination, men like Jefferson openly encouraged other nations, particularly in the Americas, to fight for self-determination and human rights. Although racism and slavery marred the national purpose, many Americans remained convinced that their country possessed a message of value for the rest of mankind. "We are the heirs of all time," wrote Herman Melville, "and with all nations we divide our inheritance."

Today America's revolutionary message remains as powerful and relevant as in an earlier epoch. In Asia, Latin America, even the Soviet Union, millions seek those very liberties that Paine, Jefferson and Adams created from revolution two centuries ago. Yet before Americans can again take up this mission, they must first fully reject the notion that the "national inheritance" can be imposed on others by intervening in their affairs. The United States, as John Quincy Adams noted in 1821, should never go abroad "in search of monsters to destroy. . . . She might become the dictatress of the world; she would no longer be ruler of her own spirit."

For, in the end, the greatness of America depends not on its force of arms, or even on the opulence of its economy, but upon the power of its message for the world. Lacking a sense of mission, the nation will probably continue to flounder, unsure even of its national identity. Only by returning to its revolutionary charter, and applying it to the realities of a post-European world, can the United States in its Third Century enjoy a resurgence equal to the great vision of its founders and the uniqueness of its people.

Notes

1: Post-European America

page

1 **World trade shares.** *Suji de miru Nihon no 100nen*, Kokuseish,a (To-kyo:1981), pp. 224–25.

1 **U.S.-Asia trade.** *The Banker*, Dick Wilson, "The Pacific Arrives," July 1985; Steffan Linder, *The Pacific Century*, Stanford University Press (Stanford:1986), p. 15; *Proceedings* "Interview with Admiral James A. Lyons," July 1986; *Global Competition: The New Reality*, President's Commission on Industrial Competitiveness, U.S. Government Printing Office (Washington, D.C.: January 1985), volume 1, p. 10.

2 **Immigration.** Leon F. Bouvier and Robert W. Gardner, *Immigration to the U.S.: The Unfinished Story*, Population Reference Bureau, November 1986, pp 8–10, 17, 27.

2 **Asian share of world economy.** Linder, *op. cit.*, p. 10; *Congressional Research Service*, Dick Nanto, "Economic Changes in the Asian Pacific Rim," August 1986, p. 2; Patricia Ann Cummins, "Japan's Economic Transition," doctoral thesis, U.S. International University (San Diego:1980), p. 51; *The World Bank Atlas, 1987*, World Bank (New York:1987), pp. 5–8.

2 **Japan.** *San Francisco Chronicle*, Linda Dourbet, "Japan's Banks in Big Leagues," July 14, 1986; *Far Eastern Economic Review*, "Once Again, Japan as Number One," May 8, 1986; *Wall Street Journal*, Peter Norman, "BIS Says Japan Has Passed the U.S. In Share of International Banking," January 31, 1986; *Euromoney*, "The World's Largest Bank Moves Into Gear," November 1986; *Los Angeles Times*, Sam Jameson, "Japan—It's Now Banker to the World," March 16, 1986; Martin Mayer, *The Bankers*, Weybright and Talley (New York:1974).

3 **Newly industrializing countries.** Linder, *op. cit.*, p. 39; *Congressional Research Service*, William H. Copper, "Export-led Development:

Asian NICs,'' p.1; *The World Bank Atlas, op.cit.*, p. 7; *Prognos Euro Report 86* (Basle:1985), pp. 10–11.

3 **"We'll overtake Britain in. . . ."** Cited in *High Technology*, Jeffrey Bairstow, "South Korea: Giants Drive Development," November 1986.

3 **China.** Nicholas R. Lardy, "Economic Relations Between China and the United States," testimony before Joint Economic Committee of the Congress, December 11, 1986, pp. 2–3; *Los Angeles Times*, August 18, 1987.

3 **Japan as customer.** Figures provided by Japan External Trade Organization, San Francisco Office; Lyons, *op.cit.*

4 **Trade with NICs.** *San Francisco Chronicle*, Frank Viviano, "Pacific Giants," May 27, 1987; Seiji Naya, "Trade and Investment Opportunities in the NICs and ASEAN Countries and the Role of the United States," testimony before Joint Economic Committee of the Congress, December 11, 1986, p. 42.

4 **China trade.** Figures cited in Lardy, *op. cit.*, pp. 2–3; *Los Angeles Times*, August 18, 1987.

4 **U.S.-Europe trade.** Naya, *op. cit.*, p. 42.

4 **European high technology.** *Financial Times*, "Technology Survey," July 9, 1987.

4 **European trade patterns.** *The Economist*, "If Not Union, Then What for Europe?" June 28, 1986; *Wall Street Journal*, Peter Gumbel, "Soviet Plan to Let in Foreign Firms Proves Frustrating in Practice," July 7, 1987.

5 **"Europeans do not. . . ."** *Financial Times*, Jean Rimboud, "The Economic Trough," February 27, 1985 (reprinted from *World Press Review*, April 1985).

5 **Eighteenth and nineteenth centuries.** E.J. Hobsbawm, *The Age of Revolution*, Mentor (New York:1962), pp. 203–204.

5 **Demographic decline.** *San Francisco Chronicle*, "Global Population and Politics Adrift," July 1, 1987; *Wall Street Journal*, Thomas E. O'Boyle, "Increase in Birthrate Is Welcome News But Considered a Fluke," September 10, 1986; *San Francisco Focus*, Frank Viviano and Sharon Silva, "The New San Francisco," September 1986; *Newsweek*, "Europe's Population Bomb," December 15, 1986.

6 **"Monster."** Franz Fanon, *The Wretched of the Earth*, Grove Press (New York:1968), p. 313.

6 **"This sort of. . . ."** Andrew Hacker, *The End of the American Era*, Atheneum (New York:1971), p. 228.

6 **Liberal observers.** Martin Weiner, *English Culture and the Decline of the Industrial Spirit*, Cambridge University Press (Cambridge:1981), p. 160.

6 **"Our governing assumption. . . ."** Walter Russell Mead, *Mortal Splendor: The American Empire in Transition*, Houghton Mifflin, (Boston:1987), p. 213.

6 **"Shift to Japanese hegemony. . . ."** Testimony of Lawrence Krause before Joint Economic Committee of the Congress, December 11, 1986.

7 **"False."** Thomas Paine, *Common Sense*, Barron's (New York: 1975), p. 80.

7 **Anglo-Saxons in 1790.** Cited in Thomas J. Archdeacon, *Becoming American*, Free Press (New York: 1983), p. 25.

7 **"Asylum for mankind."** Paine, *op. cit.*, p. 101.

8 **America has. . . ."** Cited in *Shokun*, "2005 nen wa Nihon no Tasogare," February 1987.

8 *"Underlying the nation. . . ."* Oswald Spengler, *The Decline of the West*, Knopf (New York: 1926), p. 170.

8 **"An empire for liberty."** William Appleman Williams, *Empire as a Way of Life*, Columbia University Press (New York: 1980), p. 59.

8 **"In the beginning. . . ."** Cited in Edmund S. Morgan, *Birth of the Republic: 1763–1789*, University of Chicago Press (Chicago: 1956), p. 74.

9 **"The natural system of. . . ."** Cited in Louis M. Hacker, *The Course of American Economic Growth and Development*, John Wiley (New York: 1970), p. 17.

9 **"Whether as entrepreneur. . . ."** *Ibid.*, pp. 10–11.

9 **"America is conservative . . ."** Cited in Louis Hartz, *The Liberal Tradition in America*, Harcourt, Brace and World (New York: 1965), p. 50.

9 **Chinese students.** Cited in *Newsweek*, "Free Speech Chinese Style," January 5, 1987.

9 **"Corrupting."** *Wall Street Journal*, Bernard Wysocki, "South Korean Turmoil Has Strong Element of Anti-Americanism," July 15, 1987.

10 **Koreans in America.** *Los Angeles Times*, Stephen Braun and Penelope McMillan, "700 in Koreatown Rally in Support of Homeland Reforms," April 22, 1986.

10 **"Of course one. . . ."** Interview with authors.

10 **"But in entrepreneurship. . . ."** *Harvard Business Review*, Peter Drucker, "Our Entrepreneurial Economy," January–February 1984.

10 **"Each age. . . ."** Cited in *Pacific Historical Review*, William Appleman Williams, "The Frontier Thesis and American Foreign Policy," November 1955.

11 **Japan against the West.** Stuart Kirby, *Toward the Pacific Century*, Economist Intelligence Unit, Ltd. (London: 1983), p. 41.

11 **"There is. . . ."** Linder, *op. cit.*, p. 67.

11 **Early Asian supremacy.** Nathan Rosenberg and L. E. Birdzell, Jr., *How the West Grew Rich*, Basic Books (New York: 1986), pp. 86–87.

11 **Military supremacy.** Alfred Crofts and Percy Buchanan, *A History of the Far East*, Longmans, Green and Co. (New York: 1958), p. 312.

11 **Threat to industrial Europe.** Karl Marx, *Das Kapital*, volume 1, Vintage Press (New York: 1977), p. 749, note 41 (Friedrich Engels).

12 **"The yellow races."** Cited in Crofts and Buchanan, *op. cit.*, pp. 235, 270.

12 **European racism.** Joachim Fest, *Hitler*, Harcourt Brace Jovanovich (New York:1974), pp. 55, 619, 755; Ernst Nolte, *Three Faces of Fascism*, Holt, Rinehart and Winston (New York:1969), pp. 359–64.

12 **"It took our branch. . . ."** Cited in Eldon Penrose, *California Nativism*, Rand Research (San Francisco:1973), pp. 35–36.

12 **"The racial differences. . . ."** Cited in Sam Steiner, *Fusang: The Chinese Who Built America*, Harper and Row (New York:1979), p. 181.

13 **Fear of Japan.** John Dower, *War Without Mercy*, Pantheon (New York:1986), p. 157; Homer Lea, *The Valor of Ignorance*, Harper and Brothers (New York:1909), pp. 128–28, 162.

13 **"A Japanese born. . . ."** Leonard Dinnerstein and David Reimers, *Ethnic Americans*, Harper and Row (New York:1975), p. 78.

13 **Asia-bashing.** *Wall Street Journal*, Jan Wong, "Anti-Asian Violence Grows," November 28, 1986; *Los Angeles Times*, "Man Acquitted of Rights Charge in Death," May 2, 1987.

14 **"The Germans, somehow, . . ."** *New York Times Sunday Magazine*, Theodore White, "The Danger from Japan," July 28, 1985.

15 **"Politics of imperial nostalgia."** Joel Kreiger, *Reagan, Thatcher and the Politics of Decline*, Polity Press (Cambridge:1986), p. 155.

15 **"Serious damage."** *Ibid.*, pp. 162–63.

15 **Public confidence.** Louis Harris, *Inside America*, Vintage (New York:1987), pp. 108–109, 234–36, 257–59.

15 **"The leaders. . . ."** "Meeting the Japanese Challenge," Motorola Inc., survey by Yankelovich, Skelly and White (New York:1982).

16 **"Neomercantilist business-government partnerships."** Kevin Phillips, *Staying On Top*, Random House (New York:1984), pp. 3–12.

16 **"American businessmen. . . ."** *Ibid.*, p. 5.

16 **Neoliberals.** Randall Rothenberg, *Neoliberals*, Simon and Schuster (New York:1984), pp. 201–202.

16 **"A small core. . . ."** Ezra Vogel, *Japan As Number One*, Harvard University Press (Cambridge:1979), pp. 55, 233–34.

17 **"Communitarian vision."** *Ibid.*, pp. 232–34, 245.

17 **"Advisory councils."** William Ouchi, *The M-Form Society*, Addison-Wesley (Reading, Mass.:1984), pp. 214–17.

17 **"Tilt toward big business."** Vogel, *op. cit.*, p. 116.

17 **"Baby dinosaurs,"** Mead, *op. cit.*, pp. 187–88.

17 **"The myth of the self-made man."** Robert Reich. *Tales of the New America*, Times Books (New York:1987), p. 230, p. 10, pp. 106–107.

18 **"Opportunistic individual."** *Ibid.*, pp. 150–51.

18 **"The recent progress. . . ."** Robert Reich, *The Next American Frontier*, Times Books (New York:1983), p. 17.

18 **Banning competition.** Charles and Mary Beard, *The Rise of American Civilization*, Macmillan (New York:1930), pp. 194–96.

18 **"The extreme corruption. . . ."** Benjamin Franklin, cited in Barbara Tuchman, *The March of Folly*, Ballantine Books (New York:1984), pp. 201–202.

19 **"The inevitability of contention."** James Madison, "The Federalist Number Ten," in Benjamin F. Wright, ed., *The Federalist*, Belknap Press (Cambridge, Mass:1961), p. 131.

19 **Easy prey.** Roger Brown, *The Republic in Peril*, Columbia University Press (New York:1964), pp. 14–15, 260, William Appleman Williams, *From Colony to Empire*, John Wiley (New York:1972), p. 49.

19 **"Partisans. . . ."** R. R. Palmer, *The Age of Democratic Revolution*, Princeton University Press (Princeton:1964), volume 1, p. 189.

19 **"Empire for liberty."** Williams, *Empire as a Way of Life, op. cit.*, p. 59

19 **"Leviathan which. . . ."** John C. Miller, *The Federalist Era*, Harper and Row (New York:1960), p. 151.

20 **"Recolonize our commerce."** Brown, *op. cit.*, p. 83.

20 **Early protectionism.** Arthur Schlesinger, *The Age of Jackson*, Little, Brown and Co. (New York:1945), p. 315; Hacker, *op. cit.*, p. 56; George Dangerfield, *The Awakening of American Nationalism*, Harper and Row (New York:1965), pp. 13, 149.

20 **Government intervention.** Robert Reich and Ira Magaziner, *Minding America's Business*, Harcourt Brace (New York:1982), pp. 197–98, 201; *Japanese Journal of American Studies*, Keiji Tajima, "Alexander Hamilton and the Encouragement of Manufactures," number 2, 1985.

20 **"American System."** Dangerfield, *op. cit.*, p. 19.

20 **"Reciprocity."** *Ibid.*, p. 159.

20 **Financing.** Hacker, *op. cit.*, p. 111.

20 **Government share of GDP.** W. S. Woytinsky and E. S. Woytinsky, *World Commerce and Government Trends and Outlooks*, Twentieth Century Fund (New York:1955), p. 690.

20 **The Attorney General.** James Sterling Young, *The Washington Community: 1800–1828*, Columbia University Press (New York:1966), pp. 25, 59, 73.

20 **"The last word always rests."** Alexis de Tocqueville, *Democracy in America*, Knopf (New York:1945), volume 2, pp. 306–309.

20 **Alfred Chandler.** *The Visable Hand*, Belknap Press (Cambridge, Mass.:1977), pp. 204–205.

21 **"Without aid or assistance."** Benjamin P. Johnson, "America at the Crystal Palace," in Carroll Pursell, *Technology and American Life*, MIT Press (Cambridge:1981), pp. 96–97.

21 **"Technology transfer."** Darwin H. Stapleton, "Benjamin Henry Latrobe and the Transfer of Technology," in Pursell, *op. cit.*, pp. 34–35.

21 **"I know of no. . . ."** de Tocqueville, *op. cit.*, volume 1, p. 53.

21 **Overseas financing.** Hacker, *op. cit.*, pp. 236–37, 137.

22 **"Colony of Europe."** Marx, *op. cit.*, p. 931, note 1.

22 **Immigration.** Hacker, *op. cit.*, pp. 174, 189.

22 **Imperialism.** Figures cited in Yasusuke Murakami and Yutaka Kosai, *Japan in the Global Community*, University of Tokyo Press (Tokyo:1986), p. 111.

22 **"Impulse toward expansion."** Cited in A. Whitney Griswold, *The Far Eastern Policy of the United States*, Harcourt, Brace (New York:1938), p. 338.

23 **"The East is. . . ."** Cited in Robert Freeman Smith, *The United States and Revolutionary Nationalism in Mexico: 1916–1932*, University of Chicago Press (Chicago:1972), pp. 31–32.

23 **"Our real competition. . ."** *Nation's Business*, June 5, 1925.

23 **Europe versus Asia trade.** Cited in Derek Howard Aldercroft, *From Versailles to Wall Street: 1919–1929*, University of California (Berkeley:1977); Geoffrey Bienstock, *The Struggle for the Pacific*, Macmillan (New York:1937), pp. 20–21, 45.

23 **Military statistics.** Lyons, *op. cit.*; William Manchester, *American Caeser*, Little, Brown (New York:1978), pp. 284, 669.

24 **"Europeanizing of American culture."** Laura Fermi, *Illustrious Immigrants*, University of Chicago Press (Chicago:1968), pp. 374–75.

24 **"No clear moral 'rights.' "** Cited in *Pacific Historical Review*, William Appleman Williams, "The Frontier Thesis and American Foreign Policy," November 1955.

24 **European bias.** Woytinksy and Woytinksy, *op. cit.*, p. 225.

24 **"A Slavic Manchukuo."** Akira Iriye, *Across the Pacific*, Harcourt, Brace (New York:1967), p. 291.

25 **"In the illusion. . . ."** Tuchman, *op. cit.*, p. 375.

25 **"Patterns of investment.** Chandler, *op. cit.*, p. 480; *Fortune*, "Why the Climate Is Changing," September 15, 1967.

25 **"Wary."** *Business Week*, "Business Style Aid for Japan," November 14, 1953.

26 **A weak link.** Woytinksy and Woytinksy, *op. cit.*, p. 58.

26 **"I had the impression. . . ."** Cited in *World Press Review*, Peter Hazelhurst, "Will the System Travel," October 1980.

26 **"Only the United States. . . ."** Cited in *Time*, "American Ingenuity Still Going Strong," July 5, 1976.

26 **Growth in foreign trade.** *President's Commission on Industrial Competitiveness, op. cit.*, volume 1, p. 36.

26 **China report.** *American Demographics*, Doris Walsh, "Wake Up, Wake Up," May 1987.

27 **Taiwan survey.** *Nation's Business*, Henry Eason, "Taiwan Woos American Business," June 1987.

27 **Japan in ASEAN.** *Journal of Common Market Studies*, Rolf J. Langhammer and Ulrich Hiemenz, "Declining Competitiveness of EC Suppliers in ASEAN markets," December 2, 1985; *Business Week*, "Japan's Investment Binge in Southeast Asia," November 3, 1986.

27 **India.** *Business International*, "India: Limited Avenues to an Unlimited Market," Special Report, February 1985; *Far Eastern Economic*

Review, Mohan Ram, "Thrust on Trade," December 11, 1986; *World Bank Atlas, 1987, op. cit.*, pp. 5–8; *American Demographics*, Doris Walsh, "Wake Up, Wake Up," May 1987.

28 **Third world car markets.** *Business International*, "India: Limited Avenues to an Unlimited Market," Special Research Report, February 1985; *Asia Wall Street Journal Weekly*, Maria Shao, "Toyota Investment Draws Ire of Taiwan Auto Makers," March 3, 1986; *Wall Street Journal*, Masayoshi Kanabayashi, "Japan in Wooing Auto Concerns in South Korea," July 17, 1985.

28 **Japan in Hong Kong.** *Business Week*, "By the Time China Takes Over, Japan May Own the Joint," May 25, 1987; figures provided by Hong Kong Department of Industry, special thanks to Melinda Parsons in San Francisco; estimates by Japanese Chamber of Commerce, Hong Kong.

28 **Japan in China.** Lardy, *op. cit.*, p. 49; *Business China*, May 11, 1987; *JEI Report*, "Who's China's Leading Supplier?" number 9a, March 6, 1987.

28 **"When U.S. firms. . . ."** *American Demographics*, Doris Walsh, "Wake Up, Wake Up," May 1987.

29 **"Call on the great. . . ."** Cited in Alfred Hayworth Jones, *Roosevelt's Image Brokers*, National University Publications (Port Washington, N.Y.:1974), p. 101.

2: The Pacific Crucible

page

32 **"I was dazzled. . . ."** Interview with authors.

32 **"I could not. . . ."** Interview with authors.

32 **32 percent.** Bruce Scott and George Lodge, ed., *U.S. Competitiveness in the World Economy*, William F. Finan and Annette M. LaMond, "Sustaining U.S. Competitiveness in Microelectronics," Harvard Business School Press, (Cambridge:1984), p. 183.

32 **World's largest.** Semiconductor Industry Association interview with authors.

32 **Wafer-fabrication estimates.** Confidential industry sources.

33 **"The key will be. . . ."** Interview with authors.

33 **"Declining sport."** Cited in John Naisbitt speech to Association for Humanistic Psychology, Los Angeles, September 1, 1981.

33 **"A strong manufacturing. . . ."** *U.S. International Competitiveness: Perception and Reality*, New York Stock Exchange (New York: August 1984), pp. 30–32.

34 **Second place.** *Wall Street Journal*, Peter Gumbel, "Japan Stock Market Overtakes the U.S. As World's Largest," April 13, 1987.

34 **Electronics deficit.** *Global Competition: The New Reality*, President's

Commission on Industrial Competitiveness, U.S. Government Printing Office (Washington, DC:1985), volume 1, pp. 13–16.

34 **"Economically speaking. . . ."** *Forbes*, "The Pacific Basin," November 1, 1970.

34 **"You do what. . . ."** Interview with authors.

35 **Taiwan economy.** *Business Week*, "U.S. Recovery Has Four Asian Nations Roaring Back," June 25, 1984; *Asian Wall Street Journal Weekly*, Maria Shao and James Schiffman, "Taiwan, Korea Battle for Textile Markets By Stressing High Fashion and Flexibility," April 28, 1984; *Fortune*, Louis Kraar, "Reheating Asia's Little Dragons," May 26, 1986.

35 **Taiwan's move to high technology.** *Los Angeles Times*, "Computer Piracy Creating Friction Between Taiwan and the United States," December 31, 1984; *Asian Wall Street Journal Weekly*, Maria Shao and James Schiffman, "Taiwan, Korea Battle for Textile Markets By Stressing High Fashion and Flexibility," April 14, 1986; *Far Eastern Economic Review*, Andrew Tanzer, "Asia Plugs Into the Computer," July 21, 1983; *High Technology*, Herb Brody, "Taiwan: From Imitation to Innovation," November 1986; *Image*, Frank Viviano, "Transplanting Silicon Valley," June 21, 1987.

36 **"Challenge the long-established. . . ."** Cited in *Forbes*, "Nippon Psyches Up to Fight Back," December 15, 1974.

36 **Japan's technology rise.** Stuart Kirby, *Toward the Pacific Century*, The Economist Intelligence Unit Ltd.(London:1983), p. 36–37; James Botkin, Dan Dimancescu, and Ray Stata, *The Innovators*, Harper and Row (New York:1984), p. 194; *The Economist*, "The Titans of High Technology," August 23, 1986; *JEI Report*, number 29a, August 8, 1986; *Electronic News*, "Japanese Buying Power," March 10, 1986.

36 **Korea's progress.** "Economic Miracle in Korea," Lee Hyon Song, in Lawrence B. Krause and Todao Sekiguchi, ed., *Economic Interaction in the Pacific Basin*, Brookings Institution (Washington, D.C.: 1980); *Far East Economic Review*, Reginald Child, "A Flash of Blue—and Then Back to Olive Green," June 2, 1983; *Wall Street Journal*, Kim Kihwan, "Seoul Frets as Reagan Weighs Curbs," September 17, 1984; *Forbes*, Lawrence Minard, "The Fragile Miracle on the Han," February 11, 1985.

37 **Hyundai.** *Forbes*, Marc Beauchamp, "Foot in the door," December 29, 1987.

37 **Korean electronics.** *Business Korea*, "Down But Not Out," August 1987; *Tokyo Business Today*, Peter Ennis, "Korea Battles Japan in the U.S. Market," November 1986.

37 **Korean semiconductors.** *Wall Street Journal*, Stephen Kreider Yoder, "Korean Industry Makes High Tech Strides," August 5, 1987; *Tokyo Business Today*, Peter Ennis, "Korea Battles Japan in the U.S. Market," November 1986; *Wall Street Journal*, E. S. Browning, "Seoul Seeks High-Tech Self-Sufficiency," September 7, 1984.

38 **"The less advanced end."** *High Technology*, Jeffrey Bairstow, "South Korea: Giants Drive Development," November 1986; *Los Angeles Times*, Sam Jameson, "South Korea Steps Up Activity in High Tech," August 14, 1984.

38 **"Right now. . . ."** *Ibid.*

38 **Personal computers.** Figures from Storeboard, Inc., on market shares; *Wall Street Journal*, Michael Miller, "Korea is Rushing Into the Personal Computer Business," November 6, 1984.

39 **Canton.** *China Business Review*, September–October 1985; *Los Angeles Times*, David Holley, "Canton Area Booms, Typifying Country's Liberalization Trend," September 6, 1987; *San Francisco Chronicle*, Frank Viviano, "Pacific Giants: The Overseas Chinese," May 27, 1987.

39 **Service economy.** *Business Asia*, "Business Outlook: Hong Kong," September 27, 1985; *Asian Wall Street Journal Weekly*, Marcus W. Brauchli, "Service Industries Gain Importance in Colony's Economy," March 24, 1986.

40 **Fashion orientation.** *Christian Science Monitor*, Greg Critser, "Sketching Joins Stitching in Hong Kong," September 17, 1986.

41 **"Together, Hong Kong and China. . . ."** Interview with authors.

41 **"Their older brothers. . . ."** Interview with authors.

41 **"We are perfectly placed. . . ."** Interview with authors.

42 **China's electronics industry growth.** *Electronic News*, August 10, 1987.

42 **"We will start. . . ."** Interview with authors.

43 **Leibniz and Voltaire,** James C. Thompson, Peter E. Stanley and John Curtis Perry, *Sentimental Imperialists*, Harper and Row (New York:1981), p. 8.

43 **"Admire and blush. . . ."** Cited in Sam Steiner, *Fusang: The Chinese Who Built America*, Harper and Row (New York:1979), p. 45.

43 **"The barbarians do not. . . "** Cited in William Theodore de Bary, Wing-tsu Chan, Chester Tan, ed., *Sources of Chinese Tradition*, volume 2, Columbia University Press (New York:1958), p. 428.

43 **46 million.** *San Francisco Chronicle*, Frank Viviano, "Pacific Giants," May 27, 1987.

44 **"The highest duty. . . ."** K.S. Chung, "A Confucian Octogenarian's Reflections on Life," (unpublished paper), January 15, 1987, p. 12.

44 **"Our goal. . . ."** Interview with authors.

45 **"Those who. . . ."** Cited in *Entrepreneurship: The Japanese Experience*, Yamamoto Shichihei, "Economic Efficiency and the Capitalist Ethic," Number 8, pp. 3–4.

46 **"Nothing is more. . . ."** Ryusaku Tsunoda, *et al., Sources of Japanese Tradition*, volume 1, Columbia University Press (New York:1958), p. 428.

46 **Key industries.** *Business Week*, "Japan Will Do Its Own Selling," March 30, 1930.

46 **Zaibatsu.** Frances V. Moulder, *Japan, China and the Modern World Economy*, Cambridge University Press (Cambridge:1977), pp. 186: Kunio Yoshihara, *Japanese Economic Development*, Oxford University Press (New York:1979), pp. 5, 15; Kazuo Kawai, *Japan's American Interlude*, University of Chicago (Chicago:1960), p. 148.

47 **"Second nature."** Chalmers Johnson, "The Internationalization of the Japanese Economy," (unpublished draft paper), p. 14.

47 **Return of the zaibatsu.** *U.S. News and World Report*, "The Conglomerate Way of Life," June 2, 1969.

47 **"Throughout the 1950s. . . ."** Johnson, *op. cit.*, pp. 14–15.

48 **Chaebol.** LeRoy P. Jones and Il Sakong, *Entrepreneurship in Economic Development*, Harvard University Press (Cambridge:1980), p. 271; *High Technology*, Jeffrey Bairstow, "South Korea: Giants Drive Development," November 1986.

49 **Daewoo.** *Business Korea*, ad, August 1987.

49 **Hyundai.** *Far Eastern Economic Review*, Reginald Child, "A Flash of Blue—and Then Back to Olive Green," June 2, 1983; *Journal of Japanese Trade and Industry*, Koji Matsumoto, "The *Chaebol*: Dynamic Management," number 2, 1986.

49 **Continued government backing.** *Wall Street Journal*, Stephen Kreider Yoder, "Korean Industry Makes High Tech Strides," August 5, 1987.

49 **Nationalist ethos.** *Far East Economic Review*, Andrew Tanzer, "Asia Plugs Into the Computer," July 21, 1983; *Asian Wall Street Journal*, James R. Schiffman and Mario Shao, "Korea, Taiwan View Each Other's Style with Mix of Admiration and Complexity," May 19, 1986.

49 **"I had a dream. . . ."** Woo Choong Kim, "Building a Third World Multinational," speech delivered to Association of Southeast Asian Nations Young Businessmen's Meeting, August 15, 1985.

50 **Decline of America.** *SAIS Review*, Immanuel Wallerstein, "North Atlanticism in Decline," Summer 1982, p. 22.

51 *Empress of China.* Charles and Mary Beard, *The Rise of American Civilization*, Macmillan (New York:1930), volume 1, p. 661.

51 **"World Emporium."** Manning Dauer, *The Adams Federalists*, Johns Hopkins Press (Baltimore:1953), p. 13.

51 **American traders.** Tyler Dennett, *Americans in East Asia*, Macmillan (New York:1922), p. 45.

51 **"For the purposes of. . . ."** Cited in Henry Nash Smith, *Virgin Land*, Random House (New York:1950), pp. 20–21.

51 **Whitney and Astor.** Thompson, Stanley, and Perry, *op.cit.*, p. 34.

51 **"The English seaboard."** Smith, *op.cit.*, pp. 22–26.

51 **"Access to Asia. . . ."** William Appleman Williams, *Empire as a Way of Life*, Oxford University Press (New York:1980), p. 87.

52 **Japanese and American Revolution.** *The Japanese Journal of Amer-*

ican Studies, Tadashi Aruga, ed., "Editor's Introduction: Japanese Interpretations of the American Revolution," number 2, 1985, p. 10.

52 **"Americans are of. . . ."** Akira Iriye, *Across the Pacific*, Harcourt, Brace and World (New York: 1967), pp. 34–45.

52 **Shanghai trade.** Beard and Beard, *op. cit.*, volume 1, p. 662.

52 **Nicholas Roosevelt.** *Restless Pacific*, Scribner's (New York: 1928), p. 85.

52 **"The Pacific Ocean. . . ."** *Ibid.*, p. 3.

53 **Declining Asian interest.** Louis Hacker, *The Course of American Economic Growth and Development*, John Wiley, (New York: 1970), pp. 76–77, 136–37.

53 **"The old China trade. . . ."** John K. Fairbanks, "America and China: 1840–60," in Ernest R. May and James C. Thompson, Jr., *American-East Asian Relations: A Survey*, Harvard University Press (Cambridge: 1972), pp. 28–29.

53 **Boycott of American goods.** Iriye, *op. cit.*, pp. 93–94.

53 **"Dissipated."** A. Whitney Griswold, *The Far Eastern Policy of the United States*, Harcourt, Brace (New York: 1938), p. 338.

53 **"Complete Orientalizing. . . ."** Cited in Iriye, *op. cit.*, p. 105.

53 **"An act of discrimination."** Griswold, *op cit.*, p. 351.

54 **"Pay the consequences."** Cited in Dennett, *op. cit.*, p. 581.

54 **"Was too small. . . ."** Cited in Raymond A. Ethus, *Theodore Roosevelt and Japan*, University of Washington Press (Seattle: 1966), p. 293.

54 **U.S. operations in Japan.** Griswold, *op. cit.*, p. 468.

54 **"Hung like a cloud."** *Ibid.*, p. 472.

54 **Japanese propaganda.** Thompson, Stanley, and Perry, *op. cit.* pp. 146–47.

54 **"To scores of. . . ."** John W. Dower, *War Without Mercy*, Random House (New York: 1986), pp. 4–5.

54 **Chinese revolution.** Alfred Crofts and Percy Buchanan, *A History of the Far East*, Longmans, Green and Co. (New York: 1958), p. 312.

54 **"America was the. . . ."** Cited in *Ibid.*, pp. 323, 326.

55 **"Benevolent hopelessness."** Iriye, *op. cit.*, p. 149.

55 **"Only a fraction."** Cited in Edmund O. Clubb, *20th Century China*, Columbia University Press (New York: 1964), p. 117.

55 **Ching-ling.** Sterling Seagrave, *The Soong Dynasty*, Harper and Row (New York: 1985), p. 457.

56 **Goodwill squandered.** *U.S. News and World Report*, Robert Payne, "Why the U.S. Is Failing in Asia," January 28, 1949.

56 **"The morale."** David Halberstam, *The Best and the Brightest*, Random House (New York: 1972), p. 83.

56 **"America's Indochina policy. . . ."** George Herring, *America's Longest War*, John Wiley (New York: 1979), p. 21.

56 **Ho Chi Minh,** *Ibid,* p. 1.

56 **"This desire. . . ."** Barbara Tuchman, *The March of Folly*, Ballantine Books (New York: 1984), p. 240.

57 **"It was in the power. . . ."** *UN World*, Robert Payne, "No Nation Swallows Asia," February 1949, p. 26.

57 **George Marshall.** Robert Payne, *The Marshall Story*, Prentice-Hall (New York: 1951), p. 307.

57 **"Chose to exaggerate."** Alan Wolfe, *America's Impasse: The Rise and Fall of the Politics of Growth*, Pantheon Books (New York: 1981), p. 115.

57 **"What is happening. . . ."** Cited in *Newsweek*, "Fritz on China," February 7, 1949.

58 **"Socialism of the monopolies."** Manchester, *op. cit.*, p. 495.

58 **"Anti-*zaibatsu* laws.** Kazuo Kawai, *Japan's American Interlude*, University of Chicago Press (Chicago: 1960), pp. 142–47.

58 **Corporations and conservatives.** William Manchester, *American Caesar*, Little Brown (New York: 1978), p. 494.

58 **Opposition to Occupation reforms.** *The Japanese Journal of American Studies*, Takeshi Igarashi, "MacArthur's Peace Proposal," number 1, 1981, pp. 55–61, 76–83.

59 **Japanese conservatives,** *New Republic*, Jerome B. Cohen, "Trade: A Necessity for Japan," January 24, 1955; *Business Week*, "Japan: Talking to Both Sides," April 9, 1955.

59 **Return of the *zaibatsu*.** *The Nation*, John G. Roberts, "America and the Making of Japan, Inc.," February 13, 1982.

60 **"The locomotive. . . ."** Herring, *op. cit.*, p. 74.

60 **Lack of attention.** *Atlantic Monthly*, "Japan," James McC. Truitt, June 1967.

60 **Thomas Dewey.** *Time,* "Business Abroad: Fast Drive from Japan," August 17, 1959.

60 **Lobbyists.** *The Nation*, John G. Roberts, "America and the Making of Japan, Inc.," February 13, 1982.

61 **"Hard bargain."** *Business Week*, "Japanese Businessmen," April 18, 1959.

61 **Trade deficit.** *Time*, "Pinch in Exports," August 17, 1959.

61 **"The cream of the world's technology."** Cited in *Time*, May 10, 1971.

61 **Ampex.** *San Jose Mercury*, Evelyn Richards, "How America Lost the Edge on the World Trade Battlefield," April 20–23, 1986.

61 **19 billion.** Cited in *JEI Report*, "Japan's Science Policy: An Interview with Ronald Dore of the Technical Change Center, London," number 29a, August 8, 1986.

61 **"Whenever we found. . . ."** *Keidanren Geppo*, "*Kokekara no gijutsu kaihatsu wo kangaeru*," February 1982, p. 16.

61 **"The greatest fire sale. . . ."** Cited in *JEI Report*, number 29a, August 8, 1986.

3: The Third Century Economy

page

62 "My school was British. . . ." Interview with authors.

63 "We had a good idea what to do. . . ." Interview with authors.

64 "Our goal is to build an organization. . . ." Interview with authors.

64 **United States firms in 1970.** Richard Barber, *The American Corporation*, Dutton (New York: 1970), chart 7, appendix.

64 **Profitability of American Corporations 1954–76.** John Kenneth Galbraith, *The New Industrial State*, Houghton Mifflin (Boston: 1985), p. 87.

65 "We are simply letting European business. . . ." Jean-Jacques Servan-Schreiber, *The American Challenge*, Atheneum (New York: 1968), p. 159.

65 **World market share of U.S. Corporations.** Bruce R. Scott and George Lodge, *U.S. Competitiveness in the World Economy*, Harvard Business School Press (Cambridge: 1984), p. 345.

65 **Changes Within the Fortune 500.** *Inc.*, David Birch, "The Atomization of America," March 1987.

65 **Porter study on performance of conglomerates.** Cited in the *Los Angeles Times*, May 7, 1987.

65 **ITT.** Figures from review of *Fortune*, "The *Fortune* 500," April 1974, April 28, 1986, and April 27, 1987.

66 **European performance from 1959 to 1976.** Robert Reich and Ira Magaziner, *Minding America's Business*, Harcourt Brace Jovanovich (New York: 1982), p. 14.

66 **U.S. unemployment rates in comparison with Europe today.** *Current*, Rudiger Dornbush, "European Unemployment: The Challenge of the '80s," January 1987.

66 **Comparative economic growth rates in 1960s and 1970s.** Scott and Lodge, *op. cit.*, p. 46.

66 **Comparative growth rates in 1980s.** Dornbush, *op. cit.;* "JETRO White Paper on International Trade 1985," table 3, JETRO, (Tokyo: 1985)

66 **Fall of Fortune 500 firms.** *Fortune*, "The *Fortune* 500," April 29, 1985, April 28, 1986, April 27, 1987.

66 **New firms on Fortune 500.** *Inc.*, "The *Inc.* 100," May 1986.

66 **Structure of the economy.** *Inc.*, David Birch, "The Atomization of America," March 1987.

66 **Small business job creation.** *Inc.*, David Birch, "Yankee Doodle Dandy," July 1987.

67 **Job losses at large firms.** *Inc*, Jay Finnegan, "The Entrepreneurial Numbers Game," May 1986.

67 **Revenues and profits of Forbes 500.** *Forbes*, "The *Forbes* 500," April 27, 1987.

67 **"Perhaps large corporations. . . ."** *Wall Street Journal*, Dale Jahr, "Corporate Wealth: More for the Little Guys," January 21, 1987.

67 **"A diminishing figure in the industrial system. . . ."** Galbraith, *op. cit.*, p. 58.

67 **"The world of the small retail entrepreneur. . . ."** *Ibid.*, p. 398.

68 **"It is a rare. . . ."** *Ibid.*, (1985 edition), p. 99.

68 **Gulf & Western.** Cited in *Forbes*, August 24, 1987.

68 **Study of 375 large corporations.** *Wall Street Journal*, chart in Amanda Bennett, "Growing Small," May 4, 1987.

68 **"Contigent workers."** *Forbes*, Susan Lee and Stuart Flack, "Hi ho, Silver," March 9, 1987.

68 **Large companies "entrepreneurize,"** *Inc.*, Eugene Linden, "Age of the Entrepreneur," April 1984.

68 **"We sensed the world was changing."** Interview with authors.

69 **"Size is the general servant. . . ."** Galbraith, *op. cit.*, p. 32.

69 **"Hyena . . . pride of lions. . . ."** Walter Russell Mead, *Mortal Splendor*, Houghton Mifflin (Boston: 1987), p. 189.

69 **"America's economic future depends less on. . . ."** Robert Reich, *The Next American Frontier*, Times Books (New York: 1983), p. 279.

69 **U.S. domination of microprocessor market.** *The Economist*, "High-Technology: Clash of the Titans," August 23, 1986.

69 **Early history of personal computer industry.** Paul Frieberger and Michael Swaine, *Fire in the Valley*, Osborne/McGraw-Hill (Berkeley: 1984), pp. 17, 282.

70 **"Can anyone explain. . . ."** *The Economist*, December 12, 1983.

70 **Compaq sales versus AT&T.** Figures courtesy of Dataquest, San Jose, California.

70 **Compaq sales versus Japanese producers and AT&T.** Figures from Storeboard, Inc., for business PC dealer revenue, first half of 1987.

71 **New semiconductor start-ups.** Authors' interview with Dataquest.

71 **"People have developed a mythology. . . ."** Interview with authors.

71 *Venture Economics* **figures on corporate partnerships.** Cited in *Wall Street Journal*, November 5, 1985.

71 **"If you want a new technology. . . ."** Interview with authors.

72 **Increase in high-paying jobs.** *Monthly Labor Review*, George Silvestri and Joan Lukasiewicz, "Occupational Employment Projections: 1984–95 Outlook," November 1985.

72 **JEC study.** Cited in *Newsweek*, Robert Samuelson, "The American Job Machine," February 23, 1987.

72 **Bluestone and Harrison's arguments.** *New York Times*, Barry Bluestone and Bennett Harrison, "The Grim Truth About the 'Jobs Miracle,'" February 1, 1987.

72 **Manufacturing share in economy.** Cited in *The Economist*, August 23, 1986; *Wall Street Journal*, Paul W. McCracken, "The Rust Belt's Coming Revival," March 30, 1987.

72 **Small firms account for new manufacturing jobs.** *Inc.*, David Birch, "Is Manufacturing Dead?" June 1987.

72 **Improvements in productivity.** *Los Angeles Times*, Don Conlan, "Work Ethic Works Best Under the Gun," March 10, 1987.

73 **Manufacturing growth companies.** *Inc.*, "The *Inc.* 100," May 1987.

73 **Job growth in specific industries.** *The State of Small Business: Report to the President*, Government Printing Office (Washington, DC:1985), p. 116.

73 **Yankee Group study.** Cited in *Los Angeles Times*, Tom Redburn and James Flanigan, "U.S. Firms Gain Competitive Edge," August 2, 1987.

73 **Minimills.** Interviews with authors; *Wall Street Journal*, Mark Russell, "Small Steelmakers Find Profitable Niches," January 8, 1987.

74 **Per hour steel production.** *Inc.*, George Gendron, "Steel Man Ken Iverson," April 1986.

74 **"What's at stake here. . . ."** *New York Times*, Nathan P. Hicks, "Steel Innovator's Risky Plan," August 15, 1987.

74 **"Unless you're under intense. . . ."** *Inc.*, George Gendron, "Steel Man Ken Iverson," April 1986.

74 **Service exports.** *Inc.*, David Birch, "No Respect," May 1987.

75 **Self-employment will vanish.** *Inc.*, Tom Richman, "The Hottest Entrepreneur in America," February 1987.

75 **Increase in self-employment.** *The State of Small Business: Report to the President, op. cit.*, p. xiii.

75 **Roger Boas.** *San Francisco Chronicle*, Roger Boas, "How to Turn Around S.F.'s Economy," January 17, 1987.

75 **San Francisco Jobs.** Interview with authors and materials provided by *San Francisco Bay Guardian* and Cognetics, Inc., Cambridge, Massachussetts.

76 **"Good craft people."** Interview with authors.

76 **Nation's richest city.** Wells Fargo report cited in *Los Angeles Times*, June 17, 1987.

77 **Jacob Burkhardt.** Cited in William Pfaff, *Condemned to Freedom*, Random House (New York:1971), p. 126.

77 **Stanley Baldwin.** Cited in Martin Weiner, *English Culture and the Decline of the Industrial Spirit*, Cambridge University Press (Cambridge:1981), p. 109.

77 **The Labor party.** *Ibid.*, pp. 118-9.

77 **Percentage of government share of GNP.** *Government Finance Statistics Yearbook*, International Monetary Fund, (Washington:1986).

77 **Survey of British Attitudes.** Cited in *Foreign Affairs*, Eric Willenz, "Why Europe Needs the Welfare State," Summer 1986, p. 99.

78 **"In the eyes of West Europeans. . . ."** *Ibid.*, pp. 88-89.

78 **Labor costs.** Dornbush, *op. cit.*, pp. 26-27.

78 **"Hiring an extra worker. . . ."** *Ibid.*, p. 27.

78 **New job creation.** *Inc.*, David Birch, "Yankee Doodle Dandy," July 1987.

78 **Italy youth unemployment.** *World Press Review*, John Lloyd and Charles Leadbeater, "The Changing World of Work," September 1986.

79 **Germany and France youth unemployment.** Dornbush, *op. cit.*, p. 25; Andrew Martin, *The Politics of Economic Policy in the United States*, Sage Publications (Beverly Hills, Calif.:1973), p. 9.

79 **"Likely model."** *Los Angeles Times*, Robert W. Gibson, "Britain: A Hazy Future for Economy," January 3, 1987.

79 **Ireland.** *Forbes*, Kathleen K. Wiegner, "Lessons from Ireland," September 7, 1987; *Wall Street Journal*, James M. Peery, "Ireland Is Beset by Unemployment," February 17, 1987; *The Economist*, "Ireland's Economy," January 24, 1987; *Los Angeles Times*, Tyler Marshall, "Ireland's Economy Shaken by Exodus of University Graduates," February 22, 1987.

79 **Lack of entrepreneurial ventures.** Findings of EEC report on small ventures cited in *The Economist*, November 19, 1983.

79 **"Attitudes are totally different. . . ."** Interview with authors.

80 **"Profit is a dirty word. . . ."** Cited in *Wall Street Journal*, Roger Thurow, "New Vigor Is Infusing Small Business Sector of German Economy," August 18, 1986.

80 **"I was treated. . . ."** *Ibid.*

80 **Small business job creation.** *Inc.*, David Birch, "Yankee Doodle Dandy," July 1987.

81 **"If we stick to the same policies. . . ."** *MacLean's*, Peter Lewis, "Behind Europe's Breadlines," September 22, 1986.

81 **"A weapon of future conservatism,"** Arthur Schlesinger, *The Age of Jackson*, Little, Brown, (Boston:1945), pp. 520–21.

81 **" 'Planning' as commonly understood. . . ."** Peter Drucker, *Entrepreneurship and Innovation*, Harper and Row (New York: 1985), p. 255.

81 **"The almost unquestioned assumption."** London *Financial Times*, Guy de Jonquieres, "Global Challenge Intensifies," July 9, 1987.

82 **Airbus.** *Business Week*, "Airbus Hits U.S. Plane Makers Where It Hurts," October 20, 1986.

82 **New appropriations.** *Aviation and Space Week*, December 15, 1986.

82 **Small business park.** *Wall Street Journal*, Roger Thurow, "Europe Tries to Match U.S. and Japan in High Tech," May 8, 1985.

82 **"A young man. . . ."** *Los Angeles Times*, Tyler Marshall, "West Germans' High Tech Edge Is Lost," February 1, 1984.

82 **Government spending on technology.** Mervyn Krauss, "Europeanizing the U.S. Economy," in Chalmers Johnson, ed., *The Industrial Policy Debate*, Institute for Contemporary Studies (San Francisco:1984), p. 87.

82 **Microchip spending in Europe.** *Wall Street Journal*, Roger Thurow, "Europe Tries to Match U.S. and Japan in High Tech," May 8, 1985.

82　**Microchip market share.** Figures provided by Semiconductor Industry Association, Cupertino, California.

82　**"We lag far behind. . . ."** Krauss, *op. cit.*, p. 87.

83　**"Trying to guide their economies."** Krauss, *op. cit.*, p. 75.

83　**Performance in Southeast Asia.** *Journal of Common Market Studies*, Rolf J. Langhammer and Ulrich Heimenz, "Declining Competitiveness of EC Suppliers in Asian Markets: Singular Case or Symptom?" volume 24, number 2, December 2, 1985.

83　**Technology job losses.** *High Technology*, Garrett DeYoung, "Can Europe Catch Up in the Technology Race," October 1984.

83　**"A call to catch up."** Krauss, *op. cit.*, p. 88.

83　**"If someone had. . . ."** Interview with authors.

84　**IBM market share.** Cited in *Financial Times*, Alan Kane, "European High Technology," July 9, 1987.

84　**U.S. software dominance.** *High Technology*, Garrett DeYoung, "Can Europe Catch Up in the Technology Race," October 1984.

84　**"Most of the software . . ."** Interview with authors.

84　**"We couldn't have. . . ."** Interview with authors.

85　**"Asian societies are at a turning point."** Interview with authors.

85　**"There is one more modernization. . . ."** Publisher's note, *Journal of Japanese Trade and Industry*, "Economic Development and the Confucian Ethic," March/April 1986.

86　**"The new freedom. . . ."** G. C. Allen, *A Short Economic History of Modern Japan*, St. Martin's Press (New York: 1981), p. 235.

86　**"The bureaucrats . . ."** Akio Morita with Edwin M. Reingold and Mituko Shinomura, *Made in Japan*, E.P. Dutton (New York: 1986), pp. 66–67.

86　**"Probably I would have been. . . ."** Interview with authors.

87　**"The Ministry of Finance. . . ."** Interview with authors.

87　**Two out of every three.** *Euro-Asia Business Review*, Manfred Pohl, "Japan's SMEs at Bay," October 1986, p. 14.

87　**"The big contractors. . . ."** Interview with authors.

88　**"Coordination is all right. . . ."** Interview with authors.

89　**Semiconductor industry.** *Los Angeles Times*, Donna Walters, "Japan's High Tech Industry Braces for Heavy Losses in Chipmaking Operations," May 26, 1987; *Electronic News*, David Bambrick, "Premature Erosion of DRAM Prices Changing Economics of Memory Market," April 1, 1987.

89　**"You cannot deny. . . ."** Interview with authors.

90　**Japanese firms forced into bankruptcy.** *Business Week*, "The Swollen Yen Is Weighing Heavily on Japan." May 4, 1987.

90　**"Venture business" bankruptcies.** *Wall Street Journal*, Christopher Chipello, "Japan Facing Woes with Venture Capital," August 8, 1986.

91　**"A certain freshman. . . ."** Interview with authors.

91　**Kiyonari study.** Tadao Kiyonari, "The Venture Boom in Japan" (unpublished study, Venture Enterprise Center, Hosei University), pp. 4–9.

91 **Kangyo Denki.** *Nikkei Venture*, *"Zasetsu kara no Kyookun,"* September 1986.

91 **Sord.** *Ibid.*

92 **The 46 million.** *San Francisco Chronicle*, Frank Viviano, "Pacific Giants: The Overseas Chinese," May 27, 1987.

93 **"To be small. . . ."** *Asian Wall Street Journal Weekly*, James R. Schiffman and Maria Shao, "Korea, Taiwan View Each Other's Style with Mix of Admiration and Perplexity," May 19, 1986.

93 **Reliance on Japan.** *Far East Economic Review*, Reginald Child, "A Flash of Blue—and Then Back to Olive Green," June 2, 1983.

93 **"Most of what we earn. . . ."** *Fortune*, Louis Krarr, "Korea's Big Push Has Just Begun," March 16, 1987.

93 **Need for jobs.** *Far East Economic Review*, Paul Esnor, "Caught in the Machine," September 18, 1986.

93 **Changes in government policy.** *Asian Wall Street Journal Weekly*, James R. Schiffman and Maria Shao, "Korea, Taiwan View Each Other's Style with Mix of Admiration and Perplexity," May 19, 1986; *Business Asia*, May 25, 1987.

93 **"You find the innovative jobs. . . ."** *Forbes*, Lawrence Minard, "The Fragile Miracle on the Han," February 11, 1985.

94 **Korea's debt.** *U.S. News and World Report*, "Asia's Newest Success Story," November 3, 1986.

94 **Taiwan's currency reserves.** *Business Week*, "Taiwan's Wealth Crisis," April 13, 1987.

94 **Taiwan's PC board industry.** *Electronic Business*, Philip Liu, "The rise of Taiwan's PC Board Industry," June 1, 1987.

94 **Y. C. Wang.** *Forbes*, Andrew Tanzer, "Y. C. Wang Gets Up Very Early in the Morning," June 15, 1985.

94 **"It reminded me of. . . ."** From *Keizei Taikoku no Kuro*, "Sekai no Butsuryuu wo Shihaisuru Evergreen," Nihon Hoso Shuppan Kyookai, NHK Special Report, June 24, 1987.

94 **Number of companies doubling.** Republic of China, Executive Yuan, *The Report on 1981 Industrial and Commercial Census*, (Taipei: 1982).

95 **"If you go. . . ."** *Asian Wall Street Journal Weekly*, James R. Schiffman and Maria Shao, "Korea, Taiwan View Each Other's Style with Mix of Admiration and Perplexity," May 19, 1986.

95 **"Natural system of perfect liberty."** Louis Hacker, *Economic Growth and Development*, John Wiley (New York:1970), p. 17.

95 **Family ownership in Hong Kong.** Jan Woronoff, *Hong Kong: Capitalist Paradise*, Heinemann Asia (Hong Kong:1980), pp. 115–16.

95 **Dropping size of Hong Kong companies.** *Euro-Asia Business Review*, S. Gordon Redding, "Entrepreneurship in Asia," October 1986.

95 **Family-based financing.** Hong Kong University study, data provided by Price Waterhouse, Hong Kong main office.

95 **"You can predict. . . ."** *High Technology,* Herb Brody, "Four Tigers of the Orient," Hong Kong Section, November 1986.

95 **"The Japanese state. . . ."** Interview with authors.

96 **"Obstinate" Cantonese.** Shia Shan Henry Tsai, *China and the Overseas Chinese,* University of Arkansas Press (Fayetteville:1983), p. 127.

97 **Kenneth Fung.** *Asian Wall Street Journal,* Adi Ignatius, "The Fung Family: Coping with Crisis," October 9–10, 1986.

98 **"They remain. . . ."** Interview with authors.

98 **"I started with a failure. . . ."** Interview with authors.

99 **"Our assets. . . ."** Interview with authors.

100 **"In the end. . . ."** Interview with authors.

4: The Refinancing of America

page

101 **"I feel very comfortable."** Interview with author.

102 **"We feel guilty. . . ."** Interview with authors.

103 **"In Tokyo. . . ."** Interview with authors.

103 **"I feel very. . . ."** Interview with authors.

103 **"We can't stay here. . . ."** Interview with authors.

103 **"Back home. . . ."** Interview with authors.

103 **"We have to. . . ."** Interview with authors.

104 **"We have always. . . ."** Interview with authors.

105 **Bank of America.** Marquis James and Bessie R. James. *Biography of a Bank,* Harper and Brothers (New York:1954) p. 482.

105 **"Japanese premium."** Interview with authors.

105 **Largest banks.** *New York Times,* Susan Chira, "The Japanese Bank That is Now Number One," September 6, 1986.

105 **Dominant financial power.** *JEI Report,* "Implications of Contrasting U.S. and Japanese Saving Behavior," May 1, 1987, charts 2, 3.

106 **"Largest creditor nation. . . ."** Cited in Sam Jameson, "Japan—Now It's Banker to the World," *Los Angeles Times,* March 16, 1986.

106 **Hong Kong and Shanghai Bank.** Cited in *The American Banker,* "Top Foreign Banks in the United States," April 9, 1987.

106 **"Control of the bank. . . ."** Cited in *Business Week,* "How an Unlikely Gang of Three Saved Standard Chartered," July 28, 1986.

106 **Taiwan.** *Business Week,* "Taiwan's Wealth Crisis," April 13, 1987.

106 **Loosening controls.** *Electronic News,* August 10, 1987.

106 **"If we assign. . . ."** Leroy P. Jones and Il Sekong, *Entrepreneurship in Economic Development,* Harvard University Press (Cambridge:1980), p. 306.

106 **"National one-sidedness."** Karl Marl *The Communist Manifesto,* in *The Essential Left,* Barnes and Noble (New York:1961), pp. 18–19.

106 **Britain's savings.** Earl Fry, *The Financial Invasion of the USA,* McGraw-Hill (New York:1980), p. 15.

107 **Martin Weiner.** Martin Weiner, *English Culture and the Decline of the Industrial Spirit*, Cambridge University Press (Cambridge: 1981), pp. 129–30.

107 **Meiji financial strategies.** Frances V. Moulder, *Japan, China and the Modern World Economy*, Cambridge University Press (Cambridge: 1977), pp. 184–85.

107 **Foreign trade.** G. G. Allen, *A Short Economic History of Japan*, St. Martin's Press (New York: 1981), p. 113.

107 **Net creditor.** Yoshihara Kunio, *Japanese Economic Development*, Oxford University Press (New York: 1979), pp. 38–39.

108 **Militarists.** Chalmers Johnson, "The Internationalization of the Japanese Economy" (unpublished paper), p. 13.

108 **Hong Kong finances.** Jan Woronoff, *Hong Kong: Capitalist Paradise*, Heinemann Asia (Hong Kong: 1980), pp. 174–77.

108 **U.S. financing of Taiwan.** *Columbia Journal of Business*, Chuyuan Cheng, "United States-Taiwan Economic Relations: Trade and Investment," Spring 1986.

108 **Tariffs.** *Vital Speeches*, David E. Bell, "Investment Opportunities in Asia," November 1, 1964.

108 **"We wanted the Japanese. . . ."** Cited in *Forbes*, "The Managed Yen," May 5, 1986.

109 **Temporary situation.** Johnson, *op. cit.*, p. 14.

109 **"There was. . . ."** Michiya Matsukawa, "The Japanese Trade Surplus and Capital Outflow," *Group of 30* (Occasional Paper no. 22), (New York: 1987).

109 **Imports over exports.** Patricia Ann Cummins, *Japan's Economic Transition: 1945–80* (graduate business dissertation), United States International University (San Diego: 1980), p. 41.

109 **"The Japanese economy. . . ."** *Look*, Frank Gibney, "Japan," August 10, 1965.

109 **Exports as share of GNP.** Dick K. Nanto, "Japan's Growth Formula: A Time for Reappraisal," Congressional Research Service Report, 1986, chapter 2, p. 6.

110 **"They said. . . ."** Cited in *Time*, "Showdown in Trade with Japan," July 4, 1969.

110 **Market dominance.** *Business Week*, "A Japanese Giant in Trouble," November 16, 1974.

111 **"The most socialist. . . ."** *Asian Finance*, E. Amitabha Chowdhury, "Superpower Status Hinges on Neighbors' Markets," March 15, 1987.

111 **Precious capital.** *Suji de miru Nihon no 100nen*, *op. cit*, p. 259.

111 **"Big companies. . . ."** *Fortune*, "Business Around the Globe," July 1965.

111 **$30.** Johnson, *op. cit.*, p. 17.

111 **One Japanese scientist.** Interview with authors.

112 **"Actually the CEO. . . ."** *Asian Finance*, E. Amitabha Chowdhury,

"Superpower Status Hinges on Neighbors' Markets," March 15, 1987.

112 **Japanese houses.** *Los Angeles Times*, Sam Jameson, "Tokyo Land Prices Now Outlandish," April 4, 1986.

112 **Sarakin.** *Forbes*, Richard Phalon, "The Plight of the Spendthrift in Thrifty Japan," May 20, 1985.

112 **Buying a house.** *Japan Times*, Setsuo Furihata, "Japan's Present Capitalism: An Automobile Society," May 3, 1986; *JEI Report*, "Implications of Contrasting U.S. and Japanese Saving Behavior," May 1, 1987, number 17a, p. 3.

113 **Savings rate.** *JEI Report, ibid.*, p. 3.

113 **Leverage.** *Sekai no Kigyo no Keiei Bunseki*, edited by Industrial Policy Division, Ministry of International Trade and Industry, Okurasho Insatsukyoku (Tokyo:1981).

113 **Limitations on foreign loans.** Krause and Sekiguchi, *Economic Interaction in the Pacific Basin*, Brookings Institution (Washington, D.C.:1980), p. 75.

113 **"City banks."** *Los Angeles Times*, Sam Jameson, "Japan—Now It's Banker to the World," March 16, 1986.

114 **Investment restrictions.** *Time*, "Japan: Winning the Most Important Battle," May 10, 1971; *Fortune*, Lee Smith, "Want to Buy a Japanese Company?" June 27, 1983.

114 **"Most Japanese. . . ."** *Business Week*, "The Sharp Side of the Rising Sun," September 6, 1969.

114 **Cost of capital.** William Ouchi, *The M-Form Society*, Addison-Wesley (Reading, Mass.:1984), p. 71.

114 **Capital formation.** *JEI Report, op. cit.*, 17a, p. 4.

114 **Productivity.** *JEI Report*, Paul R. Krugman and George N. Hatsopoulos, *The Problem of U.S. Competitiveness in Manufacturing*, 13a, April 3, 1987, p. 5.

114 **"Stupid."** Cited in *Business Week*, "The Sharp Side of the Rising Sun," September 6, 1969.

115 **1977 trade surplus.** Cited in *Time*, December 12, 1977.

115 **World manufacturing,** *JEI Report*, 13a, pp. 6–7.

115 **Trade surplus.** *JEI Report*, 17a, p. 8.

115 **"When I first. . . ."** Interview with authors.

115 **"More efficient."** Ouchi, op. cit., p. 73.

115 **"The challenge. . . ."** Cited in *Purejudento*, May 1987.

117 **"Is always self-defeating."** *Wall Street Journal*, Peter Drucker, "Japan and Adversarial Trade," April 1, 1986.

117 **"You can't get. . . ."** Interview with authors.

118 **Exports and profits.** *Business Week*, "Waiting for the Yen to Stop Pummeling Profits," June 1, 1987.

118 **"The technology. . . ."** *Chuo Koro*, "*Nihon no Kagaku Gijutsu wa abaunai*," February 1987.

119 **VTRs.** *Forbes*, Norman Gall, "Hold the Champagne," May 5, 1986.

119 **Silicon wafers, semiconductor equipment, cameras.** *Forbes*, Kathleen Wiegner, "Suicide in Silicon?" August 26, 1985; *Forbes*, Marc Beauchamp, "Ruined for One, Ruined for All," April 7, 1986; *Forbes*, Richard Phalon, "Phototropism," June 3, 1985.

119 **"We are. . . ."** Cited in *Toyo Keizei*, *"Keizai taikoku Nippon, Nani wo Nasubekika,"* May 9, 1987.

119 **"Small firms. . . ."** Interview with authors.

120 **"The whole system. . . ."** Interview with authors.

120 **Offshore investments.** *Forbes*, February 9, 1987; *Los Angeles Times*, May 24, 1987.

120 **560,000 jobs.** Ministry of International Trade and Industry, "An Outlook for Japan's Industrial Society Toward the Twenty-first Century," (Tokyo:1986), p. 36.

121 **Comparative rates of investment.** *Asian Wall Street Journal*, "Korean Companies Plan 42.5% Increase in 1986 Capital Spending," April 7, 1986; *Long Term Credit Bank Survey of Capital Investment* (Tokyo) April 1987; *Los Angeles Times*, Tetsuro Kikuchi, "Japanese Productivity Threatened by Aging Factories and Equipment," August 27, 1984; *Los Angeles Times*, August 2, 1987.

121 **"They've taken the view. . . ."** *Institutional Investor*, Kevin Rafferty, "Japanese Corporate Finance Goes Global," November 1986.

121 **Japanese purchases of securities.** *Institutional Investor*, January 1987.

122 **Foreign assets.** *Los Angeles Times*, Sam Jameson, "Japan—Now It's Banker to the World," March 16, 1986.

122 **"Japan is the next America."** Interview with authors.

122 **44% of investment.** *Purejidento*, May 1987.

122 **"A kind of Hitler. . . ."** Interview with authors.

122 **"United States society. . . ."** Interview with authors.

123 **"A great deal. . . ."** Karl Marx, *Das Kapital*, volume 1, Vintage (New York:1977), p. 920.

123 **"To put it. . . ."** Interview with authors.

124 **"Grander tasks. . . ."** Nicholas Roosevelt, *Restless Pacific*, Scribner's (New York:1928), pp. 107–108.

124 **"We feel suffocated."** Cited in John G. Roberts, *Mitsui: Three Centuries of Japanese Business*, Weatherhill (New York:1973), p. 268.

125 **"Japan lacks. . . ."** Mark Gayn, *The Fight for the Pacific*, William Morrow (New York:1942), pp. 182–83.

125 **Defeat.** *Newsweek*, "Japan Fronts for the West," April 13, 1959.

125 **"The continent. . . ."** Cited in George Dangerfield, *The Awakening of American Nationalism*, Harper and Row (New York:1965), p. 1.

125 **Comparisons in resources.** *Facts on the Pacific Rim*, California Department of Commerce, June 1985, pp. 6–8.

126 **"Our common perception."** Interview with authors.

126 **Europe-Asia trade.** From Stefan Linder, *The Pacific Century*, Stanford University Press (Stanford:1986), pp. 76, 80, 81.

126 **Not one European.** Cited in *Keizei Koho Center*, Japan Institute for Social and Economic Affairs, *Japan 1986: An International Comparison* (Tokyo:1986).

126 *Shayo-zoku.* G. C. Allen, *Appointment in Japan*, Athlone Press (London:1983), p. 182.

126 **"From the Japanese perception. . . ."** From *Wall Street Journal*, Art Pine, "Many in Japan Are Writing Off the West," January 25, 1982.

127 **Intraregional trade.** *The Economist*, June 28, 1986; *Euro-Asia Business Review*, Peter Praet and Christopher Stevens, "EEC Asean: Is the Door Half Open or Half Closed," July 1987.

127 **Australian trade.** Linder, *op. cit.*, pp. 78, 80; *Pacific Forecast* (supplement to the *Los Angeles Daily Journal*), Basil Teasey, "The Interdependency of Pacific Trade," July 28, 1986.

127 **"If the trend. . . ."** *Euro-Asia Business Review*, Chiang Hai Ding, "Asean-EC Relations," July 1986, p. 23.

127 **Hong Kong investment.** Hong Kong Government Industry Department, *Statistical Tables*, table 13; Jan Woronoff, *Hong Kong: Capitalist Paradise*, Heineman Asia (Hong Kong:1980), p. 177.

127 **American employment.** *USA Today*, Don Kirk, "Business future bright in Hong Kong," April 23, 1985; *San Francisco Business Journal*, Thomas York, "Americans taking over Hong Kong," July 28, 1987.

128 **"This may be. . . ."** Interview with authors.

128 **Taiwan-U.S. connection.** *Business Week*, "Where Sanctions Against Japan Are Really Working," May 11, 1986; *Current History*, John F. Copper, "Taiwan: New Challenges to Development," April 1986; *U.S. News and World Report*, November 3, 1986.

128 **Foreign investment in Japan.** Ministry of Finance table cited in *JEI Report*, "Foreign Investments in Japan: 1987 Update," 15a, April 17, 1987, table 1.

128 **China trade.** Nicholas Lardy, "Economic Relations between China and the United States," paper for Joint Economic Committee of the Congress, December 11–12, 1986; *Journal of Common Market Studies*, John Redmind and Zou Lan, "The European Community and China; New Horizons," December 1986.

128 **U.S. investment.** *Business China*, "Who is China's Leading Supplier? Japan—But Market Share Shrinks," June 22, 1987.

128 **China's transpacific trade.** Linder, *op. cit.*, p. 78; *Los Angeles Times*, June 14, 1985.

128 **"In the world economy. . . ."** *The Banker*, Dick Wilson, "The Pacific Arrives," July 1985.

129 **Japanese investment by region.** *The Economist*, "Japan Survey: By Conduct and Example," December 7, 1985.

129 **North America market share.** *JEI Report*, "Japan and Asean: Political and Economic Relations," 14a, April 10, 1987, p. 7.

129 **Long-term treasury notes.** *Los Angeles Times*, Ernest Conine, "Foreign Investment," August 3, 1987.

129 **Credit for companies.** *Dun's Business Month*, David Fairlamb, "Nomura Securities' Global Ambitions," November, 1986.

129 **"Americanization" of Nomura.** *The Economist*, "Culture Shock at Nomura New York," November 9, 1986.

129 **"The U.S. . . ."** Cited in *Asian Finance*, David Lake, "Japanese Brokers Secure a Firm Foothold in U.S. Market," March 15, 1986.

129 **American stocks and bonds.** *Ibid.; Los Angeles Times*, "Tokyo Gung-ho on Foreign Stocks," August 21, 1987; *Business Week*, "Japan, USA," July 14, 1986; *Business Week*, "Japanese Money Likely to Stay in U.S. Markets." May 12, 1986.

130 **"We have tracked. . . ."** *Forbes*, Edwin A. Finn and Matthew Schifrin, "Rationality Is in the Eye of the Beholder," March 15, 1986.

130 **Increase in direct investments.** *San Francisco Chronicle*, "The Selling of America," March 11, 1987; *Jetro Monitor*, March 31, 1985.

130 **Bartlesville.** *Piedmont Magazine*, Michelle Cruncleton, "Global Oklahoma," July 1987.

131 **"The U.S. and Japan. . . ."** Cited in *Business Week*, "Japan, USA," July 14, 1986.

131 **Korean investment.** *Business Week*, "Korea's Newest Export: Management Style," January 19, 1987.

131 **Australians.** *Asian Finance*, March 15, 1987.

131 **SPS study.** Cited in Michael A. Goldberg, *The Chinese Connection*, University of British Columbia Press (Vancouver:1985), appendix 2.

131 **Singapore venture capitalists.** Dennis Ray, unpublished research paper, "Venture Capital Evaluation in Singapore," p. 3.

131 **Over 2 billion annually.** *San Francisco Chronicle*, John Eckhouse, "California's Solid Ties to Hong Kong," November 18, 1986.

131 **"The presence of. . . ."** Quoted in *Square Footage*, "The Yen for Bay Area Real Estate," Summer/Fall 1987.

132 **"There's going to be. . . ."** Interview with authors.

133 **"If you have. . . ."** Interview with authors.

134 **Bank of Canton.** *Forbes*, "Bank of What?" April 6, 1987.

135 **Taiwan direct investment** *Los Angeles Times*, Nancy Yoshihara, "Taiwan Goes Abroad in Search of Investments," November 30, 1987.

135 **"The Taiwan Chinese. . . ."** Interview with authors.

135 **"They are usually. . . ."** Interview with authors.

135 **"The government. . . ."** Interview with authors.

5: Winning in the Asian Era

page

135 **"I was amazed. . . ."** Interview with authors.

136 **"I told them. . . ."** Interview with authors.

136 **"All the big. . . ."** Interview with authors.

137 **"Holistic concern. . . ."** William Ouchi, *Theory Z*, Addison-Wesley (Reading, Mass.:1981), p. 53.

137 **"The Japanese. . . ."** Ezra Vogel, *Japan as Number One*, Harvard University Press (Cambridge:1979), p. 235.

138 **"Prisoners of society."** Interview with authors.

138 **"Theory Z-type. . . ."** Interview with authors.

139 **"I am torn. . . ."** Interview with authors.

139 **"2000" report.** *"2000 ni okete gekidoo suru rodo shijo,"* Social Development Research Institute, March 1985.

139 **"Foreign scholars. . . ."** Interview with authors.

140 **"Executives in the big companies. . . ."** Interview with authors.

140 **"Nasty, brutish and short."** Thomas Hobbes, *Leviathan*, Collier Books (London:1969), part 1, chapter 13, p. 100.

140 **"Live lives of quiet desperation."** Henry David Thoreau, *Walden*, book 1, in *Thoreau: Walden and Other Writings*, Bantam Books (New York:1962), p. 111.

140 **"My six month commuter pass. . . ."** Cited in *Salariman*, part 2, Okami, Nihon Keizai Shumbunsha, (Tokyo:1981), p. 37; translation, with many thanks, by Leland Collins.

141 **Commitment to work.** Poll cited in *Mainichi Daily News*, Hidesuke Nagashima, "Company Loyalty Wanes," October 13, 1985.

141 **"All this loyalty. . . ."** Interview with authors.

142 **"To go to a subsidiary. . . ."** Interview with authors.

143 **"A lot of people. . . ."** Interview with authors.

143 **"The only solution. . . ."** *KKC Brief*, Hajime Karatsu, "The Deindustrialization of America: A Tragedy for the World," October 1985.

143 **"Joy of creating."** J. A. Schumpeter, "The Fundamental Phenomenon of Economic Development," from Peter Kilby, ed., *Entrepreneurship and Economic Development*, Free Press (New York:1971), p. 69.

143 **"The earning. . . ."** Max Weber, *The Protestant Ethic and the Spirit of Capitalism*, Scribner's (New York:1985), p. 53.

144 **"A set of beliefs."** Thomas Watson, Jr., *A Business and Its Beliefs*, McGraw-Hill (New York:1963), pp. 4–5.

144 **"Managerial aristocracy."** Pitirim Sorokin, *The Crisis of Our Age*, E. P. Dutton (New York:1941), p. 185.

144 **Conglomerate wave.** Seymour Melman, *Profits without Production*, Knopf (New York:1983), pp. 24–25.

145 **Discharged employees.** *Fortune*, "Why the U.S. Lags in Technology," April 1972.

145 **"The best, most innovative . . ."** *New York Times*, Modesto Maidique and Robert Hayes, "The Technology Gap," June 2, 1981.

145 **Decline of General Motors.** Cited in *Los Angeles Times*, T. W. McGarry, "Frederick G. Donner, GM Chief from 1958 to 1967, Dies," March 5, 1987.

146 **Tarrytown factory.** Melman, *op. cit.*, p. 45.

146 **"Wealth and honor. . . ."** Cited in John M. Koller, *Chinese Philosophies*, Scribner's (New York:1970), p. 265.

146 **"I always had. . . ."** Interview with authors.

147 **"Our marketing people. . . ."** Interview with authors.

147 **"The royal class."** Lee Iacocca, with William Novak, *Iacocca*, Bantam (New York:1984), p. 101.

148 **"Nobody wanted to. . . ."** Interview with authors.

148 **"When you have a child. . . ."** *Forbes*, Thomas P. Murphy, "The Art of Raising Children," May 15, 1977.

148 **"When you're dealing. . . ."** Interview with authors.

148 **"A business is. . . ."** Interview with authors.

148 **"The Japanese and IBM. . . ."** Interview with authors.

149 **"TI University."** Interview with authors.

149 **"We brought in. . . ."** Interview with authors.

149 **"We are not. . . ."** Interview with authors.

150 **Japanese manufacturers in US.** *Forbes*, Susan Lee and Christie Brown, "The Protean Corporation," August 24, 1987; *Electronic News*, "NEC Sets U.S. Winchester Production," April 4, 1986.

150 **Beating Asian competition.** *Wall Street Journal*, "How U.S. Companies Devise Ways to Meet the Challenge From Japan," September 16, 1986; *Forbes*, Geoffrey Smith, "Yankee Samurai," July 14, 1986.

150 **"The only way. . . ."** Interview with authors.

151 **"I don't have. . . ."** Interview with authors.

151 **Harmon International.** Interview with authors.

151 **"We can only. . . ."** Interview with authors.

153 **"The skills. . . ."** Interview with authors.

153 **"Resounding success."** *Forbes*, "The Pacific Basin," November 1, 1970.

153 **VCR domination.** Lionel Olmer, *U.S. Manufacturing at a Crossroads*, U.S. Department of Commerce, June 14, 1985.

153 **Alps Electric.** *Forbes*, Andrew Tanzer, "A Barbarian Personality," August 25, 1986.

154 **"When you forfeit. . . ."** Interview with authors.

154 **Anelva.** Cited in *San Jose Mercury*, Evelyn Richards. "How America Lost the Edge on the World Trade Battlefield," April 20–23, 1986.

154 **Rubinfein.** Interview with authors.

155 **LaPine.** Anthony LaPine, "Building a New Company Through Offshore Corporate Partnering," press release, April 1986, pp. 13–14;

Electronic News, "Kyocera, Prudential Bache to Buy Control of LaPine," December 22, 1986.

155 **Diaspora acquisitions.** *California Business*, Greg Critser, "East Buys West," November 1966.

155 **Korean acquisitions.** *Venture Capital Journal*, September 1966, p. 12; *California Business*, Greg Critser, "Korea's High-Tech Raiders," September 1966.

155 **Corona Data Systems.** *Los Angeles Times*, Jim Bates, "Cordata's Founder Resigns in Dispute with Korean Owners," August 13, 1987; *Electronic News*, "Cordata Co-founder Steps Down," August 17, 1987.

156 **"One thing about Orientals. . . ."** *Electronic News*, August 17, 1987.

158 **"We walked down. . . ."** Interview with authors.

158 **"If you're doing business. . . ."** Interview with authors.

159 **Companies in China.** *Euro Asia Business Review*, Nigel Campbell, "Experiences of Western Companies in China," July 1987.

160 **"The Chinese. . . ."** Cited in *International Advertiser*, "Persistent Effort in China Pays," December 1985.

160 **"I thought. . . ."** Interview with authors.

161 **"You have to. . . ."** Interview with authors.

162 **Rockwell.** *Los Angeles Times*, Donna K. H. Walters, "Patience Pays off in Korean Deals," July 10, 1987.

163 **"You've got to get. . . ."** Interview with authors.

164 **"The Japanese didn't think. . . ."** Interview with authors.

164 **"I took my camera. . . ."** Interview with authors.

165 **"The first thing you do. . . ."** Interview with authors.

165 **"The loyalty of. . . ."** Interview with authors.

166 **"The phone is fine. . . ."** Interview with authors.

166 **"When we get. . . ."** Interview with authors.

6: Making the World Nation

page

168 **"When I got on . . ."** Interview with authors.

168 **Legal immigration statistics.** Leon F. Bouvier and Robert W. Gardner, *Immigration to the U.S.: The Unfinished Story*, Population Reference Bureau, November 1986, p. 3

169 **"A permanently unfinished country."** Cited in Bouvier and Gardner, *op. cit.*, p. 28.

169 **"For older and weaker countries. . . ."** Cited in *Shokun*, "2005nen wa Nihon no Tasogare," February 1987.

169 **Hispanic growth rates.** *Advertising Age*, Ed. Fitch, "Marketing to Hispanics," February 9, 1987.

169 **Hispanics by state.** Bouvier and Gardner, *op. cit.*, p. 27.

169 **Rate of growth seven times.** Census Bureau report cited in *San Francisco Chronicle*, April 29, 1987.

170 **Growth of minorities overall.** *American Demographics*, Thomas Exter, "How Many Hispanics?" May 1987.

170 **Newly emerging post-European America.** *American Demographics*, John Kasarda, "Minorities and City Change," November 1984.

170 **San Francisco's Asians.** *San Francisco Focus*, Frank Viviano and Sharon Silva, "The New San Francisco," September 1986.

170 **Los Angeles minorities.** "Marketplace of the World," Los Angeles Area Chamber of Commerce, 1987.

170 **"Grim reality."** *Los Angeles Times*, Neil Pierce, "Our Threadbare Welcome Mat," November 29, 1981.

170 **"Unassimilated immigrants."** Richard D. Lamm and Gary Imhoff, *The Immigration Time Bomb*, E. P. Dutton (New York:1985), p. 85.

170 **"Contamination."** *Ibid.*, pp. 81, 85–91.

170 **"Bad thing."** Poll published in *Los Angeles Times*, August 24, 1986.

171 **"Will the last American. . . ."** *Esquire*, John Rothchild, "Melting Pot High," June 1985.

171 **Anti-Asian violence.** *Wall Street Journal*, Jan Wong, "Anti-Asian Violence Grows," November 28, 1986.

171 **"You have a group. . . ."** Interview with authors.

171 **"It's deliberate."** Interview with authors.

171 **"Palantine boors."** Cited in Leonard Dinnerstein, Roger L. Nichols, and David M. Reimers, *Natives and Strangers*, Oxford University Press (New York:1979), p. 23.

171 **Signers of the Declaration.** John F. Kennedy, *A Nation of Immigrants*, Harper and Row (New York:1964), p. 64.

172 **"Hordes of wild Irishmen. . . ."** Dinnerstein, Nichols, and Reimers, *op, cit.*, p. 68.

172 **Samuel F. B. Morse.** Thomas J. Archdeacon, *Becoming American*, Free Press (New York:1983), pp. 73–82.

172 **"Perhaps hopeless to think. . . ."** Leonard Dinnerstein and David M. Reimers, *Ethnic Americans*, Harper and Row (New York:1975), p. 40.

173 **Immigration Restriction League.** Archdeacon, *op. cit.*, p. 162.

173 **"This sense of dispossession."** Cited in *Los Angeles Times*, Barry Siegel, "Immigrants: Sizing Up the New Wave," December 12, 1982.

173 **Henry Goddard.** Paul R. Ehrlich, Loy Bilderback, Anne H. Ehrlich, *The Golden Door*, Ballantine Books (New York:1979), pp. 67–68.

173 **"Absolutely justified determination. . . ."** Madison Grant, *Passing of a Great Race*, Scribner's (New York:1919), p. 79.

173 **"The new immigration. . . ."** *Ibid.*, p. 89.

173 **Immigrants in World War I.** John Lescott-Leszczynski, *The History of U.S. Ethnic Policy and Its Impact on European Ethnics*, Westview Press (Boulder:1984), p. 22.

174   **Quotas.** Richard Pohlenberg, *One Nation Divisable*, Viking Press (New York:1980), p. 205; *Nation's Business* "Immigration Under the New Law," February 1925.

174   **"[Educators] have painted. . . ."** Cited in Lescott-Leszczynski, *op. cit.*, p. 65.

174   **"Jesus could not. . . ."** Cited in H. Brett Melendy, *Asians in America*, Twayne Publishers (Boston:1977), p. 233.

175   **"Hard core indigestible blocs."** Dinnerstein and Reimers, op. cit., p. 83.

175   **Immigrant wealth.** George Gilder, *Wealth and Poverty*, Basic Books (New York:1981), pp. 11, 33.

175   **"Disturbed state."** Alexander Hamilton, "Report on the Subject of Manufactures," in *Philosophy of Manufactures*, ed. Michael Brewster Folsom and Steven D. Lubar, MIT Press (Cambridge:1982), p. 93.

175   **Regional differences.** Archdeacon, *op. cit.*, pp. 11–18.

175   **Recruitment of immigrants.** *Ibid.*, p. 36.

175   **New York.** *Ibid.*, p. 48.

176   **"The man of old stock. . . ."** Grant, *op. cit.*, p. 91.

176   **Immigrants in New York.** Parmanta Saran and Edwin Eames, *The New Ethnics*, Praeger (New York:1980), pp. 91–92.

176   **Immigrants in professions.** Dinnerstein and Reimers, *op. cit.*, p. 127.

176   **Immigrants in Midwest.** Thomas Muller, *The Fourth Wave*, The Urban Institute Press (Washington, D.C.:1984), p. 2.

176   **"More efficient civilization."** Cited in Eldon R. Penrose, *California Nativism: Organized Opposition to the Japanese*, Rand Research (San Francisco:1973), p. 71.

176   **"A demographic winter."** Cited in *Newsweek*, "Europe's Population Bomb," December 15, 1986.

177   **Hispanic age.** Figures provided by Strategy Research Corporation, Miami, 1987.

177   **Relative aging among advanced nations.** *Los Angeles Times*, Jonathan Peterson, "Japan's Elderly Offer a New Market," August 2, 1985; *Los Angeles Times*, Phillip Stephens, "Some Nations Obsessed by Aging," July 6, 1986; Bouvier and Gardner, *op. cit.*, p. 19; *Wall Street Journal*, Thomas F. O'Boyle, "Increase in Birthrate Is Welcome News but Considered a Fluke," September 10, 1986.

177   **"In the next few decades. . . ."** *American Demographics*, Bryant Robey, "Locking Up Heaven's Door," February 1987.

177   **70% of immigration.** *Los Angeles Times*, Barry Siegel, "Immigrants: Sizing Up the New Wave," December 18, 1982.

178   **Rand Corporation study.** Kevin P. McCarthy and R. Burciaga Valdez, "Current and Future Implications of Mexican Immigration in California," Rand Corporation report, 1985, p. 49.

178   **"You see exhortations. . . ."** Cited in *Los Angeles Times*, Barry

Siegel, "Immigrants: Sizing Up the New Wave," December 14, 1982.

178 **10,000 Chinese engineers.** *Image*, Frank Viviano, "Transplanting Silicon Valley," June 21, 1987.

178 **Solectron and Circadian.** Interview with authors.

178 **One out of every eight.** *Wall Street Journal*, Eugene Carlson, "Regions," September 10, 1985.

178 **"Without the movement. . . ."** Interview with authors.

178 **"An outside observer. . . ."** Cited in *Wall Street Journal*, Eugene Carlson, "Regions," September 10, 1985.

179 **Los Angeles industry.** Kevin P. McCarthy and R. Burciaga Valdez, *op. cit.*, pp. 37–46.

179 **"Prohibiting employment of immigrants. . . ."** *Los Angeles Times*, Richard Rothstein, "LA's Economy Depends on Illegals," November 23, 1986.

179 **Ethnics in *Fortune* 500.** Lescott-Leszczynski, *op. cit.*, p. 139.

179 **Ethnic entrepreneurialism.** Peter Bearse and Peter Johnson, "Minority and Ethnic Entrepreneurship in the United States—1980: A Comparative Analysis," report for Minority Business Development Agency, U.S. Department of Commerce, September 1, 1986, p. 14.

179 **"Barbadian network."** Interview with authors.

180 **"West Indians love to own things. . . ."** Cited in *Los Angeles Times*, Mary Jane Smetanka, "West Indians Make Their Mark in Hartford," August 19, 1983.

180 **Hispanic business.** *Futurescan*, Security Pacific Bank, March 30, 1987.

180 **Dade County population.** Dade County Master Plan report, cited in *Miami Herald*, March 25, 1987.

180 **Miami immigrant wealth.** Luis Botifol, "How Miami's New Image Was Created," pamphlet, *Institute for Interamerican Studies*, University of Miami, 1985, p. 2.

181 **"In ten years. . . ."** Interview with authors.

181 **Los Angeles ethnicity.** *American Demographics*, Tracy Ann Goodis and Thomas J. Espenshade, "Los Angeles Rides the Wave," December 1986.

181 **Los Angeles as leader.** *Crain's New York Business*, "LA Looms as No. 1 U.S. City," December 9, 1985.

181 **Los Angeles as industrial center.** *California Business*, Benjamin Mark Cole, "Goodbye to La-la Land," May 1987.

181 **Hispanic entrepreneurs.** "Price Waterhouse 1985 Hispanic Business Survey," Exhibits II, III.

181 **Korean entrepreneurs.** Study cited in *Los Angeles Times*, June 6, 1987.

181 **"It's not social responsibility. . . ."** Interview with authors.

182 **Ethnic GNP vs. West Germany.** Numbers compiled by research

staff, *Inc.*, "Marketing the New America," August 1987; *World Bank Atlas 1987* (Washington, D.C.:1987), pp. 6–10.

183 **Senate study.** Cited in *Los Angeles Herald Examiner*, September 22, 1980.

183 **Asian income.** *Inc.*, "Marketing the New America," August 1987.

183 **Hispanic income.** *Inc.*, "Marketing the New America," August 1987.

183 **Hispanic purchasing power.** *Advertising Age*, Ed Fitch, "Marketing to Hispanics," February 9, 1987.

183 **Saint Louis.** Market research provided by KLVE Radio, Los Angeles.

183 **"People have to start realizing. . . ."** Interview with authors.

183 **"Every new group. . . ."** Interview with authors.

184 **"The guy simply. . . ."** Interview with authors.

185 **"The Ukrainian. . . ."** Interview with authors.

185 **"My father always. . . ."** Interview with authors.

185 **Von's study.** Cited in *Los Angeles Times*, Denise Gellene, "LA Grocers Cultivate Latin Buyers," May 17, 1987.

186 **Other markets.** Interview with authors; *Wall Street Journal*, Matt Moffett, "Attention to Area's Demographic Change Makes Houston's Fiesta Stores a Success," October 23, 1986; *Los Angeles Times*, Jesus Sanchez, "Ex-Produce Clerk Leads Von's Toward the Latino Market," August 31, 1987.

186 **"When we started. . . ."** Interview with authors.

186 **Upwardly mobile Hispanics.** "Ogilvy and Mather Listening Post," June 1984; figures provided by Strategy Research Corporation, Miami.

187 **"We came here. . . ."** Interview with authors.

187 **Asian economic achievement and *Los Angeles Times* study.** Marketing materials provided by *Asian* magazine, Los Angeles; *Wall Street Journal*, Ronald Alsop, "Firms Translate Sales Pitches to Asian Americans," April 10, 1988.

189 **"I think it's all. . . ."** Interview with authors.

189 **"False liberal hypothesis."** Gilder, *Wealth and Poverty, op., cit.,* p. 93.

189 **"The growth in tolerance. . . ."** Cited in David Reimers, *Still the Golden Door*, Columbia University Press (New York:1985), p. 84.

189 **Harris survey.** Louis Harris, *Inside America*, Vintage (New York: 1987), p. 189.

189 **Slamming the door shut.** *U.S. News and World Report*, "Europe's Immigration Battles," March 31, 1986.

190 **"You can't use the model. . . ."** *New York Times*, James J. Markham, "Minorities in Western Europe: Hearing Not Welcome in Several Languages," August 5, 1986.

190 **Communists against Africans.** *Los Angeles Times*, "The Continent in Turmoil," May 10, 1981.

190 **"Preserve the identity . . ."** *New York Times*, James M. Markham, "Minorities in Western Europe: Hearing Not Welcome in Several Languages," August 5, 1986.

190 **"Abused, insulted, threatened. . . ."** Cited in *U.S. News and World Report*, "Europe's Immigration Battles," March 31, 1986.

190 **British race problems.** Study cited in *Los Angeles Times*, September 18, 1987.

191 **"There's a rather nasty mood. . . ."** *U.S. News and World Report*, "Europe's Immigration Battles," March 31, 1986.

191 **"People are really. . . ."** Joel Krieger, *Reagan, Thatcher, and the Politics of Decline*, Polity Press (Cambridge:1986), p. 76.

191 **"Our Western way of life."** Jean Raspail, *The Camp of the Saints*, Sphere Books (London:1977), p. 326.

191 **"Yes, the Third World. . . ."** *Ibid.*, p. 274.

191 **"While U.S. businessmen. . . ."** From Jenny Corbett, "The European Community's Trade with Japan and Its Implications," Australia National University (Canberra:1978), pp. 53–54.

191 **"Curious racially tinged. . . ."** *Ibid.*, pp. 54–57.

191 **"The closer the cooperation. . . ."** Nicholas Roosevelt, *Restless Pacific*, Charles Scribner's Sons (New York:1928), p. 282.

191 **Pattern of protectionism.** *Wall Street Journal*, Peter Drucker, "Japan and Adversarial Trade," April 1, 1986.

191 **"Save not only. . . ."** Mary Kaldor, *The Disintegrating West*, Hill and Wang (New York:1978), pp. 23–24.

193 **"Seems to stir xenophobia."** *Forbes*, Edwin A Finn, "Achtung, Achtung Die Japaner kommen!" November 3, 1986.

193 **"The Japanese. . . ."** Cited in Dower, *War Without Mercy*, Pantheon Books (New York:1986), p. 315.

193 **"Nation village."** Frank Gibney, *Japan: The Fragile Superpower*, Meridian (New York:1980), pp. 61–64.

193 **"If everyone. . . ."** *Vital Speeches*, Norio Ouchi, "The Changing Face of Trade Policy in Japan," December 1, 1971.

194 **"Below Hungarians. . . ."** Cited in Raymond A. Ethus, *Theodore Roosevelt and Japan*, University of Washington Press (Seattle:1966), p. 130.

195 **John Dower,** *op. cit.*, p. 209.

195 **"The four races. . . ."** Saburo Ienega, *The Pacific War*, Pantheon Books (New York:1978), pp. 11–12.

195 **"The brutality. . . ."** Cited in Ienega, *op. cit.*, p. 46.

195 **"After the war. . . ."** Reprinted in *Daily News* (Van Nuys, Calif.), cited in Ian Burma, "Japanese Neonationalism," April 19, 1987.

196 **Koreans in Japan.** *Ibid.*

196 **"Please tell me. . . ."** Cited in *Look*, August 10, 1965.

196 **"Hewers of wood. . . ."** *Los Angeles Times*, Earl Cheit, "Japan's Trading Partners in Asia Have a Love-Hate Relationship With it," December 2, 1984.

196 **"The Japanese harbor. . . ."** Cited in *Time*, "Toward the Japanese Century," March 2, 1970.

197 **Korean export promotion.** *Business America*, Heather S. Jones, "Korea's Success in Automobile Manufacturing Generates Opportunity for U.S. Suppliers," August 31, 1987.

197 **Taiwan export promotion.** *Nation's Business*, Henry Eason, "Taiwan Woos American Business," June 1987.

197 **"The goal seems to be. . . ."** Interview with authors.

197 **Paoshang Iron and Steel.** *International Management*, interview with Zhu Rongii, "What China Wants Now from Foreigners," April 1986.

198 **Sales to China.** *Wall Street Journal*, Barry Kramer, "China's Stepped-up Criticism of Japan," April 22, 1987.

198 **"You cannot exploit. . . ."** Interview with authors.

199 **"Begged."** Interview with authors.

199 **"They told us. . . ."** Interview with authors.

199 **"Toshiba worries about. . . ."** *Los Angeles Times*, Sam Jameson, "Japan Sees Chao, Not Domination," August 9, 1985.

199 **Friends with foreigners.** *Los Angeles Times*, Sam Jameson, "Japan: New Ways of Thinking Promoted," December 25, 1986.

199 **"For the Japanese. . . ."** Yasusuke Murakami and Yutaka Kosai, *Japan in the Global Community*, University of Tokyo Press (Tokyo: 1986), p. 47.

200 **"Better that Americans. . . ."** Interview with authors.

200 **Japanese anti-Semitism.** *Los Angeles Times*, Stuart Lloyd Pardau, "Insularity Breeds Anti-Semitism in Japan," June 29, 1987.

201 **"Japanese are geniuses. . . ."** Interview in *Journal of Japanese Trade and Industry*, number 5, 1983.

201 **"We never dreamed. . . ."** Interview with authors.

202 **"You had the stores. . . ."** Interview with authors.

202 **Japanese passport holders.** Figures compiled by Japanese Consulate, Los Angeles, and supplied by California Coordinators, Inc., Torrance, California.

202 **International trade.** "The Sixty Mile Circle," Security Pacific Bank, February 1984, p. 9.

202 **Largest port.** *San Jose Mercury*, Steve Kaufmann, "LA, Long Beach Ports Going Full Steam," August 17, 1987.

202 **Manufacturing employment.** "Sixty Mile Circle," *op. cit.*, p. 8.

202 **"They went there. . . ."** Interview with authors.

202 **Banking center.** *Business Week*, Robert Neff, "Los Angeles Becomes the Moneybags of the West," October 27, 1986.

203 **"We are becoming. . . ."** Interview with authors.

203 **Merrill Lynch study.** Cited in *California Business*, John Nielsen, "El Norte Comes to La Jolla," September 1987.

203 **"People just come into the office . . ."** Interview with authors.

203 **"The capital of Latin America."** Cited in *Advertising Age*, John

Franklin Sugg, "Miami: Capital of Latin America," November 30, 1981.

203 **Latin visitors.** Botifol, *op. cit.*, p. 14.

204 **American blacks in Africa.** *Wall Street Journal*, Linda Watkins, "American Blacks Find Business Ties to Africa Profitable, Gratifying," November 17, 1986.

205 **Revolution's currency.** Stanford Lyman, *The Asian in North America*, Clio Press (Santa Barbara:1970), p. 86.

205 **"The first descendent. . . ."** Cited in *Los Angeles Times*, Jim Mann, "Reaction to Shuttle Loss a Milestone for Chinese," February 7, 1986.

205 **"Chinese with American citizenship."** Bernard P. Wong, *Chinatown*, Holt, Rinehart and Winston. (New York:1982).

205 **"Chinese people. . . ."** Interview with authors.

206 **"We Chinese Americans. . . ."** Interview with authors.

206 **"We tell them. . . ."** Interview with authors.

208 **"We've been building. . . ."** Interview with authors.

208 **"We will always. . . ."** Interview with authors.

7: Empires of the Mind

page
209 **"The new empires. . . ."** Cited in D. N. Chorfas, *The Knowledge Revolution*, McGraw-Hill (New York:1970), p. 53.

209 **Technological progress.** *Science and Technology Policy for the 1980s*, Organization for Economic Development, (Paris:1981), p. 15.

209 **Mass culture.** *Forbes*, Allan Dodds Frank with Jason Zweig, "The Fault Is Not in Our Stars," September 21, 1987.

210 **"Transform the belief. . . ."** Friedrich Nietzsche, *The Will to Power*, Random House (New York: 1967), p. 324.

210 **"Never continues long. . . ."** Cited in Mancur Olson, *The Rise and Decline of Nations*, Yale University Press (New Haven:1982), p. 1.

211 **Per capita incomes.** *The Economist*, "My How You've Grown," March 26, 1986.

211 **Third World GNPs.** Yasusuko Murakami and Yutaka Kosai, *Japan in the Global Community*, University of Tokyo Press (Tokyo: 1986), pp. 94–96.

211 **Manufactured goods.** *The Economist*, "My How You've Grown," March 26, 1986.

211 **Hispanic and Asian business.** *Nathan's Business*, Roger Thompson, "Small Business Report," February 1987.

212 **Poll in South Korea.** *Los Angeles Times*, Roger Conner, "Immigration in the Era of Limits," February 7, 1980

212 **Two in five.** *The Education Digest*, L. Scott Miller, "Nation Building and Education," October 1986.

212 **Asians in education.** *Change*, Richard Richardson, Howard Simmons, and Alfredo G. de los Santos, "Graduating Minority Students," May/June 1987; *Futurescan*, Security Pacific Bank, March 18, 1985; *Los Angeles Times*, July 28, 1983.

213 **"Very few."** Interview with authors.

213 **"Americans think. . . ."** Interview with authors.

214 **"The organization man."** Murakami and Kosai, *op. cit.*, p. 28.

214 **"What is happening. . . ."** *Wall Street Journal*, Mark D'Anastasio, "Soviets Now Hail China as Source of New Ideas for Reviving Socialism," September 18, 1987.

214 **Leveraged buyouts.** *Mergers and Acquisitions Magazine* cited in *Inc.*, November 1986.

215 **"When you run. . . ."** Interview with authors.

215 **Service exports.** Study cited in *Science Magazine*, July 17, 1987.

216 **"It is clear. . . ."** Cited in *Forbes*, Kathleen Wiegner, "Institutionalizing the Revolution," June 16, 1986.

216 **Birch study.** *Inc.*, David Birch, January 1988.

216 *Kanban.* *Forbes*, James Cook, "Kanban American Style," October 8, 1984; *Los Angeles Times*, Martha Hamilton, "Campbell Soup Is Taking on Japan," July 4, 1986.

216 **"The future for. . . ."** Interview with authors.

216 **"The most important thing. . . ."** Interview with authors.

217 **"Industrial companies. . . ."** *Forbes*, Andrew Tanzer, "Y. C. Wang Gets Up Very Early in the Morning," July 15, 1985.

217 **"We are devoted. . . ."** Cited in *San Jose Mercury*, Steve Kaufman, "High Tech Survivors," September 29, 1986.

218 **"I guess I'm a bit. . . ."** Interview with authors.

218 **"The long feared. . . ."** *The Nation*, Gore Vidal, "Requiem for the American Empire," January 11, 1986.

219 **"Openness has driven out. . . ."** Alan Bloom, *The Closing of the American Mind*, Simon and Schuster (New York:1987), p. 56.

220 **"World cities."** Oswald Spengler, *Decline of the West*, Knopf (New York:1926), pp. 32–33.

220 *"Cosmopolis."* Michael Grant, *From Alexander to Cleopatra*, Scribner's (New York: 1982), p. xiv.

220 **"[Alexander] was. . . ."** *Ibid.*, p. 252.

220 **Cosmopolitan centers.** Michael Grant, *The Jews in the Roman World*, Scribner's (New York:1973).

220 **Tang, Sung and Ming dynasties.** Saul Steiner, *Fusang: The Chinese Who Built America*, Harper and Row (New York:1979), pp. 28–35.

221 **Before the Tokugawa.** Francis V. Moulder, *Japan, China and the Modern World Economy*, Cambridge University Press (Cambridge: 1977), pp. 38–39.

221 **Peripheral European states.** Immanuel Wallerstein, *The Modern World-system*, volume 1, Academic Press (New York:1974), pp. 55–60.

221 **Bureaucratic centralism.** *Ibid.*, pp. 60–61.

221 **Outside influences.** J. H. Parry, *The Age of Reconnaissance*, Mentor (New York: 1984), pp. 40–41.

221 **"The miracle of toleration. . . ."** Fernand Braudel. *The Perspective of the World,* volume 3, Harper and Row (New York:1984), p. 30.

222 **"Here individuals. . . ."** J. Hector St. John Crevecour, *Letters from an American Farmer*, Fox, Duffield (New York:1904), p. 55.

222 **"World city."** Spengler, *op. cit.*, p. 59.

222 **Importer of capital.** W. S. Woytinsky and E. S. Woytinsky, *World Commerce and Government Trends and Outlooks*, Twentieth Century Fund (New York: 1955), p. 207; Earl H. Fry, *Financial Invasion of the USA*, McGraw-Hill (New York:1980), p. 45.

222 **"Instead of being. . . ."** Cited in Peter J. Buckley and Brian R. Roberts, *European Investment in the U.S. before World War I*, Macmillan (London: 1982), p. 1.

223 **"The area of optimal. . . ."** Max Weber, *Economy and Society*, volume 2, edited by Guenther Roth and Claus Wittich, University of California (Berkeley: 1978), p. 692.

223 **"American science. . . ."** Cited in Robert V. Bruce, *The Launching of Modern American Science: 1846–76*, Knopf (New York: 1987), p. 7.

224 **German scientists.** *Wall Street Journal*, Diane Coutu, "European Nations Fret Over Mounting Losses of Scientists to the United States," October 21, 1987.

224 **Nobel prizes.** *Ibid.*

224 **Royal society.** *Science*, "European Science," September 4, 1987.

224 **"America is the . . . ."** *Ibid.*

224 **Asian students in U.S.** From *Foreign Citizens in U.S. Science and Engineering: History, Status and Outlook*, National Science Foundation (Washington, D.C.:1987), pp. xi, xii, 4.

224 **5,000 Koreans.** *Los Angeles Times*, Sam Jameson, "Korea Hopes To Lure Back Scientists, Engineers," August 30, 1984.

224 **Taiwanese doctorates.** *Image*, Frank Viviano, "Transplanting Silicon Valley," June 21, 1987.

225 **"Control of the . . . ."** Sheridan Tatsuno, *The Technopolis Strategy*, Prentice-Hall (New York: 1986)

225 **"No one talks. . . ."** Interview with authors.

225 **"In one laboratory. . . ."** Interview with authors.

225 **"In the four corners. . . ."** Cited in Leo Rosten, *Hollywood*, Harcourt, Brace (New York: 1941), p. 355.

226 **European tastes.** Charles Beard and Mary Beard, *The Rise of American Civilization*, volume 1, Macmillan (New York: 1930), p. 165.

226 **"Bending the knee. . . ."** John L. O'Sullivan, "The Great Nation of Futurity," in *Manifest Destiny*, Norman Graebner, ed., Bobbs-Merrill (Indianapolis:1968), p. 19.

226 **Harper's.** Beard and Beard, *op. cit.*, volume 1, p. 790.

226 **"Day of dependence. . . ."** Cited in *ibid.*, p. 768.

226 **"These states. . . ."** John Kennedy, *A Nation of Immigrants*, Harper and Row (New York: 1964), p. 3.

226 **"The immigrants. . . ."** Cited in Lescott-Leszczynski. *The History of U.S. Ethnic Policy and Its Impact on European Ethnics*, Westview Press (Boulder, Colo.; 1984) p. 59.

227 **"Lost generation."** Beard and Beard, *op. cit.*, volume 2, p. 773.

227 **Jazz.** *Ibid.*, p. 784.

227 **"Too narrow."** Cited in Laura Fermi, *Illustrious Immigrants*, University of Chicago Press (Chicago: 1968), p. 101.

228 **"Long arm."** Rosten, *op. cit.*, pp. 359–63.

228 **Cultural dominance.** Armand Mattelart, *et al.*, *International Image Markets*, Comedia Publishing Group (London: 1984), pp. 20–22.

228 **Entertainment exports.** *Forbes*, Allen Dodds Frank with Jason Zweig, "The Fault Is Not in Our Stars," September 21, 1987.

229 **"New York has. . . ."** Interview with Luis Valdez, *San Francisco Focus*, September 1987.

229 **"Californianization of the Free World."** Kenichi Ohmae, *Triad Power*, Free Press (New York: 1985), p. xxvi.

229 **"There is nothing more. . . ."** Niccolò Machiavelli, *The Prince*, New American Library (New York: 1952), p. 49.

230 **"If the conflict. . . ."** Cited in "Dean Acheson," Gaddis Smith, from *American Secretaries of State*, Robert H. Ferrell, ed., Cooper Square Publishers (New York: 1972), p. 271.

230 **"American Century."** Cited in William Appleman Williams, *History as a Way of Learning*, Quadrangle Press (New York: 1974), p. 215.

230 **Defense of Europe.** *Atlantic Monthly*, James Chace, "Ike Was Right," August 1987.

230 **"A colossal cartel."** Cited in Mary Kaldor, *The Disintegrating West*, Hill and Wang (New York: 1978), p. 188.

230 **"Mercantilist flavor."** *The Economist*, "If not Union, What then for Europe?" June 28, 1986.

230 **Joint research projects.** *Business Week*, "NATO Pushes Eject Button on U.S. Contractors," February 2, 1987; *Business Week*, "IBM Finds A Club That Doesn't Want It As a Member," February 11, 1985.

230 **"European economic union. . . ."** Interview with authors.

230 **"Gigantic restructuring."** *SAIS Review*, Immanuel Wallerstein, "North Atlanticism in Decline," Summer 1982, p. 21.

230 **Euro-Soviet trade.** *Wall Street Journal*, Peter Gumbel, "Soviet Plan to Let in Foreign Firms Proves Frustrating in Practice," July 17, 1987.

232 **Australia.** *Fact Sheet on Australia*, "Population," Australian Infor-

mation Service (Canberra:1982); *New York Times*, Jane Perlez, "Australia Debates Touchy Immigration Issue," February 1, 1987.

233 **"Centuries of human achievement."** T. Iyenega and Kenoske Sato, *Japan and the California Problem*, G. P. Putnam (New York:1921), p. 27.

233 **Honda.** *Wall Street Journal*, Kenichi Ohmae, "Japan's Trade Failure," April 1, 1987; *Los Angeles Times*, James Risen, "Honda: The Americanization of an Auto Maker," October 12, 1987.

233 **"Venice of the East."** Chalmers Johnson, "La Serenissima of the East," paper delivered to Hebrew University of Jerusalem at workshop on "Japan Thirty Years After the Occupation," June 27–29, 1982; interviews in *Journal of Japanese Trade and Industry*, "Japan's Survival as a Trading Nation: Learning from Medieval Venice," number 5, 1983.

233 **"It is not. . . ."** Cited in Iriye, *op. cit.*, p. 64.

234 **"The opening of. . . ."** Cited in William Appleman Williams, *Empire as a Way of Life*, Columbia University Press (New York: 1980), p. 39.

234 **"We are the heirs. . . ."** Cited in Kennedy, *op. cit.*, p. 68.

234 **"In search of monsters. . . ."** Cited in William Appleman Williams, *America Confronts a Revolutionary World*, William Morrow (New York:1976), p. 59.

Index

About the Authors

JOEL KOTKIN is West Coast editor for *Inc.* magazine and the coauthor of *California, Inc.* He lives in Los Angeles. YORIKO KISHIMOTO, born in Japan and educated in America, is the managing principal of Japan Pacific Associates, a firm specializing in helping companies engaged in transpacific business. She lives in Los Altos, California.